Desiring Whiteness

"In the face of the growing consensus that racial distinctions are socially constructed, *Desiring Whiteness* has the wit to ask, 'But what makes them stick? Why do people consent to such distinctions?' Reaching beyond the narrow boundaries of the constructionist problematic, Seshadri-Crooks brings fresh insight to the workings of race and racism, and – importantly – to the ways they negotiate the psychical and social disruptions introduced by sexual difference. Historically and theoretically informative, this book will serve as a useful primer to the various positions on race, even as it offers its own forceful correctives to them."

Joan Copjec, *SUNY at Buffalo*

"When all the sophisticated analyses of the contingency of race are finished, the engima remains. That's where Seshadri-Crooks starts: 'What is it about race that we can't give up?' That is where the psychoanalytic approach is called for: to understand why we hold onto something we have convinced ourselves doesn't justify our investment. Most studies of 'race' imply that 'blackness' is its privileged sign. But that is the trick played by Whiteness. Seshadri-Crooks starts from the premise that Whiteness is the defining signifier of race. Her analysis is brilliant, rigorous, counterintuitive, and funny."

Barbara Johnson, *Harvard University*

Race is asserted to be a social construction. Nevertheless, we continue to deploy race thinking in our everyday life as a way of telling people apart visually.

Desiring Whiteness explores this visual discrimination by asking questions in specifically psychoanalytic terms: How do subjects become raced? Is it common sense to read bodies as racially marked? Employing Lacan's theories of the subject and sexual difference, Seshadri-Crooks explores how the discourse of race makes use of sexual difference in making racial identity a fundamental component of our thinking.

Through close readings of literary and film texts, Seshadri-Crooks demonstrates that race is a system of differences organized around a privileged term, Whiteness. Critiquing "Whiteness Studies," she argues that Whiteness should not be understood as the bodily or material property of a particular group, but is a term that makes the logic of race thinking possible.

Desiring Whiteness provides a compelling new interpretation of how we understand race, and will be essential reading to anyone studying race and ethnicity, postcolonialism and psychoanalysis.

Kalpana Seshadri-Crooks is Assistant Professor of English at Boston College, Massachusetts.

Feminism for Today
General Editor: Teresa Brennan

The Regime of the Brother
After the Patriarchy
Juliet Flower MacCannell

History After Lacan
Teresa Brennan

Feminism and the Mastery of Nature
Val Plumwood

The Spoils of Freedom
Renata Salecl

Ecopolitics
The Environment in Poststructuralist Thought
Verena Andermatt Conley

The Politics of (M)Othering
Womanhood, Identity, and Resistance in African Literature
Edited by Obioma Nnaemeka

Desiring Whiteness

A Lacanian analysis of race

Kalpana Seshadri-Crooks

London and New York

First published 2000
by Routledge
11 New Fetter Lane, London EC4P 4EE

Simultaneously published in the USA and Canada
by Routledge
29 West 35th Street, New York, NY 10001

Routledge is an imprint of the Taylor & Francis Group

© 2000 Kalpana Seshadri-Crooks

Typeset in Times by Taylor & Francis Books Ltd
Printed and bound in Great Britain by St Edmundsbury Press,
Bury St Edmunds, Suffolk

British Library Cataloguing in Publication Data
A catalogue record for this book is available from the British
Library

Library of Congress Cataloging in Publication Data
Seshadri-Crooks, Kalpana
    Desiring Whiteness: a Lacanian analysis of race/Kalpana
    Seshadri-Crooks.
    p. cm. – (Opening out)
    Includes bibliographical references and index.
    1. Psychoanalysis and racism. 2. Race – Psychological aspects. 3.
    Race awareness. 4. Lacan, Jacques, 1901- I. Title. II. Series.
    BF175.4.R34 S47 2001
    155.8'2–dc21   99-059598

ISBN 0–415–19254–4 (hbk)
ISBN 0–415–19255–2 (pbk)

For my mother, Sivakami Seshadri,
and my father, Venkatram Seshadri,
for giving me the courage to enjoy paradox

Contents

Acknowledgments   viii

Key to Lacan's works   x

Introduction: on looking   1

1 Deciphering Whiteness   11

2 The object of Whiteness   57

3 Whiteness and the elephant joke   79

4 Looking alike: or the ethics of *Suture*   103

5 What's in a name? Love and knowledge beyond identity in "Recitatif"   132

6 Discolorations   158

Notes   161

Bibliography   168

Index   176

Acknowledgments

It is customary, in acknowledgments such as these, to speak of being in pleasurable debt to one's friends and peers. But I must admit to suffering the agitation of rendering inadequate thanks to everyone who has supported me through the writing of this book. Among my big Others, Charlie Shepherdson has been very influential, my ideal reader, interlocutor, and house guest. Doing "Anxiety" with him and Frances Restuccia was a curiously full experience. Frances, my Lacanian colleague, has read and critiqued my work most assiduously. She has been an attentive and critical listener as I formulated my ideas; I know of no one who has more patience for growing ideas than she. Her brand of compassion is rare and rigorous, and to many very unfamiliar. John Limon vetted my argument for its logic, and has caught many a glaring inconsistency. Andrew Von Hendy read several drafts of my chapters, and very generously offered reams of notes for me to work from. Daniel Boyarin rescued me from many a moment of despair. He has offered his intellect and friendship most amply. Other friends and colleagues who read and made immensely valuable comments on early drafts of this book were Robin Lydenberg, Jean Wyatt, Chris Lane, Peter Starr, Paul Lewis, Mark Bracher and Judith Wilt. I thank them all for the patience and care with which they read what were often very rough drafts. Robin Lydenberg has been a nurturing colleague. Auditing the course she taught with Bill Richardson in the fall of 1995 on Lacan and femininity was a turning point for me. She also invited me to join the B.C-BPSI Freud reading group, from which I have profited considerably. I thank all the members of that group, and particularly Bill Richardson for sharing his knowledge so freely.

Perhaps the person without whom this book could not have had a body is Teresa Brennan. How does one thank someone who gives life to a project? She has been a rigorous but kind, tough and gentle editor all at once. Her great gift to me has been her personal enigma, which led me to do my very best for her.

Barbara Johnson has had a very great impact on the writing and revising of this book, as she has had (unbeknownst to her) on my notions of what counts as scholarship. I thank her for inviting me to present a portion of my work at her seminar at the CLCS.

Parveen Adams has offered me much encouragement on the project.

R. Radhakrishnan has watched me develop from a first-year graduate student to an assistant professor. He has read and critiqued my work, written letters on my behalf, and lent his warm and helping hand through many a rite of passage. I thank him for giving me the opportunity to speak at the faculty colloquium at the University of Massachusetts, Amherst.

I owe Marjorie Garber, Director of the Center for Literary and Cultural Studies at Harvard, a huge share of gratitude for giving me the opportunity to chair the Postcolonial Studies seminar at the Center. The CLCS has offered me and many others an intellectual support system. I would find life without the Center unimaginable.

The members of my department at Boston College have helped a great deal in giving me self-confidence. I thank them all, but particularly my mentors Rosemarie Bodenheimer, Judith Wilt, Mary Crane, Alan Richardson, Amy Boesky, Henry Blackwell and Beth Kowaleski-Wallace. To my students in the Ph.D. seminar in the spring of 1999, I owe an incalculable debt. I thank Boston College for granting me a faculty fellowship, which enabled me to take a semester's leave in the spring of 1997.

I would be remiss if I did not mention other peers and friends who have contributed in numerous ways to this project: Homi Bhabha has always made time for me despite his terrifically busy schedule. He has supported my career in ways too numerous to list here. Thanks to Raji Sunder Rajan, Don Pease, Laura Frader and Doris Sommer for their exemplary sense of integrity and generosity. Friends who have cheered me on: Jean Walton, Sangeeta Ray, Beatrice Hanssen, Asha Vardharajan, Sandhya Shetty, Parama Roy, Anindyo Roy, Judith Feher Gurewich and Samir Dayal. I owe Ken Reinhard and Juliet MacCannell a special thanks for inviting me to attend the first conference of the American Lacanian Link.

Without my family, writing this book would have had no meaning. I inscribe their names with the deepest respect and love: my dearest Paati, my sister Nirmala, her children Gautam and Janaki, my brother Kartik, his wife Anne, the much awaited Mallika, and our madcaps Chai and Norbu. And finally Robert, without whom thought would be impossible for me. He has listened, reflected, and met me in ways so stable yet surprising that I have often had to reevaluate Lacan on relationships. It would perhaps be a violation to try to alienate into words that which he presents to me.

Cover image: This sculpture is the basis of a logo for the Centre for Popularisation of Mathematics (http://www.bangor.ac.uk/ma/pa) and also of the Mathematics Division of the School of Informatics, at the University of Wales, Bangor.

Key to Lacan's works

I have utilized abbreviated title or seminar number for references to Lacan's work in the body of my text. The bibliography contains full references to the following works and others by Lacan.

E	*Ecrits: A Selection*
FS	*Feminine Sexuality: Jacques Lacan and the Ecole Freudienne*
I	Seminar I, 1953–4, *Freud's Papers on Technique*
II	Seminar II, 1954–5, *The Ego in Freud's Theory*
III	Seminar III, 1955–6, *The Psychoses*
VI	Seminar VII, 1959–60, *The Ethics of Psychoanalysis*
X	Seminar X, 1962–3, "Anxiety" (unpublished manuscript)
Seminar of 1963	Introduction to the "Names-of-the-Father Seminar" in *Television*
XI	Seminar XI, 1964, *Four Fundamental Concepts of Psychoanalysis*
XX	Seminar XX, 1972–3, *Encore: On Feminine Sexuality*
XXII	Seminar XXII, 1974–5, "R.S.I." (one session in *Feminine Sexuality*)
XXVII	Seminar XXVII, 1980, "Dissolution" (in *Television*)

Introduction
On looking

Growing up in India with a marked sense of caste identity, I found group difference to be a complex weave of practices and beliefs pertaining to a certain texture of life; it was in my experience irreducible to one's physical appearance. This is not to say that appearance plays no role in India. A glance at "matrimonial advertisements" in any Indian newspaper will demonstrate the ubiquity of physical ideals that include attributes such as being "fair"-skinned or tall. But in this thoroughly heterogeneous society (where the truth can never be told because anything is possible), the physical ideal functions as a form of preference, as an aesthetic choice, without the ontological and legal significance it has acquired in the West. Even in the more racially self-conscious north of India, where the colonialist interpellation of the elite by a so-called Aryan heritage produces those familiar symptoms of denial that Frantz Fanon (1952: 141–54) has analyzed in the context of Martinique, physical attributes do not seem so definitive, so determining of one's destiny or one's subjectivity. The size of one's nose, the degree of pigmentation, or the texture of one's hair, is not considered to be an index of ability, character or culture. Differences are marked rather by economic status, but even more by one's last name and regional and linguistic affiliations, the latter being indices of religion, caste, and what is known as "community." It is this seemingly trivial point, the indifference to "biological" difference, that radically distinguishes caste thinking, which can cut across religions, from race thinking. This distinction has not been adequately marked or theorized given the popular and simplistic absorption of caste (or *jati*) within the fourfold *varna* scheme, particularly since *varna* is often translated (from the *Satapatha Brahmana* [Srinivas 1962: 63–4]) as color, and thereby subsumed within race. The controversial translation of scripture notwithstanding,[1] caste difference is always marked by cultural accoutrements such as clothing, dialect, and one's name, but rarely, if ever, by bodily marks. Let me clarify once and for all that I am not valorizing caste, nor idealizing India as an egalitarian society. I only want to stress that in a wholly racialized society such as the US, Europe, or the Caribbean, appearance or physical attributes have come to be more starkly vested, more consequential than anything else such as family, wealth, culture, education or personal achievement. The investment in bodies may differ, and their meanings and ordering may vary according to each society, but the fundamental significance of physical attributes remains constant. It was to explain and understand this seeming irrationality at the heart of rational modern cultures (and within Western postcolonial societies) that I undertook to explore the fundamental questions that inform this book: how and why do we read certain marks of the body as privileged sites of racial meaning? How did we come to organize difference along arbitrarily chosen physical characteristics, thereby generating group formations and identifications? Why some marks like hair, skin and bone, and not others? How is it that when society organizes itself – its system of rewards and punishments, inclusions and exclusions – around appearance, appearance begins to exceed the constructs of a simple narcissism, to the point that it is always the neighbor's appearance that one is concerned with over and above one's own?

I decided to pursue these questions and some others through psychoanalysis, for it seemed to me that the investment we make in appearance is beyond simple historical or material explanation, and that it was only by exploring the psychical import of race that one could hope to understand its resilient non-sense. Taking irrationality seriously, then, I began with the observation that debates pertaining to racial theory, which have largely preoccupied social scientists and cultural critics, rarely have an impact on racial practice. Race is fundamentally a regime of looking, although race cannot be reduced to the look. By visibility, I do not mean the deployment of stereotype whereby all African Americans have dark skin, and all Caucasians are blond and blue-eyed. Obviously, the correspondence between color and race is too unstable for such simplified looking. It is common knowledge that some "black" people can be very white, and some "whites" can be very dark; identity is a question of "heritage," not skin color. Once claimed, however, heritage is ultimately marked by the body. Some small bodily mark lends authenticity to the claim of racial belonging. The discourse on racial passing offers the richest sample of such anxious fascination with miniscule but all important differences. Thus by visibility I refer to a regime of looking that thrives on "major" and "minor" details in order to shore up one's symbolic position. It is this concentration on minute difference, perfected by anti-Semitism into a mode of looking, that informs my model of visibility. In the following, I therefore focus on race as a practice of visibility rather than as scientific, anthropological or cultural theory. My premise is that the regime of visibility secures the investment that we make in "race," and there are good reasons why such an investment cannot be easily surrendered.

I suggest that Lacan's theory of subject constitution provides us with cognitive landmarks or positions by which to bring the subject of race into representation. Lacan's provocative thesis that the unconscious is structured

like a language and the general precision of his "anti-system" se
provide the requisite tools and a language with which to expl
delineate the subject's acquisition of racial identity. My use of L
psychoanalysis is not a passive "application of Lacanian concepts to issues
of race." I have tried to work with the richest aspects of the theory, and in
the process have found it necessary to wrestle with it, and to exert consider-
able force in inducing it to address race. However, the "appropriation" of
Lacan that follows does not take the expected form of ideological revision. I
have deliberately avoided the customary ideological "critique" of Lacan, nor
do I press the obligatory charge against him for neglecting the all-important
issue of race in a France that was, at the moment of his theoretical elabora-
tion, involved in a bloody colonial and racist war against the Algerians.
Attention to the person of Lacan and his political responsibility in failing to
detail a theory of race is not relevant to my project.[2] It seems much more
important to stay focused on the question of race itself, and to derive some
insight into the issues rather than to be distracted by an essentially academic
argument about the "politics of psychoanalysis." The evident fealty I
demonstrate to Lacanian psychoanalysis derives from my belief that first, in
its consistency and precision, Lacanian theory offers a vocabulary of
linguistic deciphering in relation to subject constitution that is simply
unavailable elsewhere; and second, it is important to remain tenacious in
one's intellectual pursuit, here the interrogation of the mystique of "race."
Where race is concerned too much energy is spent on talking about how we
talk about race; thus with the clamor of voices sounding off on political
correctness, hate speech, the rights of representation, etc., very little atten-
tion is devoted to analyzing what race is and why we need it.[3]

The theory of race that follows aims to supplement one of the richest
aspects of Lacan's theory, the issue of sexual difference. In using Lacan's
theory of sexual difference as the cornerstone of my analysis of race, I have
tried to evolve a procedure that does not require an analogy between sex and
race. The temptation to symmetry in translating formulas from the realm of
sex to that of race (such as sex is in the Real, therefore race is in the
Real, etc.) is great indeed. But such morphologies are, of course, inherently
non-psychoanalytical. In reading race with sex, I have tried to go beyond the
piety of asserting the specificity of each category of experience. I have
sought to discover the intricate structural relations between race and sex, to
see how race articulates itself with sex to gain access to desire or lack – the
paradoxical guarantee of the subject's sovereignty beyond symbolic
determination.[4]

I argue that the inaugural signifier of race, which I term Whiteness,
implicates us all equally in a logic of difference. By Whiteness, I do not
mean a physical or ideological property as it is invoked in "Whiteness
Studies"[5] or a concept, a set of meanings that functions as a transcen-
dental signified. By Whiteness, I refer to a master signifier (without a

signified) that establishes a structure of relations, a signifying chain that through a process of inclusions and exclusions constitutes a pattern for organizing human difference. This chain provides subjects with certain symbolic positions such as "black," "white," "Asian," etc., in relation to the master signifier. "Race," in other words, is a system of categorization that once it has been organized shapes human difference in certain seemingly predetermined ways. We will therefore have to see how this symbolic structuration is related to visibility. This is where Lacanian theory will be especially useful.

As a system of organizing difference, race is very distinctive in relation to other forms of organizations such as caste, ethnicity and nation. It is distinctive as a belief structure and evokes powerful and very particular investments in its subjects. Consider the peculiar intensification of racial identification and racial discourse even as the scientific untenability of race is ever more insisted upon by scientists and anthropologists. Even though it has now become commonplace to utter rote phrases such as "race is a construct" or "race does not exist," etc., race itself shows no evidence of disappearing or evaporating in relevance. It is common sense to believe in the existence of race. Why do we hold on to race? What is it about race that is difficult to give up?

I suggest that race should be understood in its particularity as something that is neither totally like sexual difference, which is indeterminate and exceeds language, nor purely symbolical or cultural like class or ethnicity. Race resembles class in that it is of purely cultural and historical origin, but it is also like sex in that it produces extra-discursive effects. From a certain perspective, it seems marked on the body, something inherited like sex; from a Lacanian perspective, one might even suggest (erroneously) that it seems to exceed language. The signification of class belonging, so long as it is purely a category of economic discrepancy, can be manipulated by its subjects. But the minute class makes a claim to inheritance through the language of "stock" and "blood," it lapses into "race," and this is true for all other categories of group identity. Scratch the surface of culture or ethnicity, and race will appear underneath it all to found its essence.[6] Race is historical and material as well, but unlike class it is not at all malleable. It is assumed that one cannot change one's accent and clothing and thereby change one's race. We cannot change it because race is supposedly inscribed on one's body.[7] Does that mean that it is simply a fact of nature? Is phenotype a transcendental category? In response, I suggest that we should ask why we invest in the notion of phenotype. Why do we feel that we must necessarily insist on the evidence of our eyes?

We may venture one kind of an answer using Teresa Brennan's (1993) analysis of modernity. In *History After Lacan*, Brennan presents an extended psychoanalytic and materialist critique of what she terms the foundational fantasy of modern societies: a psychotic fantasy that by

conceiving of the subject as the origin, cause, and end of know
wreaks incalculable havoc upon the environment. Such a fantasy presupposes an entirely self-contained and autonomous subject that is
characterized by the dominance of the narcissistic ego, severed from all
forms of inter-subjectivity. Perhaps we can consider race itself as a
symptom of what Brennan terms the "ego's era," when objectification and
dominance of others and of the environment are paramount. Among the
many insights she offers about the historicity of such a subject of knowledge, Brennan suggests that the dominance of the visual is a symptom of
such "social psychosis": "Visualization, whether in the form of hallucination or visual perception, observes difference rather than connection" (*ibid.*:
12). One consequence of such an intensification of visual difference is borne
out in Lacan's reworking of the Hegelian dialectic in relation to the signifier
and the look. She writes:

> the imaginary process of fixing the other is not only confined to *seeing*;
> it also involves naming. More accurately, naming is part of how the
> other is seen, as well as being part of the way out. In sum, when the
> master becomes the master, identified with and as a namer-shaper,
> released into and through a cultural linguistic tradition, the master
> simultaneously directs aggression towards the one who is seen to be
> passified. But this leaves the passified in a position where they are depen-
> dent (at the level of the ego) on the image they receive from the other.
>
> (Brennan 1993: 60)

According to Brennan, modernity is characterized by the objectification
of an other in support of one's narcissistic fantasy. This "imaginary fixing,"
she implies, also bears a relation to the symbolic order. By seizing the apparatus of a regimented look, Brennan argues, one takes possession of the
nominal function of language.[8] Language in this schema is engaged in the
service of the ego and the foundational fantasy of self-containment. In relation to "race," however, we may well invert this argument. I suggest that it is
the symbolic order of racial difference itself that governs seeing, rather than
the reverse. We *believe* in the factuality of difference in order to *see* it,
because the order of racial difference is an order that promises access to an
absolute wholeness to its subjects – white, black, yellow or brown. The relation of fantasy to the symbolic order of race must be construed somewhat
differently. The fantasy of wholeness, of being, that the signifier holds out is
not a case of narcissistic misrecognition, but is a fundamental fantasy that
determines the trajectory of the subject of "race." Thus visuality in the
realm of race should be understood as functioning in support of *and* as a
defence against the fantasy of a totalized subject. My argument is that this
fantasy of wholeness, which the signifier offers to the subject of race, is
entirely predicated on sexual difference.

Briefly, my point of departure is the Lacanian view that sexual difference is in the Real (and not, as feminists have understood it, in the symbolic). This Lacanian axiom alludes to sex as that which escapes or confounds language, which view, as Joan Copjec has pointed out, is the guarantee, not of the subject's incompletion, but her "sovereign incalculabilty" (1994: 208). Whiteness, I am suggesting, attempts to install itself in this place of linguistic contradiction – of being – where the subject fades from meaning. Such an attempt to totalize and inflate the subject can only produce anxiety. Visual difference then rescues the subject from such anxiety by reinstalling difference.

To elaborate: in Lacan's theory, the order of sexual difference, which acknowledges male and female, is organized around the non-reciprocity of man and woman. Sexed reproduction here is but the failure of Oneness that is poorly compensated for by the heterosexuality. It is an order that is predicated on the impossibility of representing the sexual relation. Lacan's aphorism "there is no sexual relation" turns on the asymmetry and non-reciprocity of the sexes. Sexual difference is marked by the impasse of signification, and the impossibility of gratifying desire, of love as *jouissance*.[9] It is missing a signifier that can organize male and female in a binary relation. In the article entitled "The subjective import of the castration complex," published in *Scilicet*, we read that "the difference between the sexes introduces a non-representable instance which is found to coincide with the point of failing that the subject encounters in the signifying chain" (Lacan, FS: 119). As Joan Copjec puts it: "Sex is the stumbling block of sense" (1994: 206); she further adds:

> When ... sex is *disjoined* from the signifier, it becomes that which does not communicate itself, that which marks the subject as unknowable. To say that the subject is sexed is to say that it is no longer possible to have any knowledge of *him* or *her*. *Sex serves no other function than to limit reason, to remove the subject from the realm of possible experience or pure understanding.* This is the meaning, when all is said and done, of Lacan's notorious assertion that "there is no sexual relation": sex, in opposing itself to sense, is also, by definition, opposed to relation, to communication.
>
> (1994: 207)

The claim that sex is in the Real pertains to the Freudian notion that

> there is only one libido, meaning that there is no psychic representative of the opposition masculine–feminine. The essence of castration and the link of sexuality to the unconscious both reside in this factor – that sexual difference is refused to knowledge [*savoir*], since it indicates the point where the subject of the unconscious subsists by being the subject of non-knowledge.
>
> (FS: 120)

I am suggesting two things: first, the order of racial difference attempts to compensate for sex's failure in language; second, we must not therefore analogize race and sex on the sexual model of linguistic excess or contradiction. The signifier Whiteness tries to fill the constitutive lack of the sexed subject. It promises a totality, an overcoming of difference itself. For the subject of race, Whiteness represents complete mastery, self-sufficiency, and the *jouissance* of Oneness. This is why the order of racial difference must be distinguished from, but read in relation to, sexual difference. If sex is characterized by a missing signifier, race, on the contrary, is not and cannot be organized around such an absence – a missing signifier – that escapes or confounds language and inter-subjectivity. Race has an all-too-present master signifier – Whiteness – which offers the illegal enjoyment of absolute wholeness. Race, therefore, does not bear on the paradigm of failure or success of inter-subjectivity on the model of the sexual relation.

The rationale of racial difference and its organization can be understood as a Hobbesian one. It is a social contract among potential adversaries secured to perpetuate singular claims to power and dominance, even as it seeks to contain the consequences of such singular interests. The shared insecurity of claiming absolute humanness, which is what race as a system manages, induces the social and legal validation of race as a discourse of neutral differences. In other words, race identity can have only one function – it establishes differential relations among the races in order to constitute the logic of domination. Groups must be differentiated and related in order to make possible the claim to power and domination. Race identity is about the sense of one's exclusiveness, exceptionality and uniqueness. Put very simply, it is an identity that, if it is working at all, can only be about pride, being better, being the best. Race is inextricably caught up in a Hobbesian discourse of social contract, where personal (or particular) interest masquerades as public good. Sexual difference, on the other hand, cannot be founded upon such a logic. The values attached to male and female are historically contingent as feminists have long suggested, but power cannot be the ultimate cause of sexual difference. Racial difference, on the other hand, has no other reason to be but power, and yet it is not power in the sense of material and discursive agency that can be reduced to historical mappings. If such were the case, as many have assumed, then a historicist genealogy of the discursive construction of race would be in order: Foucault not Lacan, discourse analysis not psychoanalysis. But race organizes difference and elicits investment in its subjects because it promises access to being itself. It offers the prestige of being better and superior; it is the promise of being more human, more full, less lacking. The possibility of this enjoyment is at the core of "race." But enjoyment or *jouissance* is, we may recall, pure unpleasure. The possibility of enjoyment held out by Whiteness is also horrific as it implies the annihilation of difference. The subject of race therefore typically resists race as mere "social construction," even as it holds on to a notion of visible, phenotypal difference.

Visible difference in race has a contradictory function. If it protects against a lethal sameness, it also facilitates the possibility of that sameness through the fantasy of wholeness. Insofar as Whiteness dissimulates the object of desire,[10] any encounter with the historicity, the purely symbolic origin of the signifier, inevitably produces anxiety. It is necessary for race to seem more than its historical and cultural origin in order to aim at being. Race must therefore disavow or deny knowledge of its own historicity, or risk surrendering to the discourse of exceptionality, the possibility of wholeness and supremacy. Thus race secures itself through visibility. Psychoanalytically, we can perceive the object cause of racial anxiety as racial visibility, the so-called pre-discursive marks on the body (hair, skin, bone), which serve as the desiderata of race. In other words, the bodily mark, which (like sex) seems to be more than symbolic, serves as a powerful prophylactic against the anxiety of race as a discursive construction. We seem to need such a refuge in order to preserve the investment we make in the signifier of Whiteness. Thus race should not be reduced to racial visibility, which is the mistake made by some well-meaning and not-so-well-meaning advocates of a color blind society. Racial visibility should be understood as that which secures the much deeper investment we have made in the racial categorization of human beings. It is a lock-and-key relation, and throwing away the key of visibility because it happens to open and close is not going to make the lock inoperable. By interrogating visibility we can ask what the lock is preserving, and why. The capacity of visibility to secure an investment in identity also distinguishes race from other systems of difference such as caste, class, ethnicity, etc. These latter forms of group identity, insofar as they cannot be essentialized through bodily marks, can be easily historicized and textualized. Nothing prevents their deconstruction, whereas in the case of race, visibility maintains a bulwark against the historicity and historicization of race. (In fact, Brennan suggests that the "ego's era" is characterized by a resistance to history.) It is this function of visibility that renders cases of racial passing fraught and anxious.

My contention that the category of race is inherently a discourse of supremacy may seem inattentive to the advances that our legal systems and liberal social ideologies have made precisely in relation to "racism" and "racist" practices. Modern civil society refuses to permit its subjects the enjoyment of supremacist rhetoric, the rhetoric of exceptionality, by distinguishing between race and racism. It draws this distinction between a supposed ontology (the study of physical or cultural differences) and an epistemology (discriminatory logic) in the name of preserving a semblance of inter-subjectivity. Race, it suggests, is a neutral description of human difference; racism, it suggests, is the misappropriation of such difference. The liberal consensus is that we must do away with such ideological misappropriation, but that we must "celebrate difference." It is understood as a "baby and the bath water" syndrome, in which the dirty water of racism must be eliminated, to reveal the cleansed and beloved "fact" of racial identity. This rather myopic perspective refuses to address the peculiar resiliency of "race," the subjective investment in racial difference, and the hyper-valorization of appearance. It dismisses these issues or trivializes them because race seems a historical inevitability. The logic is that people have been constituted for material and other reasons as black and white and that this has had powerful historical consequences for peoples thus constituted. Whether race exists or not, whether race and racism are artificial distinctions or not, racialization is a hard historical fact and a concrete instance of social reality. We have no choice, according to this reasoning, but to inhabit our assigned racial positions. Not to do so is a form of idealism, and a groundless belief that power can be wished away. In making this ostensibly "pragmatic" move, such social theorists effectively reify "race." Lukács, who elaborated Marx's notion of reification in relation to the commodity form in *History and Class Consciousness*, is worth recalling here:

> Its basis is that a relation between people takes on the character of a thing, and thus acquires a 'phantom objectivity,' an autonomy that seems so strictly rational and all-embracing as to conceal every trace of its fundamental nature: the relation between people.
>
> (1923: 89)

To arrest analysis of race at the point where one discerns and marks its historical effects is to reproduce those very relations of power that one intends to oppose. It is to render race so objective that it is impossible to conceive human difference or inter-subjectivity anew. Modern civil society engages in such reification because ultimately its desire is to keep the dialectic between races alive. It must thus prohibit what it terms "racism" in order to prevent the annihilation not so much of the "inferior" races but of the system of race itself. This is how the system of "desiring Whiteness" perpetuates itself, even in the discourses that are most pragmatically aimed against racism. The resilience and endurability of race as a structure can thus be attributed to its denials and disavowals. On the one hand, it is never in the place that one expects it to be: it disavows its own historicity in order to hold out the promise of being to the subject – the something more than symbolic – a sense of wholeness, of exceptionality. On the other hand, as a social law, it must disavow this object in order to keep the system viable and to perpetuate the dialectic: the race for Whiteness. Exploring the structure of race requires a toleration of paradox, an appreciation of the fact that it is an inherently contradictory discourse, and a willingness to see beyond relations of power in order to mine the depth of subjective investment in it.

This book is not an argument against racism and racist practices, but rather an attempt to confound race itself as bodily reference. One way in which I offer that we can undermine the notion of racial embodiment is through the exploration of an adversarial aesthetics. Chapters 4 and 5, on the film *Suture* (1993) and Toni Morrison's short story "Recitatif" (1983) respectively, attempt to delineate such an aesthetics. I suggest that *Suture*, through its abrogation of racial looking, also specifies an ethics for the subject of race. It exemplifies the possibility of traversing the fundamental fantasy of wholeness by calling into question the gestalt of racial looking. Morrison's "Recitatif" is read as a story about inter-racial love as centering on the will to ignorance, a certain "nothing to know" that is the anxious "truth" about racial signifiers. Chapters 2 and 3 outline the workings and effects of the structure of race or Whiteness. Chapter 2, "The object of Whiteness," focuses on Joseph Conrad's "The secret sharer"(1909). I suggest that the story, read through the traces of Whiteness, represents a phantasmatic realization of Whiteness to inflate the subject by effectively obliterating difference. By locating my reading at the intersection of the divide between fiction and history, I uncover the text of a realized racial fantasy. In trying to expel racial difference out of the historical account, the fictional story ends up recuperating race's excluded or illegal aspiration for sameness. If "The secret sharer" is to be read as the successful accomplishment of "Whiteness," then the next chapter on colonial discourse and jokes delineates the inevitable failure of such an aspiration. Using George Orwell's anecdotal essays of his experience in colonial territories – India, Burma and Morocco – I show how the repression of race's historicity often returns in unexpected moments of "the joke" as the uncanny encounter with one's own investment in an illegal (and for a liberal like Orwell, even repugnant) aspiration for supremacy and sameness. Chapter 1, by way of introduction, elaborates the theoretical edifice of the book as a whole. It sets the stage for the further exploration of my theory of race as a regime of visibility by working through Lacan's language of sexual difference and the moral law.

This book is a very preliminary and tentative foray into a territory that has been left uncharted. I have not found it easy to see my way clearly, and it is possible that I have not marked the simplest and most direct route through this area. There is no doubt much that remains unthought. The book is best read in a linear fashion, as the chapters build upon one another to argue for an ethics and aesthetics of racial passing that is more than imaginary – a "symbolic" passing that will alter the subject's relation to the signifier in ways that risk his/her de-subjectification as a subject of race.

Chapter 1

Deciphering Whiteness

> We have counted four human races under which all the manifold varia-
> tions of this genus are supposed to [be] conceived. But all deviations need
> nevertheless a stem genus; and either we must declare it now extinct, or
> else we must seek among those extant the one which we can best compare
> to the stem-genus. ... That portion of the earth between the 31st and 52nd
> parallels in the Old World ... is rightly held to be that in which the most
> happy mixture of influences of the colder and hotter regions and also the
> greatest wealth of earthly creatures is encountered; where man too must
> have departed the least from his original formation. ... Here, to be sure we
> find white inhabitants.
>
> (Kant, "On the different races of man," Eze edn: 47–8)

> Just talking about race means that it will always be there in residue.
>
> (Guillaumin 1995: 105)

In June of 1995, the *New York Times* reported the "anguish" of a Dutch
couple who had to confront the fact that one of their twin boys, conceived
through *in vitro* fertilization, was "black." The University Hospital at
Utrecht, which was responsible for inflicting this "anguish," called it a
"deeply regrettable mistake"; they surmised that a technician had used a
none-too-clean pipette in performing the procedure. The parents at first
denied that "something about Koen was different." Unlike his twin brother
Teun, Koen got darker as the weeks went by, which induced the parents to
visit a gynecologist and then to undergo a DNA test. The test results
confirmed that Koen's father was a "black man" from Aruba. For the
parents, the news apparently was "devastating." According to the *New York
Times*:

> They started sessions with a psychotherapist to deal with what the
> father called their "bewilderment and pain," and the questions that kept
> spinning around in their heads. How would they tell their son that he
> was not meant to exist, that he was born because of a technical error?
> Would they treat the children differently? The parents say they worry

about discrimination and that Koen will have fewer chances than his
brother. "Let's be honest, dark people have less opportunity to get a
decent job in our society," the father told *Het Parool* [the Amsterdam
newspaper]. "They have less chance to borrow at a bank."

(*New York Times*, 28 June 1995: A3)

A year later in a television interview, the parents expressed similar senti-
ments and agreed that if the "mistake" had been made with a "white" man's
sperm, they probably would not have noticed that there was "something
different" about Koen at all. In other words, there would have been no
mistake. I cite this "case" in detail as it seems exemplary of the way race[1]
works in modern societies, and also because it points to some of the lacunae
in contemporary discussions of race and the ways in which the terms of the
argument have been formulated.

Most contemporary debates over the definition of cultural identities and
psychical identifications, whether racial, ethnic or sexual, seem to lapse
invariably into the opposition between biological essence and social
construction. Where race is concerned, however, the opposition, when examined closely, is more over the terms of the debate – i.e. the deployment of the
term "race" itself – than over ontological considerations. Few if any liberally
inclined persons today will hold that "race," as it was theorized in the nineteenth century, as a concept referring to the aspirations and abilities of a
homogeneous group, is an inherited biological essence. In fact, the scientific
bases of race have been thoroughly discredited, as have the philosophical, to
the point that race is now considered a "folk" belief.[2] However, this has not
meant the disappearance of race from science.[3] It persists, for instance, in
medical literature as a means to map the demography of diseases and symptoms. But, if one applies some pressure to the medical category of race, one
discovers that it has none of the cultural valence associated with "race";
rather, it is a diffused concept that refers mostly to "human diversity" not
group essence.[4] Race is also frequently equated nowadays with the term
"phenotype" as an acceptable term to denote what are supposedly "gross
morphological differences," or (ir)relevant visible marks of skin color, hair
texture and bone structure. Nevertheless, despite (or perhaps because of) the
scientific evisceration of race as meaningful, and the narrowing of its reference to mere bodily signifiers with no signifieds, or meanings, race has never
been more reified as a factor of cultural identity. As a concept it is
acknowledged to matter in ever more important ways as it continues to
influence social legislation. In our unexamined effort to perpetuate race as
meaningful, the debate over hereditary race has today been displaced onto
questions of identity politics. Should the term race be conceived as a neutral
concept designating "human diversity," which is therefore worth salvaging
for its emancipatory power? Can or should race be separated from its
history of racist practice and doctrine? Can group identity organized along

the lines of racial difference ever overcome the pernicious exclusivism endemic to the concept? Among the most vocal figures representing the two sides of this debate within the academy in the US today are Anthony Appiah and David Goldberg.

According to Appiah (1992), any invocation of racial identity, even when it claims to be a "socio-historical" notion, and open to affiliations, etc., is always biologically grounded. In "Illusions of race" Appiah examines Du Bois' categorization of human races and his claim that the "Negro" race, "generally of common blood and language," has a special message for the world. Appiah rightly characterizes Du Bois' supposedly culturalist definition of race as produced in and as a dialectical opposition that invariably relies on the scientific or biological view which it contests. Delving into contemporary biological literature on "race," Appiah further elucidates the speciousness of genetic theories of racial difference.[5] Separating the "visible morphological characteristics of skin, hair, and bone" (1992: 35) from inherited "characterological" traits supposedly coded in genes, Appiah is at pains to disarticulate appearance, conceived as pure contingency, from destiny – pathological or political. "The truth," Appiah concludes,

> is that there are no races: there is nothing in the world that can do all we ask race to do for us. ... Talk of race is particularly distressing for those of us who take culture seriously. For, when race works – in places where "gross differences" of morphology are correlated with "subtle differences" of temperament, belief, and intention – it works as an attempt at metonym for culture, and it does so only at the price of biologizing what *is* culture, ideology.
>
> (Appiah 1992: 45)

Thus, for Appiah, invocations of racial belonging, whether Anglo-Saxon or African, are always false if not dangerous, insofar as they are grounded in an implicit biologism that is scientifically untenable. But Appiah's examination of the gene theory of races, to prove that so-called racial characteristics (such as aesthetics, aspirations, potentialities) are not heritable, overlooks an important point. Discrediting the scientific validity of race based on the relative invariability of genetic characteristics among so-called racial populations cannot in itself obliterate race or scientific interest in it. For as Colette Guillaumin suggests, scientific racial theory fixes on various localities of the body at different times, deploying signifiers that map the body according to convenience: "Rooted at first in the body or the blood, this ideology later shifted to the brain and nervous system, and has now taken refuge in the genetic and chromosome potential" (1995: 63). And at present that too has given way after *The Bell Curve* (Herrnstein and Murray 1996) to the measurement of IQ. In other words, arguing with science is only to displace race onto another locus of scientific investigation. Insofar as race is perpetuated as a meaningful category in our language, science will continue to furnish explanations of it. Arguing with race is at some level always a futile activity. As Guillaumin says with regard to such exorcising gestures: "Negations are not recognized as such by our unconscious mental processes. From this point of view, a fact affirmed and a fact denied exist to exactly the same degree, and remain equally present in our affective and intellectual associative networks" (1995: 105). It is precisely this unconscious resiliency of race that invites psychoanalytic exploration.

For Goldberg (1993), on the other hand, race is not necessarily a biological phenomenon. It is a virtually "empty concept" that articulates group identity for the sake of exclusion and inclusion and can overlap with any number of discourses on community, including ethnicity and nation. "Race has been able, in and through its intersections with other forms of group identity, to cover over the increasing anonymity of mass social relations in modernity" (1993: 81). Thus Goldberg insists that race must be grasped as a historically fluid concept that signifies differently according to the historical and material interests of the time. For him a key question is whether

> any generally abstract characterization approaching definition can be given to the concept of *race*. It should be obvious from all I have said that race cannot be a static, fixed entity, indeed, is not an entity in any objective sense at all. I am tempted to say that race is whatever anyone *in* using that term or its cognates conceives of collective social relations. It is, in this sense, any group designation one ascribes of oneself as such (that is, as race, or under the sign) or which is so ascribed by others. Its meanings, as its forces, are always illocutionary.
>
> (*ibid.*)

When using "race," Goldberg suggests, we must be clear about which signification we are employing. Quite predictably, Goldberg criticizes Appiah's view (that all references to race are always grounded in a covert biologism) as being too narrow and thus as overlooking race's productive aspect as a discourse of power (1993: 86).

> Classification, valuation, and ordering are processes central to racial creation and construction. The ordering at stake need not be hierarchical but must at least identify difference; and the valuation need not claim superiority, for all it must minimally sustain is a criterion of inclusion and exclusion.
>
> (1993: 87)

For Goldberg, race can be logically separated from racism, that is, from its legacy of racist practice. He writes:

Race has been conceptually well-placed to characterize freedom's routes, to channel freedom's mobility, and so to thrive in this age of ambiguity, for as I have made clear it is by nature (insofar as it has one) a concept virtually vacuous in its own right. Its virtual conceptual emptiness allows it parasitically to map its signification of naturalized differences onto prevailing social views ... to articulate and extend racialized exclusions. ... This prevailing historical legacy of thinking racially does not necessitate that any conceptual use of or appeal to race to characterize social circumstance is inherently unjustifiable. ... What distinguishes a racist from a non-racist appeal to the category of race is the *use* into which the categorization enters, the exclusions it sustains, prompts, promotes, and extends. ... Though race has tended historically to define conditions of oppression, it could, under a culturalist interpretation ... be the site of a counterassualt, a ground of field for launching liberatory projects or from which to expand freedom(s) and open up emancipatory spaces.

(Goldberg 1993: 210–11)

Goldberg's insistence on the emptiness of the concept of race is at first glance refreshing, in that the vacuity seems to account for the inexhaustible capacity of race to reproduce itself. However, by suggesting that "race is whatever anyone *in* using that term or its cognates" means by it, and that it is any "group designation" ascribed by oneself or by others, he elevates the term to a universal generality that evacuates it of its linguistic specificity. His view that cognates of "race," for instance, mean the same thing as "race," completely elides the hegemony of linguistic categories. It renders languages wholly commensurate with one another, and hypostasizes race itself as a "natural" element of difference that languages name in various ways. Goldberg's overtly Foucauldian emphasis on the productivity of race may appear potentially useful. However, his focus on the socio-historical formation of "racialized discourse," which refers to race as "meaning different things at different times," combined with his inattention to the specificity of language, is problematic. It serves to undermine his project, which is to argue for the political nature of "race." By universalizing race, Goldberg in effect conflates the Foucauldian notion of power itself with race as the effect and cause of discourse, thus making it impossible to pose the question of the *historicity* of "race." There is first the sociolinguistic counter-argument, also a historicist one, that we must take seriously. As Guillaumin and others have argued, the concept of race is specific to Europe and was invented in the late eighteenth to nineteenth century. Goldberg courts the danger of reifying race by universalizing it as the governing epistemological paradigm, when he ascribes racial thinking to groups that conceive their identities on the basis of other terminologies of difference (Guillaumin 1995: 61). Moreover, by separating race from racism and attempting to deliver it to a

culturalist reinterpretation, Goldberg reproduces the very problems of biologism that Appiah critiques with reference to Du Bois. But even more
importantly, by abstracting the concept from its historical or linguistic practice, Goldberg dislodges race from any mooring in history or language, thus
rendering it, in effect, a catch-all term for difference as such. Why race
should be salvaged as the only term that can offer emancipatory possibilities
despite its execrable history is never clear.

While both Appiah and Goldberg offer persuasive analyses of the
(academic) discourse of race, as representatives of what are now entrenched
positions on the race term, they fail to confront the fact that racial practice
is not fully covered by racial theory. There is a hiatus between racial theory
and practice in that the two can function quite independently of each other.
Thus to proceed as if an engagement with racial theory were to undermine
the foundations of racial practice is to misrecognize the structure of the
discourse of race. Etienne Balibar suggests that we regard "shifts in doctrine
and language [in race theory] as relatively incidental matters," given the fact
that from the point of view of the victims of racist practice, "these justifica-
tions simply lead to the same old acts" (Balibar 1991: 18). This does not
mean that race theory is irrelevant, or that we must focus entirely on racism
and racist practice at the cost of ignoring its more institutionalized forms.
Rather, as a first step, we must begin to recognize the double-edged aspect of
the rhetoric of race, where so-called theory and practice do not always coincide to produce the effect of causality. The inadequacy of critical race
theory with reference to practice is most evident in relation to cases such as
that of little Koen, with which I began. Interestingly, what is precisely at
play in this case is nature and culture, or biology and the social problems of
inclusion and exclusion that Appiah and Goldberg focus on respectively. For
instance, given Appiah's view that race evaporates with the exposure of
race's scientific or genetic fallibility, it is, interestingly enough, genetics itself
which is at the heart of this little racial "mistake." In his argument with the
Dutch-African-American philosopher W. E. B. Du Bois, Appiah demonstrates that race cannot be invoked, except through a specious use of
genetics, to define the destiny of a so-called people, or to delineate group
aspirations. However, what Koen as a Dutch-Afro-Caribbean child seems to
represent is precisely the relation between genes and destiny. At one level, we
may say that at the age of eight months, he has already been disqualified to
borrow at a bank. But more seriously, the irony of this particular case is that
genetic theory here does not serve to discredit racial identity; rather, the
DNA test establishes Koen as "black" boy (though born of a "white"
mother). Admittedly, Koen's parents are not suggesting that Koen is inherently incapable of borrowing at a bank, and neither is the DNA test a
verification of race as much as of paternity; identity and destiny here are
socially interpreted rather than genetically determined. However, the issue
remains that destiny is not uncorrelated to genetics. And no amount of

argumentation disarticulating the two will do away with the fact that because *something* is inherited as "race," your life is predetermined for you. As the Dutch parents testify, most of us continue to harbor deep-seated notions of racial inheritance, despite its scientific untenability simply due to genetic theory's claims to heritabilty as such. Some of us, as committed social constructionists, may perhaps disclaim this notion because science tells us that the relation between genes and racial identity and destiny is not one of simple predication. DNA tests can establish parentage, but they cannot establish a trans-historical racial identity. Nevertheless, the DNA test in this case does determine Koen's racial identity (and his non-creditworthiness), though not directly. The relation between genes and identity/destiny is no longer one of predication but implication. The notion of race as genetic inheritance can continue to be entertained when mediated by kinship relations: Koen's father is a "black man" from Aruba. It is a question, it seems of the signifier, of the Name of the Father, which imparts not only sexual and familial identity, but also racial. Thus the signifier establishes race at the same moment that genetics establishes kinship, and it is this synchrony that enables the simultaneous articulation of genes and identity/destiny, though not causally. None of this alters the fact that the bottom line in both arguments, whether that of predication or articulation, is of genetic inheritance. Thus I would affirm Appiah's argument that race is inextricably linked to inheritance. If we reduce the position of Du Bois and that of Koen's father into simple propositions, we see their logical similarity: "Black people (because they are born 'black') have an inherently valuable message for the world" (as this message is a factor of their racial inheritance); and "Black people (because they are born 'black') will always be poor" (which is a factor of their social inheritance based on their racial identity). Both statements leave intact the implication of race as inheritance and destiny. However, my skepticism is directed not at the contents of Appiah's argument but at its utility. Appiah's impulse to undermine race by interrogating its scientific grounds is academically valuable, but it does not address the way in which race recoups inheritance through other rhetorical means, such as articulation with kinship and recourse to visibility. It seems that, given the power of the notion of heritability as such, no amount of disputation with racial theory can dislodge the association one makes of race with inheritance. Race will continue to be articulated with kinship, with ethnicity, with culture, in ways that will require repeated purges of its claims to inheritance. Theoretical expurgations may be useful at one level, but they do not undercut the emotional force of an *ethnos* that race so effectively and resiliently enables. I argue that this effect is made possible primarily through race's ability to combine with narratives of the family and kinship in order to appear as a factor of inheritance. Race, then, derives its power not from socially constructed ideologies, but from the dynamic interplay between the family as

a socially regulated institution, and biology as the site of essences and inher-
itances. In fact, the more one attempts to render race as merely a social
construct, the more it contributes towards the naturalization of that
construct.

For instance, Balibar (1991) alludes to "neo-racism" as the audacious
naturalizing of "racist conduct" under the guise of a concrete pragmatism as
opposed to the ephemera of "abstract" anti-racism. Neo-racism or differentialist racism, according to Balibar, is a racism without races. What is
innovative about the new racism, according to Balibar, is its astonishing
"turn-about effect" which grants that while there are no biological races,
there are cultural differences that must be preserved at all costs. In an ironic
reversal of the arguments for cultural relativism, differentialist racism (with
its explicitly xenophobic agenda) argues that the "mixing of cultures" would
be fatal to humanity. As Balibar states:

> biological or genetic naturalism is not the only means of naturalizing
> human behaviour and social affinities. At the cost of abandoning the
> hierarchical model (though the abandonment is more apparent than real
> ...), *culture can also function like a nature*, and it can in particular
> function as a way of locking individuals and groups a priori into a
> genealogy, into a determination that is immutable and intangible in
> origin.
>
> (Balibar 1991: 22, original emphasis)

Thus Appiah's appeal to "communities of meaning" (1992: 45) cannot
itself escape the ossification of differences that is endemic to "race,"
anymore than his argument against racial science can undermine racial
thinking.

On the other hand, if race were merely the general marker of boundaries
between the in-group and the out-group without any necessary reference to
biology as Goldberg suggests, then we must ask about the "anguish" and
"devastation" reportedly experienced by Koen's parents. For race in all its
operational force here emerges not in the service of neat demarcations and
hierarchizations of groups, but in the moment when some anxious boundary
of inclusion and exclusion (perhaps rationalizable as nation, ethnicity, caste,
class, etc.) breaks down or becomes particularly vexed. In this case, what
should have been outside is inside, the excluded other is within the self, and
it is the self itself that has given birth to the other. It is to such a state of
"anguish" and "devastation" that we must turn to discover the workings
of race. Thus the notion that race cohabits comfortably now with nation,
then with class, or ethnicity, misrecognizes the way in which race actually
functions. If it were merely the historical construction that Goldberg asserts
it to be, then the parents' anxiety could be reduced to the pragmatic concern
they express about the boy's chances of getting a job or credit at a bank, and

as having nothing at all to do with them personally. But surely, their anxiety and devastation, their need for psychotherapy, indexes something in excess of pragmatic worry over the welfare of the boy, which could be easily allayed even by the media attention. In fact, the recourse to the language of social construction on the part of the parents – "let's face it, Dutch society is racist" – covers over that which their anxiety attempts to name. What then is race over and above that which is constructed? How does it insert itself into narratives of the family and kinship to produce the effect of inheritance? How does this sense of racial inheritance reproduce itself as common sense? How does it address the subject in his/her body and the unconscious, thus giving it a part in the familial process of subject constitution?

Racialist common sense asserts that race is a familial matter because we inherit our parents' physical features: little Koen looks different from Teun his twin brother. Thus the site where race as biological inheritance seems most insistent, and that which obsesses contemporary racialized societies, is visible difference. However insignificant it may be scientifically or philosophically, it seems to be of crucial significance psychically. This accounts for the bifurcation in the rhetoric of race between designations that are dependent upon a "theory" – philological, anthropological, or biological – of human difference such as Indo-European or Mongoloid, and the more commonplace designations of color, often correlated with cultures or nations (white, black, brown, red and yellow), which entirely flout "theory." What matters in racial practice today is visibility – the supposed evidence of the eyes – surface not depth.[6] Racial practice is ultimately an aesthetic practice, and must be understood above all as a regime of looking. It is necessary to focus on the way we reproduce the visibility of race as our daily common sense, the means by which we "tell people apart," a logic that is best enshrined in the Canadian phrase "visible minorities." To focus on racial visibility is not to suggest that race refers to brute marks on the body that are legible transhistorically and transculturally. As a first step, we must acknowledge that nothing about the body, its functions, its marks, or its sensations can be expected to carry stable meanings across time or space. It is neither "essential," something pre-given in nature, nor is it purely "cultural," comparable to other marks of difference displayed through clothing by members of religious orders, or class differences asserted through symbols by the aristocracy, or the branding of slaves and convicts.[7] Unlike these categories, race is a less determinate concept that invokes a system of classification according to "somatic/morphological criteria" which presumes that the bodily mark precedes the classification (Guillaumin 1995: 140). Though it is possible to retrace the genealogy of the visibility of race as manufactured out of purely contingent historical and material interests, these factors have only a partial explanatory power. While the visible references of race can realign visibility according to historical need, the fact of visibility itself remains constant. This intransigence is an outcome of the fact that the visible reference of race makes a claim to nature – it is about "telling," like "sex," who is this or that.[8] Unlike other forms of socially constructed difference, such as class or ethnicity, "race," like sex, appears as a fundamental and normative factor of human embodiment, something that one inherently is from birth. Thus, despite historicist arguments about its social construction, which may or may not be valid, there is a powerful *semblance* of necessity built into race that makes it ultimately intractable to constructionist claims. "Race," because it calls upon kinship, functions with almost as powerful a sense of constraint as sex, that great category of human difference whose analysis, whether biological, psychical, or cultural, is inevitably relegated to or grounded in the domain of the family. But one must be cautious about analogizing race with sex, a temptation that would greatly simplify one's analysis. To assume such symmetry would be to risk eliding the particular mode of embodiment entailed by race that only psychoanalysis can properly reveal. It would also foreclose our attempts to grasp race in its historicity, and its protean capacity to insert itself along with sex into the structure of the subject. For there is no denying the fact that race is after all a historical invention, and that like most inventions it veils the artifice of its origins. But that in itself is not interesting, for as I have already suggested, uncovering "race's" genealogy is not to address racial practice. What is confounding about race is its successful grafting to nature. Thus we must ask how race appears as the logic of human difference itself. Why do we allocate difference along certain conventional lines of looking? How do we come to be racially embodied? What is the structure of racial difference, and what insights can psychoanalysis offer in the study of the raced subject?

Argument

1   I propose the following working definition: the structure of racial difference is founded on a master signifier – Whiteness – that produces a logic of differential relations. Each term in the structure establishes its reference by referring back to the original signifier. The system of race as differences among black, brown, red, yellow, and white makes sense only in its unconscious reference to Whiteness, which subtends the binary opposition between "people of color" and "white." This inherently asymmetrical and hierarchical opposition remains unacknowledged due to the effect of difference engendered by this master signifier, which itself remains outside the play of signification even as it enables the system.

2   In order to understand how the signifier impacts the body, or how it institutes a regime of visibility, I will be interested in how race confronts its own historicity. The problem is not simply a question of race

disavowing the conditions of its historical emergence, whi/ implies that our task is to expose that process. While such ideoivь. critique is indispensable, it does not adequately account for the effects of nature that race produces. Rather than reduce race to the workings of power, I will focus on how race transmutes its historicity, its contingent foundations, into biological necessity. It is this process, a process that depends upon and exploits the structure of sexual difference, that one must grasp.

3　Lacan's theory of sexual difference as that which marks the breakdown of language, thereby indexing the subject of the unconscious as more than his/her symbolic determination, provides the analytical tools by which we may discern the subject of race. Race depends upon the sexed subject for its effectivity; the indeterminacy of the sexed subject is the fulcrum around which race turns. The signifier Whiteness attempts to signify the sexed subject, which is the "more than symbolic" aspect of the subject.

4　We infer the audacious workings of the signifier from moments when such signifying ambition fails. By focusing on moments of racial anxiety, we can discern that such affect is usually produced in relation to the subject's encounter with the historicity of Whiteness. The major consequence of such anxiety is the production of an object: the marks on the body that appear as pre-discursive. Racial visibility, I contend, is related to an unconscious anxiety about the historicity of Whiteness. This anxiety is the inevitable result of being subjected to the fraudulent signifier (Whiteness) which promises everything while disavowing its symbolic origins. These relations among historicity, the signifier, and anxiety are not necessarily causal.

A briefer statement of the argument of this book could be made as follows: Race is a regime of visibility that secures our investment in racial identity. We make such an investment because the unconscious signifier Whiteness, which founds the logic of racial difference, promises wholeness. (This is what it means to desire Whiteness: not a desire to become Caucasian [!] but, to put it redundantly, it is an "insatiable desire" on the part of all raced subjects to overcome difference.) Whiteness attempts to signify being, or that aspect of the subject which escapes language. Obviously, such a project is impossible because Whiteness is a historical and cultural invention. However, what guarantees Whiteness its place as a master signifier is visual difference. The phenotype secures our belief in racial difference, thereby perpetuating our desire for Whiteness.

We cannot reach an understanding of this all-important factor of racial visibility without clarifying the status of the signifier in the constitution of the subject. What is the relevance here of Lacan's axiom that the unconscious is structured like a language? Is he suggesting that the signifier is the foundation of the subject? It is worthwhile to sort out this issue in the context of a discussion about race, as it will lead to an insight into the difference and implication of race and sex in terms of the body. Therefore, in the following, I take up the function of the signifier in the constitution of the subject as the subject of the unconscious, situate Whiteness as the master signifier of racial difference, and then go on to pose the question of the relation between the signifier and the body, which is the proper site of our interrogation of racial visibility.

The subject and the symbolic order

What is the pertinence of Lacan's oft-repeated axiom that "the unconscious is structured like a language" to the subject of race? Does this mean that the unconscious is purely symbolic, thus rendering the subject an effect of the symbolic, here understood as the realm of culture? Race too, then, presumably, would be purely cultural, a construct, and the racialized body would be the imaginary corollary to that construction. Lacan's views of the relations between the subject and the symbolic, and of the "nature" of the unconscious itself, its various facets, have received uneven emphases in the work of most commentators. Perhaps it is not inaccurate to say that his views on the unconscious developed over the years, so that we can legitimately refer to the "early," "middle" and "late" Lacan. The Lacan of the 1950s, of the "Rome discourse" appears to stress the inscription of the subject in the symbolic order. In differentiating his theory from the tenets of ego psychology, which posited a view of the subject as autonomous, wholly integrated and self-possessed, Lacan's emphasis fell largely on the heteronomous and mechanistic order of signifiers which fundamentally constitutes, marks, and subjugates even as it distinguishes each of us as subjects. Thus the automata of the field of signifiers appears in this earlier phase to dominate much discussion of the nature of the subject. However, by Seminar VII through *The Four Fundamental Concepts* (Seminar XI),[9] Lacan seems to be focusing more than ever on the law of the symbolic order and its potential subversion by desire and the drives. Here the emphasis falls on the consequences wrought by the residue of signification, rather than on signification itself. In his later work, much of which remains untranslated, Lacan has shifted from "algebra" to topology. The emphasis is on the unconscious structure as built over or around a void, a fundamental lack (the real) that renders the subject quintessentially indeterminate. This shift in emphasis from the symbolic to the Real or, as some commentators have suggested, from the signifier (the phallus) to the cause of desire (the *objet a*) has great consequences for the understanding of sexual difference. Sexual difference and sexuality, Lacan suggested, could not be written. Insofar as the sexual relation as such is impossible, it is unrepresentable. Rather than a question of being or having the phallus (signifier or organ), sexual difference, in its radical dissociation from the signifier, is the crucial index of the indeterminacy of the subject (Copjec 1994). Without this development in Lacan's thought, it would not be possible to discern the functioning of Whiteness and its production of visibility. In what follows, I first consider the necessity of Lacan's early views on the subject of the symbolic for an understanding of racial identity. Then I go on to examine how the shift from the law of the symbolic order to the disruptive effects of the Real illuminates the status of visibility as a function of anxiety (the lack of a lack) in the structure of Whiteness.

It is not useful to conceive of the unconscious, the subjective locus of the Other or the symbolic order, as an inchoate and swirling eddy of repressed emotions and instincts. In "The agency of the letter," Lacan says: "I have alerted informed minds to the extent to which the notion of the unconscious is merely the seat of instincts will have to be rethought" (E: 147). No doubt there is room in Freud's texts for such a misdirected reading. As Lacan says: "the unconscious … [is] not a set of unorganised drives, as a part of Freud's theoretical elaboration might lead one to think when one has read in it that within the psyche only the ego possesses an organisation" (I: 66). In Seminar XI, Lacan is even more emphatic about the difference between the popular understanding of the Freudian unconscious and his own:

> The primal unconscious, the unconscious as archaic function, the unconscious as veiled presence of a thought to be placed at the level of being before it is revealed … above all the unconscious as instinct – all this has nothing to do with the Freudian unconscious, nothing at all, whatever its analytic vocabulary, its inflections, its deviations may be – nothing at all to do with our experience.
>
> (XI, 126)

The view of the unconscious as a subterranean space opposed to consciousness that is infested with an "individual's" repressed and prohibited memories and desires is, as Lacan points out in the "Rome discourse" and Seminar VII, a misreading of Freud. For Freud, it is the ideational representatives of affect, which Lacan equates with the signifier, that are properly unconscious and subject to repression, and not affects themselves which are much more evanescent.

One of the major problems of this commonplace view of Freud's psychical topography is that it produces an atomized notion of "the individual subject" (an oxymoron that Paul Smith [1988] has convincingly argued against) whose private pathology seems to resist the possibility of generalization. Not only does this view reproduce the problems of the private versus the public, but it also disengages the subject from what Lacan terms the big "Other," or the structure of language that constitutes the subject *qua* subject in the symbolic order. In short, it makes inter-subjectivity a matter of object relations between unified and wholly knowable "selves." For Lacan, Freud's "promethean discovery" (E: 34) is the emphasis on the primacy of speech and language. "Whether it sees itself as an instrument of healing, of training, or of exploration in depth, psychoanalysis has only a single medium: the patient's speech" (E: 40). Thus "what the psychoanalytic experience discovers in the unconscious is the whole structure of language" (E: 147). This radical shift in emphasis of the "meaning" of the unconscious has two immediate consequences for psychoanalysis in general that become pivotal for the analysis of race: first, it interrogates the intensely private notion of the individual as a product of personal psychology; second, this interrogation, grounded as it is in the structure of language, permits a level of generalization that opens psychoanalysis to an interrogation of the structure of language, and thus of the subject, prior to the meaning and the identities it produces. In the "Rome report," Lacan writes:

> the unconscious is that part of the concrete discourse, in so far as it is transindividual, that is not at the disposal of the subject in re-establishing the continuity of his conscious discourse. This disposes of the paradox presented by the concept of the unconscious if it is related to an individual reality.
>
> (E: 49–50)

Thus the unconscious is to be conceived not so much as an individual construct as an entity that bridges the subject to the general economy of signification. In other words, the necessary insertion of the subject into language implies his/her subjection to the general or shared universe of signifiers, which must come to represent one's desire. The important point here is that insofar as language pre-exists each of us, the subject in his or her specificity can come into existence only by borrowing the signifiers of its desire from the Other.[10] It follows then, that desire is always desire of the Other. Thus it becomes logically impossible to conceive of the atomized "individual" with an unconscious interior. On the contrary, in Lacan, the unconscious is outside rather than inside, in that it is the discourse of the Other, which is primarily meaningless, that produces subjective effects.

Given this perspective of the subject in language, the discourse of race and so-called racial identity is necessarily a function of language that situates the subject as raced within an economy of linguistic difference and meaning. It follows that the analysis of race should not be confined to the level of the ego and the ego ideal with its attendant mechanisms such as identification and introjection (and/or incorporation) of an object. In Seminar I, Lacan insists that "introjection is always accompanied by a symbolic denomination. Introjection is always introjection of the speech of the Other" (83). Thus bodily identity as well as one's own historical identity is engendered by the symbolic. What we introject as race is a signifier, a certain structure of signification, a way of slicing the world, of making meaning and of representing difference, that has its own logic or law that invests us as subjects with a semblance of coherence. My argument is that "Whiteness" should be discerned as an unconscious signifier, one that generates a combinatory with its own set of inclusions and exclusions that determine the subject. To be a raced subject is to be subjected to the signifier Whiteness. The law of Whiteness establishes race as a "neutral" description of human difference. Thus, as a mode of ordering the world, the signifier Whiteness installs a system of racial difference that is unconsciously assimilated by all raced subjects as a factor of language, and thus as "natural." In other words, Whiteness, as the inaugural term of difference, is the primary signifier of the symbolic order of race. In this sense, Whiteness is the transindividual aspect of the unconscious which subjects us all "equally" to the logic of race.

The law of the symbolic order must be grasped in its dual function as the determinant of the structure of speech and as the inexorable term of prohibition. In fact, language depends upon prohibition or a logic of exclusion, which gets manifested as cultural organization through the taboo against incest. We must therefore understand the discourse of race as a law with a certain structure, or productive capacity to organize difference founded upon a prohibition or exclusion of some sort. (I will take up the interdictory aspect of the law in the section on the racial symbolic and the moral law.) Let us here follow, very briefly, Lacan's thinking on the law as structuration in its pertinence to "race."

It is, of course, well known that Lacan derived his notion of the symbolic order from Lévi-Strauss' notion of the symbolic organization of culture. In his "Rome report," he elaborates on the relationship of language to the structure of kinship systems that Lévi-Strauss observed as a "universal" factor of social organization:

> In this structure, whose harmony or conflicts govern the restricted or generalized exchange discerned in it by the social anthropologist, the startled theoretician finds the whole logic of combinations: Thus the laws of number – that is to say, the laws of the most refined of all symbols – prove to be immanent in the original symbolism.
>
> (E: 66)

For Lacan, it is the discovery that the abstract, even meaningless, laws of number are ultimately manifested as social structure or kinship that fuels his entire theory of the Other. This Other is constitutive of the subject as the subject of language, and whose psychical organization is made possible by a fundamental prohibition. The reference here is, of course, to the structure of kinship as based on the incest taboo and the exchange of women. Lacan's emphasis here falls, in what has been perceived as a controversial move, not

on the reduction of women to signs that are exchanged on the basis of patri-
archally ordered kinship nominations (the name of the father), but on the
fact that

> this law, then, is revealed clearly enough as identical with an order of
> language. For without kinship nominations no power is capable of insti-
> tuting the order of preferences and taboos that bind and weave the yarn
> of lineage through succeeding generations. And it is indeed the confu-
> sion of generations which, in the Bible as in all the traditional laws, is
> accused as being the abomination of the Word (*verbe*) and the desola-
> tion of the sinner.
>
> (E: 66)

Thus, in establishing the relation between language and its "subjective
pivot" (E: 66) the incest taboo, Lacan, in effect, identifies a node between
signifiers and the law in its interdictory function. But what is of particular
importance to my project of delineating the structure of the discourse of
race is that this law of the symbolic is founded on a chain of signifiers whose
relation to signifieds and to cultural signs is not only arbitrary but to some
extent irrelevant. It is important to note that Lacan's formulation of the
unconscious does not trade in intrinsic meanings. He writes:

> If I say that everything that belongs to analytic communication has the
> structure of language, this precisely does not mean that the unconscious
> is expressed in discourse. *The Traumdeutung*, *The Psychopathology of
> Everyday Life*, and *Jokes* makes this transparent – nothing in Freud's
> detours is explicable unless it is because the analytic phenomenon as
> such, whatever it may be, isn't a language in the sense in which this
> would mean that it's a discourse – I've never said it was a discourse –
> but is structured like a language. This is the sense in which it may be
> called a phenomenal variety, and the most revealing one, of man's rela-
> tions to the domain of language. Every analytic phenomenon, every
> phenomenon that comes from the analytic field, from the analytic
> discovery, from what we are dealing with in symptoms and neurosis, is
> structured like a language.
>
> (III: 166–7)

The unconscious does not "express" itself through the dream, the slip, or
the joke. Rather it merely signifies the core, the residue of language which is
inexpressible in waking thought. The unconscious is discernible at another
level of speech from that of the speech of the ego; it is above all a chain of
signifiers that do not mean anything, anymore than that they refer to objects
(III: 167). If this logic is acceptable, we can extend it to say that race is
fundamentally a meaningless structure that constitutes "subjects of race"

with no potential whatsoever for any meaningful reference. The meanings we attach to racial identity, as stereotypes or as cultural history, will be structurally contingent, culturally inconsistent and ontologically incoherent. Racial identity seeks or locates its consistency on a different level – not meaning, but visibility – in order to retain paradoxically a semblance of lack or something extra-symbolic. I shall elaborate upon these points momentarily. I will for the moment look more closely at Lacan's theory of the symbolic law in its function as structure.

In his lecture on psychoanalysis and cybernetics, Lacan speaks of the game of odds and evens to ask "what is the chance of the unconscious, which in some way lies behind man?" (III: 300). Cybernetics, he suggests, has to do with conjecture, the order of binary oppositions that has an internal logic and does not necessarily convey meaning. Lacan uses the metaphor of the door – its peculiar oscillation between closing and opening – to describe the scansion of binary logic, its ordered action of a series of combinations. "The important thing here is to realise that the chain of possible combinations of the encounter can be studied as such, as an order which subsists in its rigour, independently of all subjectivity" (II: 304). The absence of inherent meaning in such a combinatory prompts Lacan to ask:

> What is the meaning of meaning? Meaning is the fact that the human being isn't master of this primordial, primitive language. He has been thrown into it, committed, caught up in its gears. ... We must marvel at the paradox. Here man isn't master in his own house. There is something into which he integrates himself, which through its combinations already governs. The passage of man from the order of nature to the order of culture follows the same mathematical combinations which will be used to classify and explain. Claude Lévi-Strauss calls them the elementary structures of kinship. And yet primitive men are not supposed to have been Pascals. Man is engaged with all his being in the procession of numbers, in a primitive symbolism which is distinct from imaginary representations. It is in the middle of that that something of man has to gain recognition. But what has to be recognised, Freud teaches us, is not expressed, but repressed.
>
> (II: 307)

The subject integrates himself into the order of meanings, which is governed by an abstract non-representational structure of material signifiers. "Man" must find confirmation of his place in the chain of signifiers, but paradoxically he is "man" because it is unavailable to him; he is marked or constituted by the signifier, which remains repressed. In relation to "race," we can assume the prevalence of a master signifier that is "introjected," that we identify with in our unconscious, and which gives us our sense of having a racial identity. We can already see how the discourse of race, insofar as it is symbolic, is already intimately related to or even dissimulates kinship and the nature of sexual difference that kinship entails. Though Lacan stresses the autonomy of the signifying chain in the constitution of the unconscious as that which carries its own logic of possibilities and impossibilities, he nevertheless underscores its subjective effects:

> While the subject doesn't think about it, the symbols continue to mount one another, to copulate, to proliferate, to fertilise each other, to jump on each other, to tear each other apart. And when you take one out, you can project on to it the speech of this unconscious subject we've been talking about.
>
> In other words, even if the word of my life had to be sought in something as long as an entire recital of the *Aeneid*, it isn't unthinkable that a machine would in time succeed in reconstituting it. Now, any machine can be reduced to a series of relays which are simply *pluses* and *minuses*. Everything, in the symbolic order, can be represented with the aid of such a series.
>
> (II: 185)

This fecund structure, marked by the play of signifiers, determines the subject's existence. This also implies that the structure, or this Other, speaks in and for the subject and remembers for him or her. The subject's memory, usually unconscious, is to be distinguished from remembering in the more narrativistic sense of the term. Lacan suggests that we

> mustn't confuse the *history*, in which the unconscious subject inscribes himself, with his *memory*. ... On the contrary, at the point we have reached, it is important to draw a very sharp distinction between memory and *remembering [rememoration]*, which pertains to the order of history.
>
> Memory has been spoken of as a means of characterising the living organism as such. One then says that a living substance, following a given experience, undergoes a transformation such that it will no longer react to the same experience in the same way as before. ... [T]here is no reason to identify this memory, a definable property of living substance, with remembering, the grouping and the succession of symbolically defined events, the pure symbol engendering in its turn a succession.
>
> (II: 185)

Subjective memory works like an automaton, marking and manipulating the subject even as it produces him or her in one's particularity. In relation to race, this model is again useful in catalyzing a major shift from essentialist, or even historicist notions of "racial memory," as hoary contents coded genetically, spiritually, discursively, culturally, in particular groups characterizing identity, to memory of race as contentless signifiers, a chain of difference reproduced mechanically by the functioning of language. How does such an understanding of the "memory" of race affect analysis? First, it must be acknowledged that the account I have given of "the subject of race" using Lacan's model of the symbolic is too deterministic. It is also incomplete. The subject is not simply the figure that emerges when all the dots are connected; the subject is also constituted or determined by the not fully inscribed page – the gaps in the chain that connect the pieces. This is a fundamental proposition in Lacan, and it is not the question of a shift in emphasis referred to earlier. What the unconscious also registers is the lack or the desire of the subject that can never be fully expressed in language. "The unconscious is, in the subject, a schism of the symbolic system, a limitation, an alienation induced by the symbolic system" (I: 196). This discovery of fundamental disjunction in the subject, that he/she merely marks a place between signifiers in a chain of signifiers, is the aim of analysis.

> The subject goes well beyond what is experienced "subjectively" by the individual, exactly as far as the truth he is able to attain. ... Yes, this truth of his history is not all contained in his script, and yet the place marked there by the painful shock he feels from knowing only his own lines, and not simply there, but also in pages whose disorder gives him little comfort.
>
> (E: 55)

In the deployment of Lacan's theory of the subject of the symbolic to "the subject of race," it is necessary to inquire what the subject of race desires. Also, what kind of access does race, as a chain of signifiers that determines the symbolic subject, have to "being," or that which is excluded by the chain? I will be suggesting that racial visibility is to be located precisely at this point of interrogation: it is the level at which race, or more properly its master signifier "Whiteness" aspires to being.

The above questions suggest that the model of the subject as determined by a chain of signifiers is necessarily incomplete insofar as it cannot account for sexual difference or more properly for the body. More questions emerge: If the unconscious is structured like a language, then how is the body constituted? If sexual difference is merely a question of the signifier, how do we account for the body's drives, or for sexuality that is often at odds with the logic of sexual difference? In relation to "race," to stop with the account of the symbolic function of Whiteness would be too premature, for it does not address the issue of visibility, or the relation of the signifier to the visible body, which is, after all, the inaugural point of this inquiry.

In order to take up in earnest the question of the body and of its constitution as raced, it is necessary to clarify the relation between the ego as body image and racial visibility. First, one must repudiate the notion that race is merely a process of specular identification, where a pre-discursive and pre-raced entity assumes a racial identity on the basis of certain familial others whose image it identifies with in a mirror relation. Such a notion is based on a simplified account of Lacan's concept of the imaginary and the mirror stage. I undertake the following discussion of the imaginary for two reasons: to suggest that insofar as the symbolic underwrites the imaginary, race must be understood as a symbolic phenomenon. It is a logic of difference inaugurated by a signifier, Whiteness, that is grounded in the unconscious structured like a language. This signifier subjects us all equally to its law regardless of our identities as "black," "white," etc. Racial visibility is a remainder of this symbolic system. Second, the process of becoming racially visible is not coterminous with the organization of the ego or the acquisition of the body image. In other words, the visibility of the body does not necessarily have to be a racial visibility. It is important that one disarticulate the two processes; otherwise racial visibility will seem to be an ontological necessity that is a universal verity of subjective existence as such.

Racial identification and imaginary ideology

> I emphasise the register of the symbolic order because we must never lose sight of it, although it is most frequently forgotten, although we turn away from it in analysis. Because, in the end, what do we usually talk about? What we go on and on about, often in a confused, scarcely articulated fashion, are the subject's imaginary relations to the construction of his ego. We talk all the time about the dangers, the commotions, the crises that the subject undergoes at the level of his ego's construction. That is why I started by explaining the relation O-Ó, the imaginary relation to the other.
>
> (I: 179)

It is commonplace to utilize Lacan's early essay on the mirror stage to analyze identification as a function of ideology. Althusser's much cited essay "Ideology and ideological state apparatuses" (1972), through its allusions to Lacan, construes ideology as a form of specularity whereby the subject (with a small s) is subjected to the capitalized Subject in a relation of mutual recognition. Althusser maps this "mirror-structure of ideology" (1972: 180) on a dual plane, and suggests that such "duplication" constitutes the *méconnaissance* that guarantees the hegemony of the ruling classes. Such an appropriation of Lacan's mirror stage could potentially be extended to resolve the conundrum of race as a (scientifically groundless) fraught looking. Insofar as racial differences are understood as being inscribed on the body as skin color, hair texture and bone structure, it seems inescapable that we should analyze race within the paradigm of identification. In fact, Lacan's emphasis on misrecognition as constitutive of the child's nascent ego as a "little other" seems to lend itself to the constructionist view of race as a "mistake" of or in the looking glass.[11] This is a powerful method of reading, and Fanon is perhaps the exemplar of such a deployment of Lacan for race.[12] In a long footnote in *Black Skin, White Masks*, he speaks of racial identification as it occurs in white and black children:

> It would indeed be interesting, on the basis of Lacan's theory of the *mirror period*, to investigate the extent to which the *imago* of his fellow built up in the young white at the usual age would undergo an imaginary aggression with the appearance of the Negro. When one has grasped the mechanism described by Lacan, one can have no further doubt that the real Other for the white man is and will continue to be the black man. The Other is perceived on the level of the body image, absolutely as the not-self – that is, the unidentifiable, the unassimilable.
>
> (Fanon 1967: 161)

Just as the white child constructs its ego ideal on the basis of an exclusion, the child in the Antilles, who looks in the mirror, also excludes its own color. Fanon contends that when Antilleans are asked to recall their mirror image, "invariably they reply: 'I had no color'" (1967: 162). "In the Antilles perception always occurs on the level of the imaginary. It is in white terms that one perceives one's fellows" (163). Further, "the Antillean does not think of himself as a black man; he thinks of himself as an Antillean" (148). For Fanon, the blackness of the Negro's body is a brute fact, and must found the subject's identification and not be displaced by identification with nation or ethnicity. Such misplaced identification for Fanon (he terms it the "mirror hallucination") is caused by the ideological power of French cultural imperialism. Ideology then pertains to the positioning of blackness: for the black child, disavowal – the inability to accept its own blackness, and for the white child, phobia – the inability to introject the other's image.

The above analysis of race, based as it is on a simple reading of the mirror stage, discloses several fundamental problems in the common-sense attitude towards racial practice.

1   If we reduce racial practice to racism, defined as power's agency to hierarchize and discriminate, we must accept race as an *a priori* fact of human difference. The concept of race as a system that fixates on arbitrary marks on the body becomes neutralized, and racism becomes the enemy. In other words, there is no possibility of interrogating the structure and constitution of the subject of race. The question "How do we become white, black, brown, or yellow?" will be foreclosed. We will fail

to discern racial practice as stemming from race rather than from racism.

2   By locating our reading of race on the *ostensibly* dual plane of the mirror relation alone, which leads to the simpler opposition now entrenched in cultural studies between the "self" and the "other," we risk confining race to a notion of the ego as false consciousness. Race, we will then be led to assert, is an illusory, narcissistic construct, and racism is an ego defense.

3   If the order of race or Whiteness pertained only to the subject's assimilation of his/her ego ideal, then race as such would seem to have nothing to do with the symbolic or the real of the unconscious, that is, with the psychical structure of the subject. It would seem to be free of the effects of the signifier, thereby rendering language "neutral" and free of "race."

As Fanon implies, racial visibility must be distinguished from the moment when the subject introjects an ego ideal as a coherent body image. But by marking the temporal difference in the constitution of the bodily ego and the raced body, we will see that the anxiety that Fanon refers to is not caused by the ideology of blackness, but by the structure of Whiteness. Less cryptically: we will see that racial anxiety, the unconscious anxiety that is entailed by the sight of racial difference, has its cause not in ideology, but in the structure of race itself, and in the functioning of its master signifier, "Whiteness." In the following, I return to the theory of the mirror stage, and examine the process of the integration of the bodily image to magnify the role of the symbolic in subtending the body image. I undertake this brief elaboration of Lacan's notion of the imaginary, which will be familiar to many readers, to clarify my claim that race cannot be mapped onto the simpler theory of misrecognition and ego identification, and that one can do so only through an inadequate understanding of the imaginary, and of the raced subject.

The most extensive discussion of the mirror stage can be found in Lacan's Seminar I, where he proposes, significantly, a "substitute" for the mirror stage in an optical experiment (I: 74). In between a concave mirror and a plane mirror, a vase out of the line of vision is inverted below a box, with a bouquet of flowers placed upright above it. The concave mirror reflects a "real" image which projects the vase upright with the flowers in the vase, with the image itself seeming to appear behind the mirror as with plane mirror images. Lacan utilizes this fairly commonplace optical experiment, in several variations, to characterize the mirror stage as both a "moment in development" and an "exemplary function," that reveals "the subject's relations to his image, insofar as it is the *Urbild* [prototype] of the ego" (I: 74, emphasis added). In other words, the mirror stage is not yet, properly speaking, the self-present moment of the total integration of the bodily ego, or what Lacan will term the ego ideal. Rather, it is a contingent moment when the primitive "ideal ego" is projected outside as the outline of a form that promises unity. It is a projection of a real image but not as yet a re-introjection of the image, which will necessarily have to be "libidinalized and narcissised" (I: 153) in an exchange with the image of the other, as the bodily ego. The ego ideal, as distinguished from the ideal ego, is the site of secondary identifications, and is a characteristic function of imaginary relations that literally enables the subject to *see* his "libidinal being" in relation to the other (I: 125–6). This is primarily because "for man the other has a captivating value, on account of the anticipation that is represented by the unitary image as perceived either in the mirror or in the entire reality of the fellow being" (I: 125). This captation by the other is also the process of the birth of the bodily ego, which is *always* mediated by desire.

> The subject originally locates and recognises desire through the intermediary not only of his own image, but of the body of his fellow being. It's exactly at that moment that the human being's consciousness, in the form of consciousness of self, distinguishes itself. It is in so far as he recognises his desire in the body of the other that the exchange takes place. It is in so far as his desire has gone over to the other side that he assimilates himself to the body of the other and recognises himself as body.
>
> (I: 147)

Identification, then, is always mediated by desire,[13] and clearly, one's own desire emerges in the Other. One consequence of this formulation is that the body is "factitious" (I: 147), insofar as human consciousness, which is bound to it, can nevertheless conceive of itself as distinct. Also, this ability of man to conceive of himself "as other than he is ... entirely structures his fantasy life" (I: 79). The body is constituted in a see-saw movement of desire. In fact, there can be no imaginary relation or ego function without desire, and when we invoke the term "desire," we are always in the realm of language and the symbolic.

The symbolic, then, is pivotal for the very existence of the mirror stage. The optical experiment that Lacan invokes to clarify the mirror stage concept emphasizes the importance of perspective. It is possible that the image may not be successfully produced if the mirror were to be inclined in one way or another. For Lacan, this is an indication of "the uneasy accommodation of the imaginary in man" (I: 140). As he says, "everything depends on the position of the subject. And the position of the subject ... is essentially characterised by its place in the symbolic world, in other words in the world of speech" (I: 80). This schema then suggests that neither the imaginary nor the mirror stage can legitimately claim an anteriority to the symbolic. Even though we tend to schematize "psychical development" chronologically, probing the structural relation of the three levels of the imaginary, the symbolic and the Real reveals that they are imbricated in one another in an inextricable fashion.

> *In other words, it's the symbolic relation which defines the position of the subject as seeing.* It is speech, the symbolic relation, which determines the greater or lesser degree of perfection, of completeness, of approximation, of the imaginary. This representation allows us to draw the distinction between the Idealich and the Ichideal, between the ideal ego and the ego-ideal. The ego-ideal governs the interplay of relations on which all relations with others depend.
>
> (I: 141, emphasis added)

The interplay of relations with others is governed by desire – a desire that is always of the Other. Desire must be understood in its mediating role between the image of the other and the consciousness of one's own body which the image engenders. That is, the subject cannot recognize his/her desire except as manifested by the other as his/her own "ideal form" (I: 176). Thus it is always alienated from the subject.

> In the human subject, desire is realised in the other, by the other. ... That is the second moment, the specular moment, the moment when the subject has integrated the form of the ego. But he is only capable of integrating it after a first swing of the see-saw when he had precisely exchanged his ego for this other desire which he sees in the other. From then on, the desire of the other, which is man's desire enters into the mediation of language. It is in the other, by [par] the other, that desire is named. It enters into the symbolic relation of *I* and *you*, in relation of mutual recognition and transcendence, into the order of a law which is already quite ready to encompass the history of each individual.
>
> (I: 177)

Insofar as the subject as ego cannot come into existence except in a symbolic relation (which always implies desire), it is logically impossible to isolate the imaginary or ego function from the realm of the signifier. Thus to speak of identification – sexual, racial, etc. – in terms of a mirror relation, as pure image, is to produce an untenable opposition between the image and the signifier, or a specious sense of "development" from the imaginary to the symbolic. Consequently, the body cannot be pure image, an ego identification produced in the mirror of error; it is, as Bruce Fink has insisted, "written with signifiers and is thus foreign, Other" (1995: 12). The signifier that constitutes the subject's body emerges from the Other as the expression of recognition or ratification of the mirror image, thereby enabling the image to be introjected. The imaginary body has a symbolic status. As a creature of desire, the subject invests in the signifier which marks it, and locates it within a matrix where "the body" is engendered in submission to the logic of the signifier. Thus to believe that we "have" particular bodies on the basis of a simple visibility is to ignore the function of the signifier in the production of the seeing subject. Thus the subject's corporeality is itself constituted as a coherent image through the intervention of the signifier. As Lacan recommends, "One should always work at the level of the alphabet" (I: 35). In other words, we must hunt down the signifier behind the image if we wish to discern the subject of race, or to put it even more precisely, we must grasp the contours of the lack that the signifier stands for, which in turn supports the body image.

The body image and the raced body

The above view of the ego and the body image raises the question of the relation of the ego ideal to race. What is the status of the master signifier of race in the constitution of the bodily ego? If we agree that the body image is constituted with the help of the signifier, then are all body images necessarily raced? Is Whiteness a founding signifier for the subject as such, and of his/her ego? Is the racial signifier necessary for the constitution of the bodily ego?

It is important that we not mistake the moment of the constitution of the bodily ego as the *necessary* moment when the body becomes racially visible. To do so would not be a sufficient departure from the erroneous belief that race is purely a question of misrecognition or identification with a mirror image. We would merely have added the factor of the racial signifier to the account of the mirror stage. There is no doubt that one can be constituted as a subject with a "unified" bodily ego without necessarily identifying with a racial signifier, or seeing oneself as racially marked. (The large point here is that race is not like sex. Not all are subject to the racial signifier.) We only have to consider the numerous accounts from literature and autobiography that enact the scene of becoming racially visible to oneself. Besides Fanon, who speaks of discovering that he is "black" during his first visit to France, there is Stuart Hall, who in "Minimal selves" says that for many Jamaicans like himself, "Black is an identity which had to be learned and could only be learned in a certain moment" (1996b: 116). This process of introjecting the signifier is repeated by other characters such as Janie in Zora Neal Hurston's *Their Eyes Were Watching God*, James Weldon Johnson's protagonist in *Autobiography of an Ex-Colored Man*, and by Oulaudah Equiano in his autobiographical narrative. There are doubtless numerous other examples that one could cite. The fact that the secondariness of race seems to apply only to so-called "people of color," and that there are rare, or virtually no instances of a so-called "white" person discovering his or her race may lead to several specious speculations such as: "black" people identify with "whites" as the latter are more powerful and define the norm. Such misidentification on the part of "blacks" leads to trauma when they discover the reality of their blackness (Fanon's thesis). Other problematic views might be that "white" people impose an identity upon those they have colonized in order to justify their dominance, or "whites" have no race or race consciousness; "whites" are not racially embodied, and this is an index of their transparency and power, etc. While some of these propositions might make some ideological sense, all of these conclusions nevertheless presume the pre-existence of "black" and "white" as if these were natural and neutrally descriptive terms. I would suggest that the difference among black, brown, red, yellow and white rests on the position of each signifier in the signifying chain in its relation to the master signifier, which engenders racial looking through a particular process of anxiety. Perhaps the more effective ideological stance may be not to raise race consciousness among so-called "whites," as scholars in Whiteness studies suggest, but to trouble the relation of the subject to the master signifier. One must throw into doubt the security and belief in one's identity, not promote more fulsome claims to such identity.

In the preceding discussion of the mirror stage, I suggested that the signifier should be understood as subtending the image, but what remains unexplained is the specificity of racial visibility and the anxiety that is attached to it. The question of racial visibility requires that one be more precise about the relation of the body image to anxiety and the function of the signifier. In race one finds one's place in the chain through the signifier, S1, S2, etc. that stands in for one through the process of naming. The signifier comes from the Other and makes a rigid reference to the subject in question. Nevertheless, to be subjected to Whiteness means that race impacts on the bodily ego as a regime of visibility. Certain marks of the body then become privileged and anxious sites of meaning. To grasp this moment of anxiety and visibility, one must turn once more to Lacan's notion of the imaginary. This time, what is necessary to note is not that the symbolic is in the imaginary, but rather the presence of the Real in the imaginary.

According to Philippe Julien (1994), Lacan's theory of the imaginary can be periodized into three phases: the first is the notion of the mirror stage as misrecognition marked by the jubilant hailing of one's future bodily coherence; second is the conception of the mirror stage and the imaginary as the demand of the child to the Other to validate its misrecognition, thus introducing the function of desire and the signifier; and the third is of the visible body image as that which is sustained by the object of anxiety. It is this last formulation of the imaginary, as elaborated by Lacan in Seminar X on anxiety and elsewhere, that is most valuable for an understanding of race.

In Seminar X, "Anxiety," Lacan revisits the concept of the imaginary to attempt "a more precise articulation between the mirror stage and, as the Rome report puts it, between the specular image and the signifier" (session

3, 28 November 1962). Interestingly, Lacan proposes that it is anxiety that will "allow us to go over again ... the articulation thus required of me" (28 November). Lacan insists in this session that the imaginary and symbolic are not to be understood as two phases of theory. He underlines the simultaneity of the subject's articulation to the small other, or the ego ideal i(o) and to the big Other, or the symbolic. He identifies "the inaugural link" between the little and big Other as emerging at that moment when the infant in its "so-called jubilatory moment," when it assumes a specular wholeness, "turns back towards the one who is carrying him. ... turns back towards the adult ... who here represents the big Other ... to ratify the value of this image" (28 November). Later in the same session, Lacan goes on to elaborate "two sorts of imaginary identifications: 1) that of o: i(o), the specular image," and "2) the more mysterious one whose enigma begins to be developed there ... the object of desire as such." Lacan's articulation of the object of desire (to be distinguished from the object cause of desire, the *objet petit a*) is a complex reworking of Freud's theory of castration anxiety. According to Lacan, during the child's so-called mirror stage, "the whole of libidinal cathexis does not pass through the specular image. There is a remainder" (28 November). This remainder is the phallus that "appears in the form of a lack, of a (minus phi)" (28 November). The paradoxical notion that the phallus *appears* as a lack indicates that something of "the subject" does not get imaged or symbolized, and this limit, which is also the mark of castration, is the object of desire. Unlike Freud, Lacan sees castration as not tantamount to anxiety as it makes desire possible. "What constitutes anxiety, is when something, a mechanism makes there appear ... at the place which corresponds to ... the object of desire, something ... [or] anything at all." In other words, when the place of the absent phallus is taken up by "something," anxiety ensues.

> Everything starts from ... imaginary castration, that there is no ... image of lack. When something appears there, it is because ... the lack is lacking. I would just like to point out to you that many things can appear which are anomalous, that is not what makes us anxious. But if all of a sudden all norms are lacking, namely what constitutes the lack – because the norm is correlative to the idea of lack – if all of a sudden it is not lacking – and believe me try to apply that to a lot of things – it is at that moment that anxiety begins.
>
> (X: 28 November)

Anxiety should not be understood as a threat to bodily integrity such as the fear of castration, but rather as "the lack of a lack." Anxiety, *contra* Freud, has an object, but it is no identifiable entity. Rather this object of anxiety is uncanny; it is a phobic object which ultimately sustains the body image. My point is that the racial body is produced in just such a process.

When the signifier of race, Whiteness, positions itself in the place of the minus phi as the object of desire, that is when its historicity is most apparent and productive of anxiety. This is because Whiteness, by attempting to signify that which is excluded in subject constitution, the more-than-symbolic aspect of the subject – the fact that he/she is not entirely determined by the symbolic or the imaginary – produces anxiety. There is a lack of a lack as it appears in that place that should have remained empty. It is a false door opening *not* onto a nowhere, but to an all-too-concrete wall. This anxiety then produces the uncanny object of race, the arbitrary marks on the body, namely hair, skin and bone. These marks then are properly the desiderata of race; they serve the function of the *objet a*. Uncanny and phobic, they make desire possible again by producing lack on another level. The difference between the visible body as an ego function, and the visible body as a function of Whiteness or racialization, can be understood as the difference between seeing and being seen. The subject of the imaginary is constituted as *seeing* by the signifier, whereas the subject of race is constituted as *seen*, the subject of the gaze, through a certain logic of the signifier. If racial identity is produced by the signifier, racial visibility is produced as a remainder, a phobic object, in order, paradoxically, to give consistency to the signifier. Racial visibility is always a function of anxiety, but one's place in the chain may determine what form that anxiety may take. Consider for instance, the Third Reich, where the system of race is installed as the promise of being. The lethal result is, of course, the policy of anti-Semitism that finds its locus in that most anxious regime of visibility that finds its object in minute and arbitrary bodily marks. By providing a psychical account of the regime of visibility, I suggest that we view the logic of anti-Semitism not as a "racist" aberration of difference, but as the kernel of all racial practice as a mode of looking.[14]

Race, sex and the moral law

My guiding question so far has been: why and how do we read certain marks of the body as privileged sites of racial meaning? The above proposition that Whiteness produces the bodily mark of race through the mechanism of anxiety requires that one specify more clearly the relation between race and sex. To suggest that the signifier Whiteness appears in the place of the object of desire is to assume a relation between race and sex in the constitution of the body. It is thus necessary to analyze this relation, and to do so we must return to that second interdictory aspect of the law of the symbolic order – the moral law – which in psychoanalysis is theorized exclusively in connection to the issue of sexual difference and sexuality. My method is not to work an analogy between sex and race, but to discover the ways in which race conjoins with sex to gain access to desire or lack – the paradoxical guarantee of the subject's sovereignty beyond symbolic determination.

Lacan discusses the moral law in the context of the ethics of psychoanalysis and its various aspects: his stunning exposure of the law's underside through the juxtaposition of Kant and Sade, the function of the superego, the mechanism of sublimation, and the dialectic of drive and desire. But here, I am interested only in that aspect of the law as it pertains to the body, particularly in its interdictory force as the Name of the Father, or the prohibition of incest. Insofar as this interdiction can be understood as providing a theory of the body, it serves as an entry into the topic of racial visibility.

In his "Guiding remarks for a congress on feminine sexuality" (1958), Lacan insists that while the somatic and the psychic are continuous, the organism and the subject are not. The organism, for Lacan, pertains to chromosomal and hormonal elements and to reproduction; it is the object of biology, but not of psychoanalysis. For the latter avows that the subject's unconscious, which possesses "a sexual reality," is not impacted by the organism and its functions. The organism is not characterized by "sex" in the psychoanalytic sense of the term. "Sex" pertains to the constitution of the body which is largely a psychical process. It would be a serious error to assimilate Lacan's notion of the organism to the "sex" of the sex-gender nexus that preoccupies feminism and queer theory. Cultural critics focused on uncovering relations of power mistake Lacan's notions of the organism on the one hand and sexuality on the other for sex and gender respectively, thus eliding his notion of sex altogether. Nothing can be further from his teaching. The simple binary between sex and gender in these discourses that plays out as nature vs. culture, essence vs. construct, pre-discursive vs. symbolic, etc. does not hold in Lacan's theory, where "sex" is neither nature nor culture. To "deconstruct" the sex-gender nexus as Judith Butler does, would be, in the realm of psychoanalysis, to misunderstand "sex." For Lacan, "sex" is neither pre-discursive nor symbolic. It is "the point of failing that the subject encounters in the signifying chain" (FS 1985: 119). According to the author of "The Subjective import of the castration complex" (FS 1985), "sex" (or sexual difference) can be grasped only in the context of drive theory and the function of the part: the part object and the partial drive. It is at the intersection of the circulation of the partial drive around the object, and the subject's own production of the part object, as that which is lost in its submission to the Other, that sex is figured as the singular libido, which Freud termed "the masculine libido." The libido is masculine because

there is no psychic representative of the opposition masculine-feminine. The essence of castration and the link of sexuality to the unconscious both reside in this factor – that sexual difference is refused to knowledge [savoir], since it indicates the point where the subject of the unconscious subsists by being the subject of non-knowledge. It is from here that what cannot be spoken of sexual difference gets transposed into the question with which the Other, from the place of its lack, interrogates the subject on *jouissance*.

(FS 1985: 120)

The sex of the body then is discerned only retroactively after the cut of the signifier, but crucially as that which is unavailable to the signifier. The libidinal, polymorphous body is thus wholly indeterminate, with a potential for *jouissance* that directly bespeaks the lack in the symbolic order. By inserting this third indeterminate element between organism and sexuality, Lacan indexes the body in its radical otherness, as that aspect of the subject that is beyond symbolic determination and is in the real.

Sexuality, on the other hand, though it too cannot be reduced to gender, pertains to the subject's symbolic position *vis à vis* the object and as determined by the cut of the signifier. Thus masculinity and femininity do not correlate to anatomy, though anatomy could intersect problematically with signification, particularly in imaginary symbolization where the organ is barred as phallic symbol that acts as the signifier of the other's desire, as "pre-disposition" (VII: 307–9). Masculinity and femininity would pertain to particular ways in which subjects make the sexual relation fail. As Lacan elaborates in *Encore* (Seminar XX): to take up a masculine position is to pursue the *objet a*, while to take up the place of the woman would be to pursue the phallus or enjoy the lack in the Other. The key point here is that psychoanalysis gives us three terms, not two: organism, sex, and sexuality, and they do not fit into the neat opposition between nature and culture. In psychoanalysis, though the somatic and the psychical are continuous, they are not identical. My concern here is the disjunction between sex and sexuality.

The dehiscence between the body and sexual difference is caused by the function of castration – the Name of the Father or the incest taboo. This is the moral law that causes the disjunction between sex (the radically Other body) and sexuality (the symbolic body) by forbidding a certain *jouissance* which is made possible by the fact that the law itself cannot provide a guarantee as to its meaning, the ultimate signifier of the Other's desire. The paradox of *jouissance*, Lacan suggests in the Ethics seminar, emerges from this lack. I shall not dwell on the familiar process of castration: its institution of the subject in the symbolic as a sexed subject, its harnessing of desire in the service of the symbolic order through the mechanism of fantasy (which maintains the distance between subject and *objet a*), and its inadvertent production of real desire for the lost object, the residue of the symbolic order. I want to delineate here, in shorthand, three aspects of the moral law directly pertinent to my thinking about race.

First, the moral law as the prohibition of incest, subsists at the node between the Real and the symbolic. It is, as Lévi-Strauss pointed out, universal and cultural. It is cultural insofar as it is the cause of sociality as such. Cultures may configure kinship differently, but what is universal is the deployment of prohibition between certain members of the family. Psychoanalysis attempts to account for that aspect of the prohibition that functions as a moral imperative. Insofar as it constitutes sociality, the prohibition is also responsible for the constitution of the subject as the subject of the law.

Second, psychoanalysis in its exploration of the function of prohibition reveals that the law, even as it constitutes the subject in the symbolic order, cannot provide a guarantee of its meaning, based as it is on the dead father. The law thus speaks with a forked tongue. By prohibiting *jouissance* it discloses the subject's potential for it. The ego ideal may persuade the subject to the supreme good, but the superego reveals that supreme good of the subject as nothing but the wish for that which is forbidden.

Third, the law, through its interdiction, makes possible kinship relations by legitimating certain alliances and refusing others as immoral and transgressive. Without the moral law, we would not be able to find our place in the symbolic order as subjects.

If we turn to the law that organizes race or the racial symbolic, we discover that it too subsists as a force of interdiction. In *The Elementary Structures of Kinship* (1969), Lévi-Strauss observes in passing that "incest proper ... even combines in some countries with its direct opposite, interracial sexual relations, an extreme form of exogamy, as the two most powerful inducements to horror and collective vengeance" (1969: 10). The taboo against miscegenation, which underpins other interdictory practices such as segregation, and various forms of discriminations, behaves like the prohibition against incest by organizing kinship relations, punishing transgressions, and offering subjects a place in the racial order. However, a closer examination of the racial interdiction will reveal that it does not so much bear a resemblance to the prohibition of incest, as it relies upon it. In fact, the prohibition against miscegenation varies considerably from the prohibition of incest. As Lévi-Strauss himself suggests, miscegenation laws combine with incest laws only "in some countries." It is thus a purely cultural and therefore wholly symbolical law; one may even say that at most it is a juridical rather than a moral prohibition. It does not appear at that node between the Real and the symbolic as the fundamental cause of sociality and subjectivity.

Insofar as the racial law is purely symbolic, to be a raced subject is to be symbolically determined. The racial symbolical cannot be said to be missing a signifier. Rather it supplies a master signifier (Whiteness) that appears in the place of the object of desire (that must remain absent for desire to be possible). Insofar as it is purely symbolical, the racial "law" cannot in itself bespeak the subject's, or more properly the body's, potential for that Other *jouissance*, which emerges at the site of a lack in the symbolic order. The law of race is not lacking; it supplies its own guarantee by equating Whiteness with being. Thus the doubled aspect of the moral law that makes possible an enjoyment even as it forbids it in the name of the good should not be thought as having a parallel in the law of race; rather the racial symbolic calculates its success, as we shall see shortly, upon the doubleness of the moral law. Also, racial law does not have the moral authority of the incest taboo. Its good, expressible only as purity, and eugenic health, cannot lend itself to the structure of the categorical imperative that characterizes the moral law. The good or the morality of race does not so much slide into its opposite, as itself being subject to continual interrogation as a good. The law of race is groundless, without a foundation of truth, but it is not indeterminate. Thus we can say that the moral law, insofar as it can provide no guarantee of its meaning, indexes the radical indeterminacy of the subject, while the racial law in its function as social or symbolic determinacy (Whiteness is its guarantee) is necessarily groundless (a function of citation) but not indeterminate. We can deconstruct race as performativity, but not "sex." The moral law given its own lack renders sex unknowable.

Finally, it is in its bearing on kinship that the racial symbolic discloses its parasitic dependence upon the moral law. The prohibition of miscegenation must be understood not as a law that resembles the incest taboo, but rather as one that threatens it. The law of race undoes the moral law. In the racial realm, the taboo against incest plays no role, as those racially other can never be admitted or acknowledged within the family structure. In slave regimes, particularly the type that prevailed in North America, slave women, we may recall, were fair game for their owners. The master could cohabit with his slaves, and the children he bred upon his slaves, with absolute impunity. The strict separation between those who were kin (racially similar people) versus slaves (racially dissimilar people) rendered the incest taboo void à propos the latter group. The slave owner could play out his fantasy of the primal father of the original horde whose murder Freud posits at the origin of the moral law. *Thus the racial symbolic, and the taboo of miscegenation make incest, "or the time before the moral law," possible even as it upholds the law at another level.* If the incest taboo dictates who one may or may not cohabit with or marry, it presupposes the boundaries of the family, whereas the racial symbolic intervenes at a more fundamental level and presents a selected view of the family which considerably limits the effectivity of the moral law. The threat that miscegenation poses to the moral law explains the horror and fear that Lévi-Strauss alludes to as one of the inducements to collective vengeance. All raced subjects have cause to fear miscegenation as it could render the moral law inoperative.

However, one would imagine that the voluntary act of marrying one's slave or racial other, thus defying the power of the law of race to define the boundaries of the family, and thereby giving the racial other a symbolic status, would allay that fear. But as we know, that is hardly ever the case. Racial intermarriage can be just as reviled as cohabitation, if not even more, by all races involved. The logic on both sides is, perhaps, that one can cohabit with "them" but one does not have to go so far as to marry one of "them." Moreover, we cannot attribute the fear of the "black" mother whose son or daughter is "dating" someone "white" or the horror of the "white" parent confronted with a "black" son- or daughter-in-law merely to social causes. But even less does it make sense to say that the parental fear stems from the possible breakdown of the incest taboo. Marriage after all is at hand, and along with it kinship relations. The fear stems then not from the horror of suspending the incest taboo which pertains to cohabitation, but from the fact that the law against miscegenation is more than its prohibition of marriage and cohabitation; its essential function is to deny legitimacy. Here it behaves just like the incest taboo; it refuses in a purely arbitrary fashion to grant symbolic status to certain kinds of unions and their issues. You may marry your slave mistress, call her Mrs., acknowledge her children as your own, but the logic of race will, could, may always say: she is still a whore and the children nothing but bastards. The fear of miscegenation, then, is not allayed by marriage because its threat is always the loss of one's symbolic status. *The prohibition of miscegenation should above all be understood as the tenacious refusal to grant legitimacy in order to preserve the possibility of incest.* Whiteness puts itself in the very place of being; it attempts through a purely symbolic mandate to signify the very thing that is lacking in the moral law. However, insofar as it too addresses itself to kinship, it seems to bear a resemblance to the moral law, but this is a very superficial resemblance, for its *raison d'être* is to escape or even circumvent the moral law, even as it upholds it ferociously at the level of the racial family. This ferocious defense is best disclosed in the anxiety generated by the white woman who cohabits with a black man, for it will not be so easy to deny legitimacy to the children of such a union. Such a child already marks its presence in the family, and demands symbolic status, thus rendering the expulsion of the mother as the only viable and melodramatic solution.

How then does the racial law pertain to the body? I have suggested that the moral law engenders the body in its radical otherness as sex, and sex is discernible only as the misfire of the symbolic order. What about the racial body, the body that appears as the alibi of a certain regime of visibility? Though race in its invocation of embodiment seems universal, given its material foundations and cultural delimitation as a discourse, it is also wholly bound by the field of signification. The concept of race, as a chain of meanings that privileges certain parts of the body, is not transcultural. Unlike sexual difference, which is founded on the real-symbolic law of the prohibition of incest, *the law of racial difference is thoroughly historical and historicizable*; besides, its interdictory force is ambiguous and fungible. Nevertheless, there are some objections that one could pose to the above discussion that one must take up.

First, the fact that the racial law suspends the incest taboo: it could be asserted that if race can nullify the incest taboo, and make *jouissance* possible, then it must be "real sex" – the sort that no subject of castration can properly have or be. Second, it can also be asserted that race does have transcultural effects that do not pertain to discourse: namely the visible marks of the body that seem to precede signification. We can then ask: Are the racial marks of the body such as texture of hair, pigmentation, bone structure, indices of something unknowable like "sex" that make language fail? Does language fall into contradiction with itself at the point of race? Does it hit something Real, which cannot be grasped and understood by language?

One must make one's way through these questions carefully. I want to argue two things simultaneously:

1   Race is entirely captured and produced by language. The racial symbolic is not lacking; it is not missing a signifier that wholly and adequately captures the compass of the raced subject. This is because, though the law of racial difference may seem identical to the voluptuous law of sexual difference that produces enjoyment by forbidding it, the enjoyment is purely imaginary. The fact that the racial law can suspend the law of incest should not be construed as the *jouissance* engendered by the lack in the symbolic order. Its *jouissance* is wholly of the phallic type, and insofar as its interdiction is a symbolical one, it cannot have any real purchase on the body in its radical otherness. As a symbolical law, race has no access to the body in its otherness. Not only does it have no "real desire" of its own (there is no specificity to the desire of the raced subject other than its "desire" to symbolize totality), it effectively blocks access to desire and lack by attempting to fill that place with the signifier. The racial symbolic is a success story.

2   The notion of the success of the racial symbolic is consistent with the indeterminacy of the subject as such whose cause is *not* socially immanent. I rely here on Joan Copjec's formulation in *Read My Desire* (1994), but would like to add another step to her argument. Copjec asserts that it is the sovereignty of the subject, its radical incalculability that serves as a bulwark against "racism" and preserves difference as such. She too argues that race is symbolic, but she does not examine the relation of symbolic difference to the incalculable difference of the subject. I would suggest that the incalculability of the subject is not in and of itself a bulwark against racism (here construed as the noncoercive preservation of differences), rather, it can serve as an alibi for race to articulate itself with and as sex. In other words, the symbolic origin of the raced subject is articulated (as we saw with the incest taboo) in relation to lack, and the racial signifier Whiteness attempts to signify that impossibility. It is this dangerous and illegal articulation that we must prise apart in order to preserve the sexed subject as the failure of the signifier.

How does race articulate itself with sex? How does it produce extra-symbolic effects? I would suggest that race aims for the body in its otherness[15] by disavowing its own historicity. For what the racial symbolic promises the subject is precisely access to being. Whiteness offers a totality, a fullness that masquerades as being. Thus for the raced subject, to encounter the historicity of Whiteness is particularly anxiety-producing. In other words, the cause of the raced subject is its own disavowed historicity. I refer not so much to the fact that race is *historiciz-able* (that it has at its origin some historical, cultural or social cause) but rather to the phenomenon of its *historicity* (which is the delimitation of race as a regulative norm at the expense of its natural universality) that radically exposes the subject to its own linguistic limit. To encounter one's subjectivity as an effect of language, and not as an enigma, is anxiety-producing not because one is reduced to a construct (what would that really mean experientially?) but because it implies the foreclosure of desire and the possibility of being. It is to discover that the law of racial differ-ence is not attached to the Real. What the raced subject encounters, in a given moment of anxiety, is the law as purely symbolical. This is to confront the utter groundlessness of the law of racial difference, to discover that the question of one's being is not resolved by Whiteness, but that Whiteness is merely a signifier that masquerades as being and thereby blocks access to lack. To pose the question of being in relation to race is to face that there is not one. It is here that we must situate social and juridical laws against discrimination as well. Like the prohibition against miscegenation, our legal prohibitions, couched in the language of respect for difference, ultimately serve to protect the paradox of Whiteness. The paradox is that Whiteness attempts to signify the unsignifiable, i.e. humanness, in order to preserve our subjective investment in race. The Other of race, in short, is not lacking; there is no "hole" where being could be promising *jouissance*. All of race is expressed and captured by language.

Thus the raced subject experiences anxiety, which is a consequence of encountering the lack of a lack. It is as if the jigsaw puzzle were complete, but there were still a piece left over for which there is no place. Anxiety is an affect, according to Lacan, that appears when there is no possibility of desire, when there is a "lack of a lack." For the raced subject, the anxiety experienced by its encounter with historicity produces an object. Anxiety, Lacan maintains,

> is not without an object ... the object *petit a* is what falls from the subject in anxiety. It is precisely the same object that I delineated as the cause of desire. For the subject, there is substituted, for anxiety which does not deceive, what is to function by way of the object *petit a*.
>
> (*Television*: 82)

The *objet a* that race produces is a lethal object, its own disavowed historicity, produced out of the lack of a lack – a phobic object that tries to make the barred Other, the desire of the symbolic, exist. This phobic *objet a* I suggest is localized as the pre-discursive mark on the surface of the body. The effect of "nature" that race produces emerges from its anxiety, its disavowal of its own historicity. This is the peculiarity of race which is neither in the Real, like sex, nor wholly discursive, like class or ethnicity.

To recapitulate: race has no Other *jouissance*, no lack, no barred Other. Its symbolical origin, however, does not render it simply historical for it relies for its effectivity on a phobic object that exceeds biological and historical explanations of identity. What this means is that one encounters the limits of one's subjectivity as an effect of language, and the question of being as not so much that which escapes articulation, but as one that is extinguished or foreclosed. Thus what the study of race offers to psychoanalysis is a view of historicity that is not only about the ungraspable, non-signifiable limit, but about the horrific confrontation of the subject with its own signifying totality, the anxiety of suffering the recognition that there is no enigma to racial difference or to the raced subject. Thus what we see repeatedly in cases of racial anxiety is the attempt to constitute that enigma through an object that has no real consistency. An analysis of the prohibitions of miscegenation and incest reveals the intricate entwinement of race and sex as a struggle waged in the subject for a desire that can never be its own.

The historicity of Whiteness

I have argued so far that racial identity is made possible through the introjection of a master signifier of a system of differences – Whiteness. Whiteness produces the bodily mark and thus engenders racial practice by disavowing its own historicity in attempting to signify the "ground" of the subject itself. In constructing this argument, with the intention of exploring how a concept that is purely cultural and historical can nevertheless appear as a bodily fact, I have assumed Whiteness in its historicity to be the master signifier of the logic of race without any explanation of this heuristic choice. In the following, I present what I acknowledge to be a highly speculative genealogy of Whiteness. I take this intellectual risk in order to begin a long overdue discussion about the historicity of Whiteness in its capacity to produce extra-discursive effects – the marks of the body, a certain effect of visibility. Why did Whiteness emerge at a particular historical moment? How did it produce a regime of visibility that presented race as a factor of human embodiment? What is the relation of Whiteness as master signifier to the identity of "white" people who are supposed to possess Whiteness?

In Teresa Brennan's (1993) theory of the foundational fantasy of Western modernity, as informed by what she terms the "logic of denial" (1993: 171), the denial of the agency of objectified entities such as nature, the mother,

God, and even the father, provides a historical scaffolding for an analysis of Whiteness. She suggests that it is historical thinking itself that is eroded by the foundational fantasy which is materialized through a particular mode of production narrative:

> "History", as the sense of the sequence of past events, is increasingly moulded by the extent to which a foundational psychical fantasy makes itself materially true, and by its consequent material effects on the individual psyches that entertain the fantasy. That is why grasping the fact that the fantasy has become a material narrative across time is so critical, if so difficult. It is critical in creating a monolithic view of history which has a material basis in the present, but which had to cover all sorts of local differences to attain supremacy. Even so, these differences still erupt, in uncovering what the written record has not included hitherto. In this respect, scholarship, as the uncovering and correcting of what has been omitted or distorted, is always anti-foundational.
>
> As we have seen, the materialization of the narrative is also critical in creating, and then undermining, the historical sense as such.
>
> (Brennan 1993: 178)

Thinking of Whiteness historically thus entails thinking through its historicity – the material effects of race as political, existential and historical fact – and the traumatic Real of such history that insists upon symbolization. One historicist way of approaching Whiteness is to regard it as the *unconscious* core of what Samir Amin has termed Eurocentrism (Amin 1989).

According to Amin, Eurocentrism is a characteristically modern formation and is to be distinguished from other "banal" ethnocentrisms which merely testify to the "limited horizons" (Amin 1989: vii) of most cultures. As a specific determinant of modernity, Eurocentrism "implies a theory of world history and, departing from it, a global political project" (75). As an offshoot of the ideology of capitalism which demands a universalism "at the level of scientific analysis of society as at the level of elaboration of a human project capable of transcending its historical limits" (103), Eurocentrism exists in a tension between the global aspirations of capitalism and the particularism of Enlightenment race theories. Amin suggests that the "real contradiction" (105) between the culture of Enlightenment, which narrativized the superiority of Europe and the universalism of capitalist aspiration, is finally reconciled in the notion of race, which sets up Europe or the "eternal West" (89) as the standard for the world to emulate. Balibar's critique of Eurocentrism parallels Amin's, but he quite rightly suggests that the universalism of humanist Europe is itself subtended by a racial logic insofar as the latter applies "pseudo-biological notions to constitute the human race and improve it or preserve it from decline" (Balibar 1991: 59).[16]

It is, however, the reinvention of Europe – rational, humanist, secular, individualist, progressive – with roots in classical Greece, that is of crucial significance for an understanding of the structure of race. In other words, it is the nineteenth-century shift from biological to philological views of race that truly secures Eurocentrism. Amin inveighs against the northern European "myth of Greek ancestry" (1989: 90) as "constitut[ing] the core of the Eurocentric dimension of capitalist culture" (XI). The claim to Greek rationalism certified the uniqueness of Europe's capitalist triumph while simultaneously producing the Oriental world as its opposite (91). Drawing on Martin Bernal's seminal and controversial work *Black Athena* (1987), Amin argues that the new racialized Europe, by successfully excising the Afro-Asiatic roots of ancient Greek language and culture, misappropriated Greece from its Levantine context:

> In fact, up to half of the Greek language was borrowed from the Egyptian and the Phoenician tongues. But linguistics invented a myste-rious "Proto-Aryan" language to take the place of this borrowing, thereby safeguarding a myth dear to Eurocentrism, that of the "Aryan purity" of Greece.
>
> (Amin 1989: 93)

For Amin, the "racist hypothesis" (1989: 94) secures the artificial continuity between classical Greece and contemporary Europe: the co-optation by linguistics of sociobiological classificatory models to propose the opposition between the Indo-European and the Semitic (Hebrew and Arab) families of languages, which constitutes the hegemony of dominant Eurocentric ideology. This node in Amin's analysis – the postulation of the Proto-Aryan language as the kernel of the Eurocentric nexus of universalism, capitalism, and racism – is the locus of what I have identified as the primary signifier of the discourse and system of race: Whiteness. As the hypothetical center of Aryanism, this Ur-language can be construed discursively as the signifier of race, the structuring One of racial classification and visibility. The power of this signifier should not be underestimated; it is more than the evocation of a hegemonic and transcendental ideal (or signified) for the world. In fact, Amin's view (and it is one shared by Edward Said and Martin Bernal) that Eurocentrism is a resolutely tendentious ideology that installs the racist dichotomy between the European "self" and the Oriental "other," cannot fully account for the autochthonous nature of the concept of race. The structure of Eurocentrism aims at a universal logic of differ-ence, and we cannot discern this logic if we remain fixed on Eurocentrism as an ideology or a transcendental signified. What Eurocentrism discloses is the functioning of a new logic, a logic that is founded on race as a system that not only establishes hierarchy, but one that organizes human groupings in general. This logic, this chain of relations is made possible by a transcendental signifier – Whiteness. Whiteness functions as the signifier that engenders an "array of associations" among culture, language and nation. What is important here is the manner in which Whiteness as the signifier of race installs itself as the irreducible element in the organization of human difference and diversity, thus setting up an equivalence between language and race, which then gives way to language and culture, language and nation, language and authenticity. The modern system of race, which functions as a regime of visibility, can only be founded in the moment when language gets territorialized and biologized. Eurocentrism, which is an ideology, is only a manifestation of such a logic; (corporate) multiculturalism can be understood as another. In other words, both Eurocentrism and multiculturalism, though politically opposed to each other, covertly share the logical assumption of an organic relation among language, culture and biology.

The relation of Whiteness as the master signifier to so-called "white" people should be examined. There are two popular modes of analyzing Whiteness that are often run together, from which the present theory of Whiteness as a signifier should be distinguished: first, there is the comparatively young field of "Whiteness studies" that posits a notion of Whiteness as a property of a group of people, and as an outcome of negations, born out of oppositions; and second, there is the older notion that racial practice emerges out of encounters with different "races." In the American context, Roediger (1994), for instance, suggests that "in its production of identity through negation ('We are not Black'): and in the record of behavior it has called forth, Whiteness in the US is best regarded as an *absence* of culture" (n. 21, 196). Such an argument about the fundamental vacuity of Whiteness should not be conflated with the notion that racial logic emerges in the European encounter with non-Europeans during the period of geographical exploration. The latter deduction is problematic in that it assumes races as having an existence prior to racial practice. It thus effectively hypostasizes the logic of race. It is perhaps more to the point to discern the ways in which, as a geographically localized peoples, Europeans were always already subjected to the regime of racial looking prior to their encounters with so-called "black" and other "peoples of color." In other words, so-called people of color can be said to have been racialized by a specifically self-constituted group, called "white people," that is characterized by its subjection to the law of racial difference. The "contact zone" is already racialized and inscribed within a racial symbolic by the signifier of Whiteness, which largely functions to subsume and homogenize incommensurable differences. Whiteness, as the structuring principle of race, emerges through a splitting; in other words, it emerges not through a conflict with the alien and the external, but through an internal conflict among national, class and ethnic forces.

Hannah Arendt (1973) in a chapter entitled "Race thinking before racism" provides an explanation of the origins of race, and its two ideological modes.

Arendt's intention is to revise the popular view of race as a concept with German origins to locate its genesis instead in revolutionary France. Though she begins by suggesting that race is a competing doctrine with class struggle and nationalism, the core of her argument is that race was invented as an aristocratic ideology to counter the threat of emerging national consciousness. In its anti-nationalistic, pan-aristocratic focus, race sought to justify the claims of the ruling classes against those of the inferior classes. It is to Comte de Boulainvilliers, "a French nobleman who wrote at the beginning of the eighteenth century and whose works were published after his death" (1973: 162) that Arendt attributes this invention. She writes: "In order to regain uncontested primacy for the nobility, Boulainvilliers proposed that his fellow-noblemen deny a common origin with the French people, break up the unity of the nation, and claim an original and therefore eternal distinction" (162). The "historical claim" (164) was that the aristocrats represented the conquerors of France who were of Germanic rather than Gallic or native French origins. According to Arendt, the irony is that "Frenchmen were to insist earlier than Germans or Englishmen on this *idée fixe* of Germanic superiority" (164–5) that was given final shape by Comte de Gobineau in the nineteenth century.

If French racial thinking was anti-nationalistic, then German race thinking, which developed later than the French after the defeat of the Prussian army by Napolean's forces, was a weapon to induce national pride among Germans. As an ideology aimed at uniting the masses, race thinking, Arendt suggests, was egalitarian and merely nationalistic. Arendt is eager to defend German nationalism from charges of racism, and contradictorily even from race thinking. She concedes that "organic naturalistic definitions of peoples are an outstanding characteristic of German ideologies and German historism" (1973: 166). But she also insists in the next sentence that these definitions are not yet "actual racism," by which she means the assertion of the inherent inequality of human races. Her argument, mounted as it was in the 1950s as a study of totalitarianism, is persuasive if only due to its boldness and novelty: it flies in the face of common knowledge. But perhaps it is her very defense of Germanism (read particularly in the light of her rather ignorant comments about Africans in the next chapter[17]), that invites a closer reading of her rhetoric. The key sentence is the following: "As long as common origin was defined by [German nationalists as] common language, one can hardly speak of race-thinking" (166). What Arendt misreads here as mere linguistic patriotism is, of course, the moment of the naturalization of language as race and territory. Without the linguistic basis, race could never obtain the "folk" consistency that it continues to have. Surely, it is the notion of a particular language and language groups as expressive of the "genius" of particular geographically localized peoples that is at the foundation of race thinking? Physiognomy is, of course, enlisted in the service of such a homogeneous perspective, so that it becomes the index and guarantee of racial difference, but it could never be, even according to Arendt's own thesis, the origin of race thinking.

Since it is with the birth of comparative grammar that language could be thus essentialized, perhaps we should review, rather cursorily, the German investment in the notion of the proto-Aryan language, which I have suggested is the locus of Whiteness. While I possess neither expertise nor even much familiarity with the field of comparative grammar or philology, I here turn to Raymond Schwab's magisterial *The Oriental Renaissance* (translated in 1984) as potential guide through this heavily guarded scholarly terrain. Schwab suggests that the notion that the ancient languages of Greek, Latin, Avestan and Sanskrit were once related and perhaps emerged from a common source predated the concept of the Aryan. He cites Volney as an early theorist of the idea (1984: 174), and also attributes William Jones (the pre-eminent Orientalist and founder of the Asiatic Society of Bengal) with having suspected the possibility of a familial relation between the Oriental and Germanic sources. However, it is with the rise of comparative grammar in 1816, as pioneered by Franz Bopp and taken up by Schlegel and Klaproth, that the particular concept of modern Aryanism, or what was popularly known as Indo-Germanism, emerged as an explicit principle of discriminatory logic. As Schwab states:

> the explosive element inherent in a certain manipulation of linguistics was ignited when Germany came into contact with Avestan and Sanskrit. In 1823, Klaproth calmly awarded his Indo-European fatherland the appellation Indo-Germanic. This was the beginning of a single adventure which was to lead Europe and civilization far astray.
>
> (Schwab 1984: 184)

Klaproth's appropriation of the Indo-European as the Indo-Germanic, in other words the assumption of German as the purest surviving form of the original Aryan language, and of Germans as "the chosen people," Schwab suggests, "insured Germania birthrights and race-rights for the very near future" (1984: 184). This is the decisive moment, when a new genealogy of the Indo-European is invented (the effective excision of the Afro-Asiatic roots of Greek and Latin) with the consequent demotion of the neo-Latin languages to a secondary status, and the valorization of Germanic languages, especially German, as the superior and pure Aryan tongue expressive of the genius and authenticity of "the people." The emergence of Aryanism or race in the context of an intra-European rivalry between the Germans and the French is a historical fact that has not gained much influence among theorists of "race." So fixed have these scholars been on the repercussions of this ideology as racism, that they have failed to discern its structure as one that emerges in an internal splitting of "the European" through the investment of language by biology and territory. Schwab attributes what is essentially an Orientalist appropriation to "political intrigue whose objective was to recapture the first Renaissance from the Latins by undisputedly possessing oneself of the Orient" (186). Aryanism then is a rivalry (or race) among so-called "whites" for absolute claims to Whiteness. It emerges, not as Amin, Said and Bernal argue, in deliberate and tendentious opposition to the Orient or Africa, but in distinction from the various other "lower" races of Europe – the Latins, the Celts, the Slavs, or in H. F. K Gunther's (1927) classification, the superior Nordics from the Mediterranean, the Dinaric, the Alpine and the East Baltic.[18] It was a method of contesting the hegemony of Europe (which would of course by the 1830s seem to guarantee the hegemony of the world) on the basis of ethnicity and nation. Thus, while I agree with Arendt that race thinking is an intra-European ideology, I also want to credit the common knowledge about race, that it is ultimately founded in notions of Aryanness – the genius of Boulainvilliers notwithstanding.

To continue the present procedure of reading Arendt sympathetically, but against the grain, I suggest that a footnote she provides to the key sentence quoted above is also worth noting. The sentence one may recall is: "As long as common origin was defined by common language, one can hardly speak of race-thinking." In the footnote she adds: "Even Fichte, the favorite modern scapegoat for German race-thinking, hardly ever went beyond the limits of nationalism" (1973: 166). Thus if Fichte is to be regarded as the philosopher *par excellence* of nation and language, then by the very terms of common knowledge, which Arendt rejects, he must also be the voice of race as I have been speaking of it.

Let us take up Fichte's *Addresses to the German Nation*, delivered in 1807–8. These famous lectures clearly adumbrate the themes of Aryanism which were formed from the clay of German nationalism.[19] As one may recall that the addresses were given during the period of the great Napoleonic incursions into Prussia; the defeat of Jena and Auerstadt was followed by Berlin, and Fichte apparently had to flee Berlin for Königsberg in East Prussia. France was still in occupation of the city when Fichte returned to Berlin to deliver his lectures. What is interesting for my purposes is the fact that Fichte's attack on France and his attempt to rouse the German people to patriotism were couched entirely in linguistic terms. Distinguishing between the Germanic Teutons and the "other" Teutons, the neo-Latins, Fichte offered a theory of the origin of languages that doubled Herder's earlier theory of the *Sprachgeist* – the spirit of the language as something inhering in nature. For Fichte, too, language was "a force of nature" that has nothing arbitrary in it (Fichte 1979: 61). The continual development of a given language with fealty to its original spirit was the epitome of the authenticity of "the people," and German was, of course, just such an authentic and pure language, in contradistinction to the neo-Latin languages which Fichte suggested were completely severed from their original sources:

> The German speaks a language which has been alive ever since it first issued from the force of nature, whereas the other Teutonic races speak a language which has movement on the surface only but is dead at the root.
>
> (Fichte 1979: 68)

The "deadness" of living neo-Latin languages, in fact, makes all comparisons with German impossible as these languages, according to Fichte, are not of "equal rank" or value (1979: 69). Going on to compare the "consequences of the difference" between the Germans and other Teutons in his fifth address, Fichte suggests that "all the evils which have now brought us to ruin are of foreign origin" (84). These evils pertain to the degeneration of the German national spirit, the valorization of everything foreign, the deprecation of all things German, and artificiality: "Naturalness on the German side, arbitrariness and artificiality on the foreign side, are the fundamental differences" (83). For Fichte, Germans were distinguished by their love of freedom, independence of spirit, and high moral seriousness, and these qualities were for him best manifested in Martin Luther, the quintessential German man who spearheaded the Reformation. It would be easy to read Fichte's addresses as exemplary of a certain cultural nationalism and ethnic particularism, and by a stretch of imagination, even as a precursor of Gobineau and Chamberlain, the great apologists of "race." But it is important to remember that Fichte's use of race is not in terms of white vs. black, or even European vs. non-Europeans, or Teutons vs. Celts – the grand binaries that inform race theory – but Germanic Teutons vs. other Teutons. Fichte's claim to German superiority is above all coded by class – he attributes all the gains of medieval Germany to the burghers (105). His primary objective is to claim the title of "the people" as a synonym for "Deutsch" (108). It is in this move to appropriate a very bourgeois notion of the "ordinary" man as quintessentially German that perhaps the crux of Aryanism lies. In the line of thinking that traces German superiority to its language, its closeness to the proto-Aryan language, the consequent originality of the German people, their purity and their moral seriousness and spirituality, freedom becomes the prerogative of "original men" who live for "higher purposes" (139). Germany then is a synecdoche for Europe: "As Germany sinks, the rest of Europe is seen to sink with it, if we regard, not the mere external appearance but the soul" (105). In this synecdochal relation between Germany and Europe, and Germany and "the people" who truly have the right to be free, is also the synecdoche with humanness:[20]

So, let there appear before you at last in complete clearness what we
have meant by Germans. ... The true criterion is this: do you believe in
something absolutely primary and original in man himself, in freedom,
in endless improvement, in the eternal progress of our race, or do you
not believe in all this ... ? All who ... have an inkling of freedom and do
not hate it, but on the contrary love it, all these are original men; they
are, when considered as a people, an original people, *the* people simply,
Germans. All who resign themselves to being something secondary and
derivative, and who distinctively know and comprehend that they are
such ... they are an appendix to the life which bestirred itself of its own
accord before them or beside them; they are an echo resounding from
the rock, an echo of a voice already silent; they are, considered as a
people, outside the original people, and to the latter they are strangers
and foreigners. In the nation which to this very day calls itself simply *the*
people, or Germans, originality has broken forth into the light of day.
... Whoever believes in spirituality and in the freedom of this spirituality, and who wills the eternal development of this spirituality by
freedom, wherever he may have been born and whatever language he
speaks, is of our blood; he is one of us, and will come over to our side.
Whoever believes in stagnation, retrogression, and the round dance of
death ... or who sets a dead nature at the helm of the world's
government, wherever he may have been born and whatever language he
speaks, is non-German and a stranger to us.

(Fichte 1979: 126–7)

Ultimately, Fichte's rhetoric carries him away from his own original
source of authenticity – language – to a specious universalism. It is specious
because what is at stake here is the claim to originality: the German as the
original, free, and thus only authentic human being. This is not an argument
for the universality of German culture – there is no assimilationist principle
at work here; in fact, Fichte speaks of closing the circle (126). The goal here
is to install the particular at the center of a general notion of humanity, the
approximation of the German with the human or "the people" itself. And it
is this core conflation of the Aryan as human that characterizes the function
of Whiteness: a signifier that not only inaugurates a system of differences,
but one that attempts to signify the impossible, a core notion of humanness,
or being itself – the subject beyond symbolic determinacy – that founds the
anxious regime of visibility.

In locating the emergence of Aryanism in an intra-European rivalry for
hegemony over Europe, I suggest that there are at least two consequences for
our understanding of the structure of race: First, contrary to the popular
notion in critical race theory and postcolonial studies, racial thinking does
not emerge in the simple binary opposition between White and Black,
or Occidental and Oriental. Rather, what we see is the autochthonous

emergence of a notion of "the original people" grounded in a linguistic theory, which begins by making subtle distinctions among the Teutons, which properly inaugurates the hierarchical thinking about "races" within Europe.[21] Whiteness, as the transcendental signifier, or standard of a system of differences, makes every term within the chain refer back to it, and it is in the race to approximate and appropriate Whiteness that racial practice is born.

The discourse of Whiteness is above all, to use Guillaumin's terms, "auto-referential" rather than "altero-referential." Guillaumin writes:

> The auto-referential system, centered on the Self, was historically the first to be put in place; it coincided with the pre-eminence of the aristocracy, to whom its race symbolism was specific. ... Their eyes remain fixed on their own existence which, both in their own minds and in reality, regulates the course and symbolism of social activity. It is perhaps legitimate to see in this system a form of ethnocentrism. ... However, "aristocratism" is not yet racism because unlike racism, it is not founded on a belief in its own "naturalness".
>
> Altero-referential racism is centered on the Other, and seems to arise only in egalitarian societies. A fundamental trait of such a system is the occultation of the Self, of which people have no spontaneous awareness; there is no sense of belonging to a specific group.
>
> (Guillaumin 1995: 50)

Guillaumin's terms are useful not so much in distinguishing between pre-modern and contemporary notions of race, as she suggests, but rather in discerning the emergence of race through the self-splitting referred to earlier. Guillaumin's failure to discern the notion of Whiteness as the organizing principle of Eurocentrism (as distinguished from "banal ethnocentrisms") enables her to exonerate both ethnocentrism and aristocratism as not "true racism." But proper attention to the crucial element of class at play in Whiteness reveals that it is not about aristocratism, but about "the people" – the *volk*, with precisely the sense of its "own naturalness" that Guillaumin disavows as an element in auto-referential systems. I would also suggest that the altero-referential system does not so much displace but is founded on the auto-referential notion of Whiteness. Thus the discourse of race as we understand it today is an effect of that internal splitting that we identified earlier as the cause of race. The structure of race is totalizing, and attempts to master and overcome all difference within its boundaries. The dichotomy of self and other is within Whiteness in the competition over who properly possesses Whiteness, or sovereign humanness. H. F. K. Gunther's (1927) classification along physiognomic lines is a part of the logical nucleus of racial visibility grounded in "the narcissism of small differences" that grounds racial visibility. Thus in Gunther's classification, "other" European races such as the Mediterranean can carry the "Negro strain," or the Tartar may carry the "Asiatic." The signifier Whiteness is about gaining a monopoly on the notion of humanness, and is not simply the displaceable or reversible pinnacle of the great chain of being.[22] However, one must not forget that as the unconscious principle or the master signifier of the symbolic ordering of race, Whiteness also makes possible difference and racial inter-subjectivity. It orders, classifies, categorizes, demarcates and separates human beings on the basis of what is considered to be a natural and neutral epistemology. This knowledge is also the agency that produces and maintains differences through a series of socially instituted and legally enforced laws under the name of equality, multiculturalism, anti-discrimination, etc. Anti-racist legislations and practices, in other words, work ultimately in the service of race, which is inherently, unambiguously, structurally supremacist. The structure of race is deeply fissured, and that is discernible in the constitutive tension, or contradiction between its need to establish absolute differences, and its illegal desire to assert sameness. In fact, race establishes and preserves difference *for* the ultimate goal of sameness, in order to reproduce the desire for Whiteness. As Foucault might have put it, race separates in order to master. However, unlike the technologies of power that Foucault so painstakingly detailed, the analysis of race cannot be exhausted through its historicization. Race produces unconscious effects, and as a hybrid structure located somewhere between essence and construct, it determines the destiny of human bodies. It is our ethical and political task to figure out how destiny comes to be inscribed as anatomy, when that anatomy does not exist as such.

Chapter 2

The object of Whiteness

Most men represent pieces and fragments of man: one has to add them up for a complete man to appear. Whole ages, whole peoples are in this sense somewhat fragmentary; it is perhaps part of the economy of human evolution that man should evolve piece by piece. But that should not make one forget for a moment that the real issue is the production of the synthetic man; that lower men, the tremendous majority, are merely preludes and rehearsals out of whose medley the whole man appears here and there, the milestone man who indicates how far humanity has advanced so far. It does *not* advance in a single straight line.

(Nietzsche, *The Will to Power*: 470–1)

Everything that is colour is merely subjective – there is no objective correlative in the spectrum to enable us to attach the quality of colour to the wavelength, or to the relevant frequency at this level of light vibration. There is something objective here, but it is situated differently.

(Lacan, Seminar XI: 97)

In his remarkable essay, "The whiteness of the whale," in *Moby Dick* (1851), Melville reflects on the sublimity and horror of Whiteness. In a sentence that runs to forty-seven lines, Melville lists the universal veneration of the color white and ends with the observation that "there yet lurks an elusive something in the innermost idea of this hue, which strikes more of a panic to the soul than that redness which affrights the blood" (Melville 1981: 179). The breathless syntax of the over-long sentence lists the virtues of Whiteness, including the "pre-eminence" of the white man who is given "ideal mastership over every dusky tribe," and is punctuated finally by the terror of Whiteness. Melville's description brilliantly demonstrates the obsessive self-citations of Whiteness as the generative core of a system of difference. Melville ends the chapter by associating the horrific and panic-inducing qualities of Whiteness with formlessness and annihilation:

Is it that by its indefiniteness it shadows forth the heartless voids and immensities of the universe, and thus stabs us from behind with the thought of annihilation, when beholding the white depths of the milky way? Or is it, that as in essence Whiteness is not so much a color as the visible absence of color, and at the same time the concrete of all colors; is it for these reasons that there is such a dumb blankness, full of meaning, in a wide landscape of snows – a colorless, all-color of atheism from which we shrink?

(Melville 1981: 185–6)

The striking phrase "the visible absence of color" refers to Whiteness as the simultaneous presence and absence of a certain substance. It is precisely the indefiniteness, the ambivalence, the mute meaningfulness, the colorless, all-color of Whiteness that fascinates and mesmerizes the subject as the promise of being itself. For Melville, it is the absent cause of perceptible hues of nature which are but "the subtile deceits, not actually inherent in substances, but only laid on from without" (186). This cause is the "great principle of light" which "for ever remains white or colorless in itself, and if operating without medium upon matter, would touch all objects, even tulips and roses, with its own blank tinge – pondering all this, the palsied universe lies before us as a leper" (186). Whiteness here is the great and immanent absence that sustains the system of chromatism; it actually enables one to see, even as it presents a threat to ordinary vision. As the cause of color, of visibility itself, Whiteness as light is beyond mere perception; he who looks upon it would, in Melville's terms, end as "the wretched infidel [who] gazes himself blind" (186). Melville's notion of Whiteness as the formless and dangerous essence of visibility is wholly compatible with the view of Whiteness as the master signifier of race that I have been delineating so far. In the last chapter, my emphasis was on the capacity of Whiteness to engender the structure of racial difference. Here, I will focus on the lethal and illegal fantasy of sameness and mastery that Whiteness offers as the real yet concealed motivation for the maintenance of race.

The master signifier makes difference possible, but it is also excluded from the play of signification that it supports. In Lacan's terms, we could propose that the dual character of Whiteness, as support and panic-inducing kernel, exists in a relation of "extimacy" (Lacan's term for the paradox of the excluded interior) to the symbolic system it engenders. This signifier, in its awesome and terrifying aspect, discloses itself as something inassimilable to the very system that it causes and upholds. In our terms, Whiteness engenders the scale of human difference as racial embodiment, but this ostensibly "neutral" system of differences is organized around the exclusion of Whiteness, particularly the terror that it presents as pure and blinding light, which would annihilate and erase difference. I argue that this "terror" should be understood as the *raison d'être* for race itself – the will to preeminence, to mastery, to being – which must necessarily be prohibited by social and juridical law. This ineffable and excluded power of Whiteness, as that which makes perception possible but is itself the blinding possibility beyond the visible, should be explored as the "lure" that fuels and perpetuates racial visibility while holding out a promise of something beyond the empirical mark.

I suggested in the previous chapter that the visible bodily marks of race serve to guarantee Whiteness as something more than its discursive construction. Whiteness, I argue, attempts to signify being, but this audacious attempt is impossible because of the simple fact that Whiteness is only a cultural invention. This impossibility, based on the historicity of Whiteness, generates anxiety. But anxiety in race identity is endemic insofar as Whiteness tries to fill a space which must remain empty, or unsignified. This is where so-called ordinary visible difference, telling people apart on basis of bodily detail, comes to sustain the regime of race. If we can find a non-discursive basis (the marks on the body) for our faith in race, then the function of Whiteness, as the unconscious promise of wholeness, is preserved. Our investment in phenotype actually serves a dual function. On the one hand, it allows the co-existence of race as social construction, which serves to defend against the *jouissance* of Whiteness. On the other, it preserves that fantasy of wholeness by valorizing phenotype as something pre-discursive. In this chapter, I explore the lethal fantasy at the core of race, which is the possibility of transcending or reaching beyond the visible phenotype. It is the possibility of being itself, where difference and lack are wholly extinguished. As the master signifier of race, Whiteness maintains the structure of (visible) difference – the chain of metonymic substitutions – which locates the subject as desiring (thus eternally lacking) Whiteness. The fantasy of encountering Whiteness would be, for the subject of race, to recover the missing substance of one's being. It would be to coincide, not with a transcendental ideal, some rarefied model of bodily perfection, but with the "gaze," that void in the Other, a piece of the Real, that could annihilate difference.

The Lacanian view about our general sense of visual reality or conscious perception is that it is itself subtended by our drive to search, recognize and recover the object of desire. In other words, what we take to be the evidence of our eyes, the fruit of our active looking, is largely caused by an unrecognized and underlying need to encounter that which Lacan terms "the gaze." The gaze is "that which always escapes the grasp of that form of vision that is satisfied with imagining itself as consciousness" (XI: 74). It is beyond reality and visual perception which, as Freud established, are founded on language and thought. The gaze is of the order of the Real, because it directly addresses lack – the lack in the Other and the lack in the subject. Encountering it would be lethal, insofar as it is contingent on the subject's constitutive lack or castration (XI: 73), the subject as *manqué à être* (or subject as a want-to-be.) To encounter the gaze would be to relinquish one's subject status, to give up meaning for being. The gaze promotes the fantasy of wholeness, but at the price of one's distinctive subject status. The gaze thus causes desire, it is the consummate version of the *objet petit a*, and more importantly it is the object of the scopic drive. Translated or extended to the sphere of race, it is Whiteness as being itself that functions as the lure – the gaze that causes desire and is at the center of the drive's trajectory. Put more starkly, it is our drive for supremacy, for the *jouissance* of absolute humanness, that sustains our active looking. Setting aside the *historical* fact that such a goal is impossible because race has no purchase on the body's *jouissance*, or in anything beyond its own cultural origins, we must nevertheless take up the persistence of the fantasy of Whiteness.

How does the totalizing fantasy of encountering the gaze play out in relation to the socially protected system of differences? What would it mean to localize that drive in an object and to encounter it in order to complete oneself as human? What would be the consequence of such an encounter, if it is at all possible, other than the annihilation of the subject? Joseph Conrad's "The secret sharer" presents such a fantasized encounter with the gaze. Read symptomatically, the story exemplifies the logic and desire of Whiteness, and the lethal enjoyment that it offers as satisfaction of the drive for supremacy. The reading I undertake is not primarily concerned with the meaning of the narrative; rather, I am interested in showing that to be a subject of race is a pathological state, because where race is concerned, it is the signifier itself that is the symptom.

At the center of Joseph Conrad's "The secret sharer" is the captain/narrator whose initial uncertainty locates him as the quintessential subject of psychoanalysis, as a self-doubting and tormented subject of affect. The text can be read as a phantasmatic "progression" on the captain's part from uncertainty to certainty, from questioning the inadequacy of the law, the fact that it is lacking, to a fantasized encounter with the object that can plug the lack in the law. The tale can be translated in racial terms as the captain's felt sense of lack in relation to the symbolic order of Whiteness, which forbids pursuit of the very thing that causes it to exist, followed by his transgression of such prohibition to attain the impossible fullness that the social-juridical law of race explicitly forbids. It is the fantasized encounter with a sense of wholeness, his coincidence with the gaze that provides the captain with an answer to his uncertainty, that will permit him to take up command of his ship once more.

The reading that I am proposing is ironic on at least two levels. Theoretically, in Lacanian terms, encountering the gaze would not provide satisfaction or wholeness. As Lacan pointed out in his discussion of alienation and separation, such an encounter would be impossible. The subject emerges in the field of the Other as the effect of the signifier. Thus on the one hand the *vel* of alienation establishes that one can only either have meaning (as subject in language) or being (non-meaning). On the other hand, the subject's intersection with the Other also means that one is constituted as a subject through what Lacan calls "the superimposition of two lacks" (XI: 214). In every communication, the subject invariably asks, "*He is saying this to me, but what does he want?*" (XI: 214, original emphasis). There is something lacking in the Other's speech, which echoes the subject's own sense of loss. In short, a subject can never coincide with the Other, or the *objet petit a* that stands in its place. To coincide with the *objet petit a* can only mean the annihilation of the subject. Simply put, it would be the realization of the death drive. The other level of irony pertains to Whiteness as the object cause of desire and the object of the drive. The assumption made by every subject of race that Whiteness is a transcendental signifier that promises absolute wholeness and being is false. It is false not because such an assumption is "merely a fantasy." The *objet petit a* is after all the cause of fantasy, and fantasies are neither true nor false; they are simply fundamental to the subject. The fantasy of Whiteness is false because it is not fundamental; in fact, it is a fantasy about the fundamental fantasy that has no real effects. In reality, Whiteness is not transcendental as it is culturally produced; it cannot offer being or *jouissance* because it has no impact on the "real" body. The Other of race is not lacking; it does not present a real enigma to the subject. Unlike sexual difference, there is nothing fundamentally irresolvable about race or its master signifier. Nevertheless, in the following, I read Conrad's story as if the theoretical objections to the realization of such a fantasy did not matter. I do so primarily because such a reading will permit us to glimpse the heart of Whiteness, which is often shrouded by prohibition and elevated into an enigma.

The secret of Whiteness

"The secret sharer" is an exemplary text for psychoanalytical exegesis. As Barbara Johnson and Marjorie Garber (1987) have shown, the short story lends itself to a variety of psychoanalytical approaches depending on one's persuasion. In fact, we can say that Conrad's story is situated at the very juncture of fundamental questions about subjectivity that have proven to be such a fertile point of departure for Freud. As Lacan states *à propos* the project of psychoanalytic interpretation: "The major term, in fact, is not truth. It is *Gewissheit*, certainty. Freud's method is Cartesian – in the sense that he sets out from the basis of the subject of certainty" (XI: 35). Conrad's "term" in this story is the subject of certainty as well – the nameless captain narrator who radically doubts his command and himself. The captain's narration begins with an expression of a profound sense of being an outsider: "what I felt most was my being a stranger to the ship; and if all truth must be told, I was somewhat of a stranger to myself" (368–9). In addressing his own radical self-division, which neither speech nor the imaginary have worked fully to cover over, the captain installs himself as the questioning subject. Since he is sharply aware of his lack, the captain's desire for certainty is typically expressed through a process of thought and meditation. Addressing uncertainty, or what Lacan would call the subject's sense of self-division, is of course the common element of the Cartesian and Freudian procedures. However, Lacan's particular appropriation of the Cartesian subject is worth noting, for it will illuminate the consequence of the captain's shifting locations in the story.

In "Science and truth," Lacan asserts that the subject of science, i.e., the Cartesian subject, is the basis of the subject of psychoanalysis as well. Referring to the practice of psychoanalysis as a science, he says that there is

> a certain moment of the subject that I consider to be an essential correlate of science, an historically defined moment, the strict repeatability in experience of which perhaps remains to be determined: the moment Descartes inaugurates that goes by the name of *cogito*.
>
> (Lacan 1965–6: 5)

Lacan suggests that modern science brought radical changes to subject positions, and this epistemological break is embodied by the Cartesian subject – the punctual subject who arrives at certainty of his own existence through thought. For the subject of science, or the Cartesian subject, thought, knowledge, and self-certainty are securely interlocked as truth. Psychoanalysis too, must transform the analysand, the subject who suffers (doubt), into the subject of thought. The psychoanalytic technique of free association, where the metonymic slippage of the unconscious is brought into speech, overlaps with the Cartesian meditation. However, what becomes crucial for psychoanalysis is the non-correlation between thought and certainty. The subject does not arrive at certainty; rather, it appears or emerges: "the subject of the unconscious manifests itself, that it thinks before it attains certainty" (XI: 37). In other words, the thoughts produced by the unconscious do not deliver certainty to the analysand. On the contrary, free association, unconscious slips, dreams and jokes are apt to be doubted, even dismissed by the analysand. Thought can manifest the subject, but the subject may continue to doubt. Thus according to Lacan, the analysand's doubt becomes the point of certainty on the part of the analyst.

> And who would not have doubts about the transmission of the dream when, in effect, there is such an obvious gap between what was experienced and what is recounted? Now – and it is here that Freud lays all his stress – doubt is the support of his certainty.
>
> (XI: 35)

Certainty, then, is situated not in the analysand, or his/her thinking, but outside in the analyst. It is at the point where the subject doubts his own speech or fears that the analyst may be misled that Freud locates the "I am," because here one can be assured "that a thought is there, which is unconscious, which means that it reveals itself as absent" (XI: 36). Lacan elaborates:

> It is here that the dissymmetry between Freud and Descartes is revealed. It is not in the initial method of certainty grounded on the subject. It stems from the fact that the subject is "at home" in this field of the unconscious that the progress by which he [Freud] changed the world for us was made.
>
> (XI: 36)

The subject of the unconscious departs in significant ways from the Cartesian subject insofar as he/she is a subject not of knowledge and truth but a subject in language. The language in which unconscious thoughts are expressed demonstrates that the subject is merely an effect of the signifier. The signifier causes him to appear in a signifying chain, and without it he is nothing, not a subject at all. Therefore the production of thought leads not to a certainty of one's being as in Descartes, but to the confrontation with one's otherness – the unconscious as the intimate other. The subject of psychoanalysis is one who doubts or suffers the loss of his being. His symptom emerges from that which is outside signification; Lacan says that "the symptom is first of all the silence in the supposed speaking subject" (XI: 11). The task of the analyst, who discovers the certainty of the subject's other location in the moment of his/her doubt, is to discover the signifier's relation to the substance of his silence, the material symptom, or the manifestation of his/her suffering. To bring the symptom, the silence, into signification is a form of a cure (XI: 11), but paradoxically, it is the fact that we must alienate our need into a linguistic demand that produces desire, the desire for being, the desire to recuperate the object that will satisfy one's lack. It is the analysand's disposition towards the object (which could be fear of satisfaction, or fixation, etc.) that determines his choice of neurosis and the symptom. This unobtainable object pursued by the analysand is properly the basis of fantasy. Thus the question that the subject poses about his being, the interest he takes in his self-division, is caught up in the network of desire and fantasy which sustains and protects the symptom.

> I propose that the interest the subject takes in his own split is bound up with that which determines it – namely, a privileged object, which has emerged from some primal separation, from some self-mutilation induced by the very approach of the real, whose name, in our algebra, is the *objet a*.
>
> (XI: 83)

The speaking subject suffers from the unconscious thought that he has lost some primal object necessary to his being. While the pursuit of this object at a safe distance from satisfaction sustains the subject in desire, it is the unconscious strategies or symptoms evolved by the subject to obtain satisfaction that cause suffering. In the case of the captain in "The secret sharer," it is the coincidence with the object that is presented as an ostensible "cure." It is this inversion that I suggest is characteristic of the structure of race. For the subject of race, it is the signifier itself that is the symptom, rather than the cure for the symptom. In other words, Whiteness, with its repressed promises of being, is the thing which produces the symptoms – the will to mastery, sameness, totality, etc. Bringing that repressed aspect of Whiteness into signification is to put the fantasy of sameness to practice, as we will see in the case of Leggatt in "The secret sharer." In the following, I analyze the captain's "progress" from being the preoccupied subject of alienation and doubt to a self-identical and totalized subject of Whiteness. I suggest that such a reading is possible only if we are willing to situate our analysis in the node between so-called history and fiction. In undoing the opposition between the two modes of narrative, we will be able to discern the lineaments of the fantasy that motivates and sustains the system of race.

The nameless captain of Conrad's narrative, who is initially the quintessential subject of doubt and affect, suffers from a particular type of object. This object which seems to hover just beyond his vision, seems to be the gaze as *objet petit a*, the lost object of desire and its cause. The initial section of the narrative, up to the arrival of Leggatt, is largely an account of the movements of his eyes. The opening paragraph of the story, which marks the captain's scopophilia, makes it clear that there is nothing for his eye to feed on:

> On my right hand there were lines of fishing-stakes resembling a mysterious system of half-submerged bamboo fences, incomprehensible in its division of the domain of tropical fishes, and crazy of aspect as if abandoned forever by some nomad tribe of fishermen now gone to the other end of the ocean; for there was no sign of human habitation as far as the eye could reach.
>
> (Conrad 1966: 367)

The description here is of a confused seascape, neither order nor disorder, but somehow both. The fishing stakes seem to allude to a system of categorization that does not have a clear sense of purpose or function. These opening lines situate the captain's restive eye, his intense state of desire as a lack of something, his mood of questioning. In the introduction itself, the narration goes on to establish the captain's profound sense of being looked at but with no possibility of a reciprocal glance. For instance, there is the early moment when the captain, in his state of intense self-estrangement, refuses or cannot bring himself to meet the glance of his second mate – a potential moment of intimacy over their mutual contempt for "Whiskers," the chief mate (368). The chief mate – whose level of doubt and certainty expressible only as "bless my soul, sir! You don't say so!" – is the banal counterpart or caricature of the captain's own more recondite skepticism. Described as being of "a painstaking turn of mind" (369), the chief mate's laborious questioning of the quotidian, accompanied by an unbending will to establish absolute causality – to account for everything – contrasts with the captain, who seems above all to be determined by his desire, or what Lacan terms "the cause" that escapes symbolic reckoning. It is a desire we become aware of in the opening passages of the narrative through his questing eye, his desire to look, to search, recognize and recover, as Lacan would put it, the *objet a* which will resolve his doubt. His "roaming" eye scans the "monotonous" horizon, focuses on glimmers of light, and follows the tug until it is out of sight. "And then," he says, "I was left alone with my ship, anchored at the head of the Gulf of Siam" (367). His sense of aloneness with the ship, he says, left only the "sky and sea for spectators and judges" (368). Moreover, with the sudden onset of the tropical night, "with all that multitude of celestial bodies staring down at one, the comfort of quiet communion with her was gone for good" (368). The captain's sense of being seen but by nothing in particular seems to induce in him a desire to localize that gaze, which at the moment seems not to have an object status. Inevitably he finds his spot – the ship *Sephora* (which Leggatt the fugitive deserts) anchored inside the islands.

> There must have been some glare in the air to interfere with one's sight, because it was only just before the sun left us that my roaming eyes made out beyond the highest ridge of the principal islet of the group something which did away with the solemnity of perfect solitude.
>
> (368)

It is, of course, the *Sephora* as the point of the gaze which finally expels the object in the guise of Leggatt the chief mate, who has dived overboard to escape punishment for having murdered, in a moment of extremity, an insubordinate crewman. It is inevitable that we read Leggatt as the *objet a* substantialized as the gaze.

Let us examine this designation of Leggatt as the *objet a* a bit more closely in the light of Lacan's comments regarding the gaze. When the captain first glimpses Leggatt, he is a bright flash of light:

> I saw at once something elongated and pale floating very close to the ladder. Before I could form a guess a faint flash of phosphorescent light, which seemed to issue suddenly from the naked body of a man, flickered in the sleeping water with the elusive, silent play of summer lightning in

a night sky. With a gasp I saw revealed to my stare a pair of feet, the long legs, a broad livid back immersed right up to the neck in a greenish cadaverous glow. ... He was complete but for the head. A headless corpse!

(371)

Leggatt arrives first as a point of light and as headless. The captain's fascination with that point of light which solicits his look is the quintessential scenario of the gaze. I shall take up the headless aspect later and focus here on the subject in relation to light and the gaze. It is in relation to the "point of light" that Lacan elaborates the notion of the eye of the subject as the receptacle or screen that responds variously to this marking by light and thus constitutes its desire.

> It is not in the straight line, but in the point of light – the point of irradiation, the play of light, fire, the source from which all reflections pour forth. Light may travel in a straight line, but it is refracted, diffused, it floods, it fills – the eye is a sort of bowl – it flows over, too, it necessitates round the ocular bowl, a series of organs, mechanisms, defences.
>
> (XI: 94)

This mutually constituting relation between light and the eye that receives the light permits Lacan to delineate the subject of the gaze as something other than "the place of the geometral point defined by geometric optics" (95).

It maybe worth recalling here that Lacan distinguishes between two systems: geometral or flat optics which posits a subject of representation, and another which "turns *me* into a picture" (XI: 105). Geometral, or flat optics, is associated with the self-identical subject of the Cartesian meditation (XI: 85). Vision in this mode pertains to images. "This function is defined by a point-by-point correspondence of two unities in space" (XI: 86). It is the establishment of this correspondence that permits the emergence of anamorphosis. Lacan's example of Holbein's famous painting *The Ambassadors*, with its anamorphotic skull, exemplifies the lack or desire of the subject inherent in the notion of self-consciousness. In response to a question about the relation between the gaze and desire, Lacan replies:

> If one does not stress the dialectic of desire one does not understand why the gaze of others should disorganize the field of perception. It is because the subject in question is not that of the reflexive consciousness, but that of desire. One thinks it is a question of the geometral eye-point, whereas it is a question of a quite different eye – that which flies in the foreground of *The Ambassadors*.
>
> (XI: 89)

On the other hand, there is the non-geometral system which posits the subject as represented rather than representing; it is that "which turns *me* into a picture" or where I "turn myself into a picture under the gaze" (XI: 105–6). The two systems are not opposed; rather they are superimposed and represented schematically in Lacan's chiasma or dihedron. The latter system, however, pertains directly to the lacking subject of desire, or the gaze. Such a subject is, above all, distinguished by its looked-at-ness. "In the scopic field, the gaze is outside, I am looked at, that is to say, I am a picture" (XI: 106).

The gaze, a concept which Lacan borrows and reworks to some extent from Merleau-Ponty, and Sartre, is that which situates the subject as always already "given to be seen," which indicates "the pre-existence of the gaze – I see only from one point, but in my existence I am looked at from all sides" (XI: 72). Thus the gaze locates the subject as a screen, or as a receptacle for the gaze. It makes the subject visible in the field of light. Lacan's famous anecdote of the sardine can floating on the waves refers to the subject as that which is absent in the picture. The light looks at the subject, and paints a picture in its eye, thereby establishing a sense of dimension. The subject itself, then, is a screen, or a blot in the landscape, while the gaze is that which "grasps" or "solicits" the subject (XI: 96–7). "In the matter of the visible," Lacan says, "everything is a trap" (XI: 93). The gaze involves the lure, not as deception, but even more as the masquerade of sexuality (XI: 100, 107). Lacan elaborates the relation of the gaze specifically to the sexual aim thus:

> From the outset, we see, in the dialectic of the eye and gaze, that there is no coincidence, but on the contrary, a lure. When in love, I solicit a look, what is profoundly unsatisfying and always missing is that – *You never look at me from the place from which I see you.*
> Conversely, *what I look at is never what I wish to see.*
>
> (103)

If Leggatt represents anything at all, it is the fantasy of absolute coincidence between the eye of the captain and the gaze of his other. Legatt who emerges as the point of light, not only embodies the gaze as that which refers to the captain's being (the object always delivers a sense of being, however illusory, to the subject) but also as that which the captain "imagines in the field of the Other" (XI: 84), the something which eludes vision. The captain's fantasy more specifically is that of being united with the *objet a*, the thing from which the subject must separate in order to constitute itself. Rather than being absent as the thing that is lacking in the subject, Leggatt promises presence and possession of the object of desire. As a luminous and alluring thing, who delivers a sense of being to the captain by filling his lack, Leggatt represents the captain's scopic drive and its object. The captain's first concern, naturally, is not to lose him – again (Melville 1981: 372).

Leggatt's relation to the captain is that of the "extimate" *objet a* who resolves the latter's meditation on the certainty of his own existence, and his relation to the law. "Extimacy" is a term introduced by Lacan, but fully elaborated upon by Jacques-Alain Miller (1986) to designate the paradoxical status of the "Real in the symbolic," or the manner in which the Other of language is engaged in its lack. In relation to the system of race, extimacy refers to the illegal desire of Whiteness to overcome difference and to plug the lack that sustains the inter-subjective relations of race. The notion of the extimate object as the cause of desire is used to denote that the most intimate and hidden aspect of the subject is also that which is most foreign and other to ourselves. Miller, in fact, refers to the analytic relationship as extimacy, both in its externalization of the interior, and insofar as it involves the most intimate confession on the part of the analysand, but to one who is not really one's friend. "The analyst, on the contrary, is precisely extimate to this intimacy" (Miller 1986: 77). In Miller's theory, even though extimacy is schematized spatially in the figure of the torus (the doughnut-shaped circle), it is a relational notion where the function of the object in relation to the Other, and to the barred or divided subject, alters in accordance with the location of lack. Thus that which is extimate to the subject is designated as such in relation to another term – the Other or the barred subject. Miller offers three major schemas that help map the various locations of the extimate in relation to language and the subject. The first schema posits that the Other of language can act as a cover of the extimate in relation to the split subject. In this case, the extimate is identified with the unconscious itself. Miller suggests that the Other of religion is one such cover of the object in the barred or lacking subject. In the second major schema, it is the *objet a* that is the extimate part of the Other. It functions as the other of (or in) the Other; it is the alterity of *jouissance*, which the Other cannot tolerate. Miller situates "racism" in this schema as the calling

> into play a hatred that is directed precisely toward what grounds the Other's alterity, in other words, its *jouissance*. ... Racism is founded on what one imagines about the Other's *jouissance*; it is hatred of the particular way, of the Other's own way, of experiencing *jouissance*.
>
> (Miller 1986: 79)

In a third schema, the *objet a* can be extimate in an antinomic relation to the Other, where it can erupt through the signifier to evacuate the Other, such as the word "Bomb!" that can as an illocutionary speech act empty the Other. The object here is "incompatible with the presence of the subject" (Miller 1986: 82). I suggest that Leggatt occupies all of these positions at one point or the other in his extimacy to the captain. Admittedly, the second schema seems most relevant to our thinking about race in "The secret sharer," because it identifies the extimate object as the "neighbor's" *jouissance*, the way he takes his satisfaction, which affronts the Other, and thus gives rise to (racial) hatred. However, for reasons discussed below, race and the alterity of the neighbor, either as a racial other, or as one's own intimate otherness, that Lacan elaborates through the axiom "Love thy neighbor" in Seminar VII, seem not to be the cause of the captain's self-doubt, or of Leggatt's homicidal tendencies. If anything, the narrative seems to elide both these forms of inter- and intra-subjectivity altogether. In fact, both the captain and Leggatt seem to identify with the *jouissance* of the object in its alterity to the Other. It is a relation that is more akin to the antinomy that Miller delineates through the "Bomb!" example, where the object literally evacuates language or the Other and the subject of representation. Leggatt and the captain occupy positions that are in opposition to "the law of the signifier." As Miller reminds us, this law "is indeed the very law of 1–2, and in this dimension, there is a kind of democracy, an equality, a community, a principle of peace" (1986: 79). Miller's notion of the antinomy of the object to the Other of language will be taken up in the following discussion about racial inter-subjectivity. In relation to the captain, however, it is Leggatt's position of extimacy as the grand Other that acts as a cover for the extimate object (which corresponds to Miller's first schema discussed above) that is particularly valuable in discerning the captain's fantasy of Whiteness. Let us take up the specifics of how Leggatt as *objet a* addresses the law of the racial inter-subjectivity.

The share of Whiteness

How does the imposition of Lacan's notion of the gaze as embodied in Conrad's Leggatt relate to the structure of Whiteness as the contradictory establishment of human differences for the illegal desire of sameness? At first glance, it may seem that Conrad's story has nothing whatsoever to do with race or even the structure of Whiteness. However, as Bruce Harkness (1962) has so carefully documented, Conrad's story is based on a "racial" incident. In his edited case study of "The secret sharer," Harkness reprints a brief analogue – an excerpt from Basil Lubbock's *The Log of the "Cutty Sark"* (1924) and two newspaper reports from *The Times* relating to the incident that inspired Conrad's story. Lubbock's log, as Harkness points out, was not Conrad's source. However, the *Cutty Sark* was the original tea clipper which was commissioned in 1880 by the American Navy to deliver Welsh steam coal to their fleet off the coast of Japan. It was on that fateful voyage that the chief mate murdered a crewman who had refused to obey his orders. The murderous chief mate escaped under mysterious circumstances, and a rumor sprang up that he had swum away to freedom. Conrad apparently heard the story as a "sea yarn," and his alteration and interpretation of the story exposes the workings of the structure of Whiteness at the core of reality. According to Lubbock, the chief mate was no "parson's son" – a gentleman, as Conrad portrays him, who had been schooled on the *Conway* (a training ship) – but a "regular bucko of 'Down East' style – one of those hard-fibred, despotic characters which were more common in the virile days of sail than in these luxurious days of steam" (Lubbock 1924: 39). The crew was apparently made up of a motley collection of nationalities "5 Englishmen, 3 Danes, 3 niggers (two of them steam-boat men) and 2 Greeks and an Italian" (40). Lubbock, despite his own offensive terminology, clearly implies that the chief mate John Anderson harbored an antipathy towards the three "black men," especially one John Francis "who was particularly incapable and clumsy" (41). The animosity between the two men apparently grew over the latter's insubordinate language. Lubbock charts the development of their hostilities, and describes the fateful day when the chief mate, enraged by Francis' refusal to obey an order, seized the capstan bar that Francis had raised against him and "brought it down on the man's head with such a force that John Francis dropped senseless to the deck" (45). The consequence of the murder was that Anderson was "retired" to his cabin, with Captain Wallace himself taking up his watch. However, "whilst the *Cutty Sark* lay off Anjer awaiting her belated orders, the mate took the opportunity of persuading his kind-hearted captain to help him escape" (46). According to Lubbock, Anderson was smuggled out by boat to an American ship, the *Colorada*, whose captain was "only too glad to get hold of a man-handler of such reputation" (46). The "real" story, however, had another piece to it: Anderson's escape apparently irked the crew to the point of near-mutiny against the captain, who was himself so afflicted by guilt that he committed suicide by jumping overboard. According to *The Times'* report, Anderson was spotted by a crewman two years later and was indicted for Francis' murder. The judge apparently meted out "exemplary punishment": Anderson was sentenced to seven years' penal servitude.

Lubbock's story, of course, purports to tell the truth of Conrad's fictional account. We could set the record straight in our reading of Conrad by arguing that the implied author's valorization of the "bully mate" discloses his own secret desire to "vent his spite" against blacks. In other words, it would be quite easy to derive a ready answer to the question regarding the functioning of race in this story: Leggatt as the "object cause of desire" represents the captain's racist fantasies, which he must come to terms with before he can fully assume the authority of his command. Leggatt's disappearance at the end of the story can be read as the captain's acknowledgment and divestment of his racism and his assumption of a strong and healthy ego, which permits him to steer the ship to safety. This is such an obvious and satisfactory conclusion that the Lacanian apparatus of anxiety and racial visibility, the *objet a* and the gaze, seems unnecessarily complicated and redundant. However, we can settle on this reading only if we agree on the following points: that the novel is not so much about race but racism, which is to assume that race is a descriptive property of individual groups who are then symbolized in discriminatory ways in the novel through particular use of metaphors and similes; that one can overcome racism by acknowledging and coming to terms with it, without unsettling one's subjectivity as raced in any way; that the division between the historical record of the *Log* and Conrad's story is that of truth vs. fiction; that the arrival at certainty necessarily entails the strengthening of the ego as the road to good health, and furthermore that "health" signifies the assumption of authority or any of the above. The main objection is that while such hypothetical conclusions may explicate the captain's "psychology," it is unlikely that it would illuminate the structure of race, the function of the signifier Whiteness in the constitution of the raced subject, or the lethal core of Whiteness which is my prime concern. On the other hand, if we situate our reading between so-called truth and fiction, and repudiate the closure offered by the certainties of the ego, we will find that the object as represented by Leggatt represents something beyond the genocidal fantasies of racism. In fact, Conrad's elision of the racial aspect of the story must be read in relation to the certainty that the captain arrives at, as the ostensible point of health at the end of the narrative. Also, the issue of Whiteness as productive of a regime of visibility that passes as common sense will remain unaddressed if we banalize Leggatt as the captain's "alter ego."

Recognizing Whiteness

Let us recall the captain's state of mind – he is looking for certainty, he wants to heal the fundamental split that constitutes him at the level of the subject and its ego. In other words, the captain's heightened sense of alienation, his doubts about his existence, and his being locate him as the typical analysand who desires to coincide with the object (the excluded material) in the hope of obtaining satisfaction. The object (the unanalyzable cause behind the unconscious) is thought to cover the gap or the split that lies at the heart of subjectivity. As the *objet a* of fantasy, then, Leggatt promises a "cure" for the captain's alienation – and that is the absolute recognition of the captain as a subject in the Real (a totalized being) rather than the symbolic. In other words, Leggatt represents the fantasy that one need not accept lack (or castration) in order to exist, the fantasy of fullness without risking one's status as a subject. Thus, if recognition is the key term, we realize that Leggatt, as the fantasy object, invokes the theme in at least two ways.

There is a sense in which, according to Lacan, the gaze is an object cause of desire because it is the lost *jouissance* of the parental gaze that delivers a recognition to the child in an excess of pleasure. It is this excess that the subject now seeks to reproduce in his desire for the gaze. As Lacan says in his "Rome discourse": "man's desire finds its meaning in the desire of the other, not so much because the other holds the key to the object desired, as because the first object of desire is to be recognized by the other" (E: 58). It is in this sense that Leggatt is the gaze – he promises a sense of being to the subject and the primary recognition that will allay the captain's uncertainty. As the captain puts it with regard to the initial encounter between the two: "A mysterious communication was established already between us two – in the face of that silent, darkened, tropical sea" (Conrad 1966: 373). As the object, Leggatt in fact has a versatility which promises to address every gap and fill every split in the captain's psyche. When he first arrives, he appears headless, recalling Lacan's "acephalic" subject of the drives.

> The object of the drive is to be situated at the level of what I have metaphorically called a headless subjectification, a subjectification without subject, a bone, a structure, an outline, which represents one side of the topology. The other side is ... a subject, through his relations with the signifier, is a subject-with-holes (*sujet troué*).
>
> (XI: 184)

On another level, Leggatt is not so much the captain's misrecognized mirror image, his ego ideal, so much as the misrecognition itself. Rather than promising unity, he arrives as the "body in pieces" that will address the captain's fragmentation. Leggatt addresses his own demand for recognition to the captain, thus placing them in a relationship of perfect reciprocity or the impossible relationship of love. "As long as I know that you understand," says Leggatt, "but of course you do. It's a great satisfaction to have got somebody to understand. ... It's very wonderful" (Conrad 1966: 396). Speaking of his arduous swim towards the captain's light, he acknowledges his need to be seen:

> "When I saw a man's head looking over I thought I would swim away presently and leave him shouting – in whatever language it was. I didn't mind being looked at. I – I liked it. And then you speaking to me so quietly – as if you had expected me. ... It had been a confounded lonely time. ... I wanted to be seen, to talk to somebody, before I went on."
>
> (381)

In mirroring the captain's split between his ego and his self, Leggatt as the captain's "intelligent double" (388) delivers a recognition that perhaps only an analyst, who is posited as "the subject supposed to know," the *objet a* of the analysand, can be imputed to deliver.

Before I take up Leggatt's function as the "cure," I shall examine the theme of recognition as it pertains to Whiteness. Leggatt's own desire for recognition is, of course, at the core of his reason for deserting the ship. His "fight unto death" with the insubordinate crewman who refused to obey his orders invites a Hegelian reading as the contradiction of forces for mastery over the other in order to attain self-consciousness and freedom.

Significantly, Leggatt has no direct memory of the fight. His recounting of the story is itself secondhand, for he suggests that in his rage, at that moment of extremity in the midst of a storm, he had no consciousness of the "fight" itself:

> "They say that for over ten minutes hardly anything was seen of the ship … It was clear that I meant business … I understand that the skipper, too, started raving like the rest of them. … They had rather a job to separate us, I've been told."
>
> (375)

His apparent loss of consciousness is restored only with the murder itself. Conrad only vaguely alludes to the "fact" that the struggle revolved around "racial hatred" as Lubbock claims. Leggatt claims that his antagonist was "black in the face," suggesting more the dire effects of the fight than "racial difference" as such. At another point, the captain's mate ("Whiskers") says that the story he has heard about the *Sephora* "beats all these tales we hear about murders in Yankee ships," to which the captain replies, "I don't think it beats them. I don't think it resembles them in the least" (389). This repudiation of the "racial" element of the story, I contend, inscribes it at a different level, a level that is proper to disclosure of that pathological core, the extimate thing at the heart of Whiteness.

Leggatt's description of the crewman and the captain's reaction to the "fight" is of crucial importance here. In referring to his victim, Leggatt shows no remorse whatsoever for having killed him. "I've killed a man," he says, and trails off in his customary aposiopetic manner: "When I say a man," thus calling the "man's" humanity into question. Leggatt's rhetoric, his inability to finish any sentence, indicates the extent to which his opponent is regarded as beyond symbolic representation – inhuman and thus unsignifiable. More explicitly, he says later:

> "There are fellows that an angel from heaven – And I am not that. He was one of those creatures that are just simmering all the time with a silly sort of wickedness. Miserable devils that have no business to live at all. But what's the good of talking! You know well enough the sort of ill-conditioned snarling cur."
>
> (374)

The crewman's lack of individuality, his group designation as "one of those creatures," suggests that the struggle could be understood as precisely for recognition and mastery. The "fight," then, is not one of racial hatred; there are no "men" here, only opposed forces where survival alone can establish the humanity of the winner. It's not a question of the "best man winning;" rather, it is a question of the man winning over the beast – culture over nature. And necessarily in a "fight" of this sort, the other must be annihilated for the winner to survive. Thus upon closer examination, we see that this particular "fight unto death" does not end, as in the Hegalian scenario, with the sublation of the contradiction between master and slave. In that instance, the slave submits to the master and thus acquires the greater self-consciousness of the two through his labor. What we see instead is the complete annihilation or negation of the other, with the master surviving as pure self-consciousness or "being in itself," "for itself" wholly self-sufficient without need for recognition from the "slave" in question. The logic that poses the choice as "kill or be killed" is not the same as the choice between "your freedom or your life." The latter is founded on the dialectical relation that establishes the subject within the ambit of the symbolic law, while the latter is the logic of Whiteness; it is not so much about survival, but about the *jouissance* of absolute preeminence. The struggle that establishes the symbolic position of the master and the slave would in racial terms also establish difference and the mediating social and juridical laws. It is in this sense that Conrad's inscription of the story at a more primeval level must be understood as a repudiation of the inter-subjective order of race which is supported by the law of the symbolic order, while at the same time being coterminous with the core notion of Whiteness, which annihilates all differences and attempts to attain absolute humanness through the signifier Whiteness. In other words, the symbolic order of race is predicated on this possibility, which it must exclude in order to keep the fantasy of such enjoyment alive. The symbolic law of race in this instance, then, is representative of that aspect of the law that demands the acceptance of one's lack.

The captain of the *Sephora* is the representative of the law who, in this text, would enforce the system of racial order and its attendant values of racial tolerance, equality and justice. Conrad's reworking of the "historical" tale is significant for an understanding of his view of the law. The "historical" captain of the *Cutty Sark*, Captain Wallace, was, according to Lubbock's account, jovial and popular and every bit in command of the ship. Lubbock attributes a confident decisiveness to his personality (1924: 42) which is in striking contrast to Conrad's Captain Archbold, whose very name is an uncertainty throughout the narrative. In Conrad's text, Archbold is a vague and "muddled" man, above all lacking in decisiveness. Easily frazzled and deeply riddled with anxiety and terror by the gale he had to weather, Archbold is represented as possessing a "spiritless tenacity," being "densely distressed" (Conrad 1966: 385). Recounting the crisis during the storm, Leggatt expresses his utter contempt for him thus:

> "I assure you he never gave the order. He may think he did, but he never gave it. He stood there with me on the break of the poop after the main topsail blew away, and whimpered about our last hope – positively

whimpered about it and nothing else – and the night coming on! To hear one's skipper go on like that in such weather was enough to drive any fellow out of his mind. It worked me up into a sort of desperation. I just took it into my own hands and went away from him, boiling, and ... "

(Conrad 1966: 390–1)

Despite his general state of perplexity, however, Archbold proves to be obdurate about dispensing (legal) justice and punishing Leggatt for his crime. This is apparent in the conversation between the captain and Archbold:

"You were very anxious to give up your mate to the shore people, I believe?"

"He was. To the law. His obscure tenacity on that point had in it something incomprehensible and a little awful; something, as it were, mystical, quite apart from his anxiety that he should not be suspected of 'countenancing any doings of that sort.' Seven-and-thirty virtuous years at sea, of which over twenty immaculate command, and the last fifteen in the *Sephora*, seemed to have laid him under some pitiless obligation."

(386–7)

Conrad's characterization of Archbold as tenacious about the letter of the law, to see justice done and refuse to countenance murder under any circumstances, stands in marked contrast to the "historical" Captain Wallace, who was supposedly a "kind hearted" man and permitted his murderous mate to escape. Archbold's problem, according to both the captain and Leggatt, is that unlike Captain Wallace he was incapable of embodying the law and thus mastering it. Exceptional circumstances call for exceptional judgments, but Archbold is too much the "lawyer," a man who is manipulated, even duped by the law. From this perspective, he is charged with the most flagrant sin of all – pusillanimity. In fact, it is such weakness and submission to the letter of the law that is implicitly designated as the cause of the general malaise in "culture." As for the lack of support for Leggatt from his shipmates, not only do they respond with the slavish insistence that the law be followed to the tee, but it is their inability or refusal to discriminate between "miserable devils" who do not deserve to live, and human beings who do, that is the cause of Leggatt's frustration. For Leggatt, the task would be to remove the blindfold of Justice and to let her see that not all are equal before the law – the claim to humanness is an exclusive one, and is attained by one who has the ability to annihilate difference.

Archbold's subservience to the law is also indicated by his compliance with the order of domesticity. In fact, Leggatt implies the lack of the skipper's "manliness" thus:

"Devil only knows what the skipper wasn't afraid of (all his nerve went to pieces altogether in that hellish spell of bad weather we had) – of what the law would do to him – of his wife, perhaps. Oh, yes! She's on board. Though I don't think she would have meddled. She would have been only too glad to have me out of the ship in any way."

(378)

Leggatt's slide from the law to the wife as twinned forces of authority makes explicit his contempt for the rules and niceties of society as such. When we are finally presented with Archbold in the flesh, the captain represents him thus:

He mumbled to me as if he were ashamed of what he was saying; gave me his name (it was something like Archbold but at this distance of years I hardly am sure), his ship's name, and a few other particulars of that sort, in a *manner of a criminal* making a reluctant and doleful confession. He had had terrible weather on the passage out – terrible – terrible – wife aboard, too.

(385, emphasis added)

In fact, Archbold mentions the wife again in the same tone of "criminal" accountability: "I've been at sea now, man and boy, for seven-and thirty years, and I've never heard of such a thing happening in an English ship. And that it should be my ship. Wife on board, too" (386). Earlier, Leggatt had already set the manliness of the voyage in sharp contrast to the domestic scene when he ironically suggests that his story would make a "nice little tale for a quiet tea-party" (375). Thus Archbold's consideration for his wife is, in some ways, to be construed as a betrayal of the tacit masculine code of sailing, a code which cements the deep homosocial bond between the captain and Leggatt. Domesticity in this story, and in many of Conrad's nautical tales, is not only opposed to the realm of total masculine self-sufficiency available only in those lawless spaces beyond England and Europe, but it is tantamount to emasculation. Thus to be law-abiding is to be less of a man; it is to acknowledge difference (racial and sexual) and thus lack. Therefore the enjoyment of Whiteness, not unsurprisingly, also connotes a certain sexual self-sufficiency that we may well term "masculine *jouissance*." In the graph of sexual difference that Lacan presented in Seminar XX, this is the place of the One who is not subject to the paternal metaphor. In other words, this is the position of the father of the primal horde who is postulated as a being prior to the institution of the moral law (the prohibition of incest) and who is characterized by his fullness, his ability to know no lack, or prohibition of his desire. To occupy the masculine position in symbolic difference, as a necessarily lacking subject (barred S) is to have such an exceptional One inscribed at the level of one's unconscious. To attain the place of the unchallenged master, to transcend lack at the level of one's racial identity to the point of annihilating difference, is also to overcome the cut that engenders sexual difference. In fact, this is the very state of fullness that Whiteness attempts to signify: not only the mastery of humanity, but of sexuality. It is essentially an androcentric fantasy that femininity, due to its inherent incompleteness, would necessarily militate against.

Leggatt's attitude to the law is emblematic of his attachment to that androcentric and totalitarian fantasy of Whiteness: "Do you see me before a judge and jury on that charge? For myself I can't see the necessity" (Conrad 1966: 374). Again:

> "You don't suppose I am afraid of what can be done to me? Prison or gallows or whatever they may please. But you don't see me coming back to explain such things to an old fellow in a wig and twelve respectable tradesmen, do you? What can they know whether I am guilty or not – or of *what* I am guilty, either? That's my affair."
>
> (396)

It is very important to both Leggatt and the captain that it be understood that the objective of the former's desertion is not to escape punishment but to refuse the authority and thus place himself beyond the law. When Archbold suggests that he may have to report a suicide (387), the captain gives him no encouragement whatsoever, though logically this would end the manhunt for the fugitive and bring the case to a close. Rather than mislead Archbold into giving up the pursuit, the captain prefers to play deaf, ostensibly to enable Leggatt to hear everything that is being said. But his pretense can be read symptomatically too, as the contumacious rejection of Archbold's discourse of legal correctness.

In conclusion, I suggest that we view Leggatt as the extimate object that provides the fantasy of overcoming castration and maintaining one's subject status in the symbolic. Leggatt positions himself beyond the law, as the extimate core of the law which exposes its lack. How, then, does Leggatt function as an *objet a* delivering recognition, or more properly as the "pathological cure" for the captain? Leggatt's appointing himself beyond the Law is also very much in antinomy with the law, insofar as he almost successfully evacuates the Other when he drops off the side of the ship. The captain, in trying to ease Leggatt's escape, steers his ship precariously close to the black hills of Koh-ring, thereby endangering his entire crew, the ship, and his command. Language, words, speech are all expunged at that moment when Leggatt drops into the sea: "Such a hush had fallen on the ship that she might have been a bark of the dead floating slowly under the very gate of Erebus" (402). The problem that insists upon us as readers is the question of how such an object, which Miller asserts is incompatible with the presence of the subject, insofar as the object cancels the subject, can provide a "cure" for the captain. It is inevitable that we read the story as the delineation of the impossible fantasy at the core of "Whiteness." An important reason why this tale should be read as a "fantasy," not of the captain as a character in the text, or of the implied author Conrad, but of the discourse of race itself, is that it is ultimately a fantasy about transgressing the law in relation to race. The story's construal of Archbold as the tenacious executor of the law also valorizes the mere juridical prohibition against racial domination into the moral law (the commandment against murder) that makes desire possible. Let us recall that the historical John Anderson, according to Lubbock, was permitted to escape by the "kind hearted" Captain Wallace, and that when he was finally captured his sentence was far from being commensurate with his crime. Thus when read by the traces of Whiteness, "The secret sharer" can be interpreted as a story about the successful reaching of the goal of Whiteness – the *jouissance* of absolute mastery and fullness. While the inevitable failure of such a goal could produce anxiety, and the captain is often on the brink of such an affect, it is here presented as triumphant. Finally, as the thing that will fill up the lack in the law, Leggatt promises a fantasy of completion of almost "psychotic" fullness to the captain. Thus in the end, driven by Leggatt's white hat – the spot of light on the surface of the current – the gaze of Whiteness saves the ship as it guarantees certainty to the captain. This time the captain's "yearning stare" in seeking the *objet a* alights not on something expelled from the Other, but on something that is his very own: "What was that thing? ... I recognised my own floppy hat. It must have fallen off his head ... and he didn't bother. Now I had what I wanted – the saving mark for my eyes" (403). The object has been fully (impossibly) introjected as his own, investing him with a certainty that no subject of the symbolic can properly have. The captain's certainty is not to be confused with the imaginary sense of unity in overcoming one's fragmentation. Rather, it is the certainty of having Whiteness as the "object of desire" (of recognizing or fantasizing a lack in the symbolic order of race), of possessing it in and *as* his unconscious, that permits him to take up the command of his ship again with renewed vigor.

Chapter 3

Whiteness and the elephant joke

> A German, an Englishman ... and a Negro were once commissioned to write on the subject: *The Elephant*. The German spent ten years in research ... and produced a twenty volume work entitled: *An Introduction to the Study of the Elephant*. The Englishman bought the latest hunting equipment, went to Africa, and after five years of hunting in the jungle produced ... a highly illustrated work, *How to Shoot the Elephant*. ... The Negro simply retired to his home and wrote a letter to the *Times* on the subject: "The Elephant and the Race Problem."
>
> (*The Book of Negro Humor* [1966] ed. Langston Hughes: 255–6)

> Think for a moment in the real. It is owing to the fact that the word *elephant* exists in their language, and hence that the elephant enters into their deliberations, that men have been capable of taking, in relation to elephants, even before touching them, decisions which are more far-reaching for these pachyderms than anything else that has happened to them throughout their history. ... Besides, it is clear, all I need do is talk about it, there is no need for them to be here, for them to be here, thanks to the word *elephant* and to be more real than the contingent elephant-individuals.
>
> (Lacan, Seminar I: 178)

> The closer we get to psychoanalysis being funny the more it is real psychoanalysis.
>
> (Lacan, Seminar I: 77)

It is to Hannah Arendt (1973) that we owe the remarkable insight that the practice of imperialism entailed the development of two "devices" – race and bureaucracy. Arendt's great achievement is her delineation of the convergence of these two discourses, which she suggests were independently discovered, but begin to dovetail with the progress of domination. Arendt characterizes the discourse of race as "the emergency explanation of human beings whom no European or civilized man could understand, and whose humanity so frightened and humiliated the immigrants that they no longer cared to belong to the same human species" (Arendt 1973: 185). Bureaucracy, on the other hand, she suggests, was founded on "legend," the "quixotic" (210) notion of the white man's burden to slay the dragon of primitive superstition, which deteriorated rapidly into boyhood ideas of adventure as selfless service to the cause of Empire (209–10). Arendt's analysis of bureaucracy is particularly illuminating for an understanding of the relationship of colonial discourse to the order of Whiteness (or race). Citing the influential colonial administrator Lord Cromer as a model of the colonial bureaucrat who articulated a "theory" of bureaucracy, Arendt argues that his gradual persuasion to the method of a "hybrid form of government" entailed the governance of subject territories through what he termed "personal influence," without accountability to a legal or political policy or treaty. Cromer's perspective, which was to prove definitive for colonial rule in general, recommended that the bureaucrat, who worked anonymously behind the scenes, be freed from any form of accountability to public institutions such as Parliament, the law courts or the press (214). Such a form of bureaucracy, Arendt suggests, through her reading of Cromer's letters and speeches, was the outcome of his realization of the essential contradiction of colonial rule, the impossibility of cultivating democracy, and in his own words, of governing "a people by a people – the people of India by the people of England" (cited in Arendt 1973: 214). Thus the transformation of the administrator as (the great English) apostle of the rule of law to one who "no longer believed in the universal validity of law, but was convinced of his own innate capacity to rule and dominate" (221), meant that the surreptitious exertion of violence, termed "administrative massacres" (216) in lieu of the "civilizing mission," was now a "realistic" alternative for containing the natives. But such a subversive efflorescence at the very heart of the great project of freeing the natives from the shackles of their "cruel superstitions" brought bureaucracy in opposition to the foundations of colonial law. It is at this moment, of the loss of faith in the so-called English ideals of parliamentary democracy and rational government, that Arendt marks the convergence of the device of bureaucracy with the practices of race. This does not mean that she proposes adherence to English ideals as a norm from which colonial discourse has deviated. If anything, Arendt's thesis is that every discourse of progress always carries within it its own negation in the form of a "subterranean" current. In her preface to the first edition of *The Origins of Totalitarianism*, she writes that her book assumes that

> progress and Doom are two sides of the same medal; that both are articles of superstition, not of faith …
>
> The conviction that everything that happens on earth must be comprehensible to man can lead to interpreting history by commonplaces. … The subterranean stream of Western history has finally come

to the surface and usurped the dignity of our tradition. This is the reality in which we live. And this is why all efforts to escape from the grimness of the present into nostalgia for a still intact past, or into the anticipated oblivion of a better future, are in vain.

(Arendt 1973: vii–ix)

Arendt's analysis of the confluence of colonial bureaucracy and race enables us to discover the contradictions built into colonial discourse. It is these contradictions that Homi Bhabha (1994) elaborates as structural ambivalence – an ambivalence that splits the discourse between official claims to the rule of law as a rationalization of colonial power and its practical underside – that is the impossibility of "justice" in an inherently unstable and disoriented political situation. While Bhabha pinpoints this ambivalence under various terms – mimicry, sly civility and hybridity – what is significant is the fact that the contradiction within the order of race – as the institution of difference and the desire for sameness – is best discerned in the field of colonialism. As a concrete utilization of the logic of "race," colonial discourse, as the agency of a naming and an ordering of difference, inevitably produces, or more properly is founded upon, a residue, namely what Arendt terms bureaucracy, the material practice entailed by the "desire" of Whiteness for absolute mastery. But bureaucracy must not be understood as a simple and correctable error of colonial discourse; rather, it must be understood as the "symptom" of the inherently contradictory claims of the rhetoric of colonialism (the impossibility of the rule of law) engendered as it is by an impossible desire. Slavoj Zizek's formulation of the symptom is useful here; he suggests that it is in a given discourse "the point of exception functioning as its internal negation" (1989: 23). And basically, for the symptom to function as the necessary contradiction, the subject must have no knowledge of its logic. The unconscious aspect of Whiteness guarantees just such a non-knowledge, while its illegal desire, articulated in the symptom of lawless bureaucracy in the scene of colonialism, supported by the latent equation of Whiteness with humanness, remains repressed and unacknowledged only to return in an uncanny encounter.

My literary example in the last chapter, Conrad's "The secret sharer" (1966), illustrated the fantasy of Whiteness fulfilling its promise and delivering a lethal enjoyment that logically and existentially would be impossible. Such an assertion then raises the question of that impossibility – how is it encountered, and with what consequences? What does it mean for Whiteness as wholly symbolic or bound by language (in the sense that race is "successful" and is not missing a signifier) to fulfill or attempt to fulfill its promise as the master signifier? What is the consequence of its failing to do so because of its "success"? How does historicity expose the "success" of race? How does the anxiety that ensues at such exposure manifest itself? How can we map or discover such a successful failure? Since we are dealing here with the unconscious function of the signifier in the constitution of the subject of race, it is incumbent on us to turn to the formations of the unconscious, i.e., dreams, parapraxes, slips of the tongue, jokes, etc. Jokes, and humor in general, are a particularly useful site for probing the working of the signifier, as they are less particularized than dreams and the lapses of speech, and since they can only be told in a public context, inter-subjectivity is an indispensable element to them. Jokes need at least three people, and exploring this triangular relation in the context of colonialism may lead us to discern the anxious function of Whiteness. In the following I use George Orwell's anecdotes of his experience as a policeman in Burma and as a visitor in Morocco as texts of the failure of Whiteness. Orwell's pieces are particularly useful because in their attempt to be confessional, to speak the truth about difference and prejudice under the guise of a liberal faith in race, they display an anxiety that divulges all.

In Seminar X, Lacan discusses the notion of the *unheimlich*, or the uncanny, as the object that appears in anxiety. In Seminar XI, it is the effect of the missed encounter with the real – the tuche beyond the automaton of the chain of signifiers. Thus the particular connection that I am suggesting between jokes and the uncanny is, at some level, already anticipated by Lacan in his pairing of tuche and automaton. Automaton refers to the automatism of the signifying chain, a feature that Freud had already isolated as an intensified aspect of the joke. In jokes, automatism refers to the almost mechanical emergence of signifiers, thus disclosing the truth of the subject. We may recall the joke that Freud tells about the marriage broker who, in order to allay the prospective groom's suspicion that the bride's family had perhaps borrowed their finery, says: "Who would lend these people anything?" thus exemplifying "the insistence of the signs ... governed by the pleasure principle" (XI: 53–4). Tuche, on the other hand, is that which "lies behind the automaton" (XI: 54), and Lacan speaks of it as the real, as the cause of repetition. In more Freudian terms too, we can establish the relation between the jokes and the uncanny, or the automaton and tuche, to illuminate the ambivalence of Whiteness. Thus in the following I read Freud's texts through a Lacanian lens to discover the no doubt surprising proximity of jokes and the uncanny; this proximity in turn is deployed as an interpretive tool for a reading of George Orwell's essay or short story, "Shooting an elephant," in which I contend a dangerous joke is on the verge of being cracked.

Uncanny jokes

In his *Jokes and their Relation to the Unconscious* (1905c) and his 1928 essay on humor, Freud draws analogies between jokes and dreams on the basis of their shared process of *entstellung* or distortion. This process, which takes the form of condensation and displacement, he suggests, is characteristic of joke and dream work. Also in his 1919 essay on the uncanny, Freud relates the uncanny to dreams, but he does not note the undeniable resemblance between jokes and the uncanny. However, Lacan's analysis of anxiety, as elaborated in Seminar X, provides the key that clarifies the nexus of relations among anxiety, the uncanny, and jokes. It is his delineation of the object of desire as it plays out in anxiety that aids my formulation of these connections. Moreover, it is only through a pursuit of the particular anxiety generated by the disavowals of "race" in the fraught space of the colonial encounter, that properly discloses the implication of these mechanisms. I shall begin by attempting to grasp the adjacency of the uncanny and jokes in Freud's text before I turn to Lacanian anxiety. To do this it is necessary to attend to language and the transformation of the signifier, which one must recall is Freud's primary basis for the theories of the uncanny and of jokes.

Much of the weight of Freud's argument about the uncanny rests on the etymological ambiguity between *heimlich* and *unheimlich*, "the meaning of which develops in the direction of ambivalence, until it finally coincides with its opposite" (Freud 1919a: 226). Freud elucidates the point at which the two terms meld into each other – the fine line between familiarity and strangeness as an index of the deep relation between the uncanny and dreams. This particular ambiguity translates quite well into the English language, but interestingly, English offers yet another point of potential convergence between canny and uncanny, which though not immediately obvious, proves quite useful for my purposes. One of the meanings of "canny," according to the *Oxford English Dictionary*, is sly humor used by the English for Scottish humor. On the other hand, we also note that the same source gives us "mischievous and malicious" as synonyms for uncanny. In other words, there is another point at which the canny and uncanny slide into each other and that is tendentious humor, or in the words of the *OED*, "sly and malicious mischief." Thus it is not too far-fetched for us to pause at this particular definition of the canny and uncanny as humor insofar as it too, in the form of jokes, bears, according to Freud an uncanny resemblance to dreams based upon their common source in the unconscious. The resemblances between the mechanisms of the uncanny (in its meaning as unhomeliness – *unheimlich*), or at least aspects of it, and aspects of jokes are numerous. But the most important feature in Freudian terms is the shared mechanism of surprise: it ensues as the process of saying something forbidden in tendentious jokes (Freud 1905c: 106), and as the eruption of that which should have remained hidden in the uncanny (Freud 1919a: 225). A quick inventory of resemblances would include other structural connections, such as doubleness, repetition compulsion, the rediscovery of something very familiar (Freud 1905c: 121; 1919a: 245), ignorance about the source of affect, automatism, and intellectual uncertainty about a given object of the uncanny and that of jokes.

Lacan invokes the notion of the uncanny as one of the many things that can appear at the site of anxiety; it is a site he specifies where everything can appear, which accounts for the impossibility of arriving "at a satisfying, unitary formulation of all the functions of anxiety in the field of our experience" (X: 5/12/62). However, there is a more overt insinuation in his comments (about the uncanny and anxiety) of the possible adjacency between jokes and the uncanny. In Seminar X, he remarks:

> Just as I approached the unconscious by the witticism, I will approach anxiety this year by the Unheimlich, it is what appears at this place. This is why I have written it for you today: it is the $(-\Phi)$ [minus phi], the something which reminds us that what everything starts from is imaginary castration, that there is no – and for good reason – image of lack. When something appears there, it is because, if I can express myself in this way, that the lack is lacking. Now this may appear to be simply a joke, a concetti (?) which is well placed in my style which everyone knows is Gongoric.
>
> (X: 28/11/62)

What can be a joke or conceit according to Lacan is his notion that anxiety is caused when an uncanny object appears in the place that should have been empty, when there is a "lack of a lack." Thus it is the surprising excess of both his ornate "Gongoric" style and the appearance of an uncanny object in a place that marks castration that is "funny" – a joke, a possible conceit. It is this very excess that I am on the track of in attempting to grasp the immoderate movement of colonial discourse as a bureaucracy.

Freud, on the other hand, does not remark on the structural connections between the uncanny and jokes, but he does, in his essay on the uncanny, make a seemingly irrelevant joke: "There is a joking saying," he says, that "love is home-sickness" (Freud 1919a: 245). The joke revolves not so much around the subject of the joke sentence, i.e., love, but rather the object of the sentence: homesickness, or more precisely home (*heim*), which Freud suggests should be understood in its full spatial sense as also standing for nation. "Whenever a man dreams of a place or a country and says to himself, while he is still dreaming, this place is familiar to me … we may interpret the place as being his mother's genitals" (1919a: 245). For Freud too, the joke emerges from the uncanny excess of the answer to the potential question, not what is love, but what is home (sickness)? That is, in the fact that "woman's genitals" is not mentioned directly, but must be deduced. I seize upon this moment in Freud's text primarily because it represents a peculiar juxtaposition of the uncanny with the humorous – in fact, it is rather difficult to differentiate what is humorous from what is uncanny in this expression, which reinforces my point about the excessive presence of the joke within the uncanny, or the excess of the uncanny object that is itself a joke.

George Orwell's anecdotal essay "Shooting an elephant" (1953a) begins with an overwhelming sense of homesickness – a sentiment that Freud jokingly has already placed within the realm of the uncanny. But homesickness of this sort apparently has little to do with nostalgia, and everything to do with a hatred for his present contradictory situation. Orwell's homesickness has been described sympathetically by Raymond Williams as a "complicated" response. "He was stuck ... between hatred of the empire he was serving and rage against the native people who opposed it and made his immediate job difficult" (Williams 1974: 3). What is particularly interesting about Orwell's anecdote is the way in which explosive, uncontrollable laughter hovers menacingly in the margins of the text. The principal anxiety that Orwell feels pertains to laughter: the excessive, horrific laughter of the Burmese natives. When he is tripped on the football field, "the crowd yell[s] with hideous laughter" (Orwell 1953a: 148). They also stand around street corners and jeer at him. For Orwell, these are moments when the enjoyment of the natives threatens the potential evacuation of his subjectivity. In the present of Orwell's text, we hear no laughter whatsoever – sighs and gasps, perhaps, but no laughter. However, the irrepressible threat of laughter throughout the essay powerfully implies the circulation of an unarticulated and unspeakable joke in the text – the telling and sharing of which, Orwell signifies, could potentially dislocate him as a subject.

Colonialism, jokes and the comic

Insofar as we cannot assume that jokes play the same function or emerge from the same source in all situations, it is necessary to inquire into the place of the joke in the colonial context. While Orwell's anecdotes express an anxiety over native laughter, it does not immediately follow that his anxiety is related to an uncanny joke. In fact, we can simply state that laughter can be uncanny in and of itself, and that Orwell's refusal to be the subject of such laughter is the natural impulse of an authority figure to police the strange as it were. However, if we stay our analysis at the point of laughter without inquiring into the projected source of it, then we will not be able to gain much insight into the functioning of Whiteness, its failure to signify totality, and the affect of anxiety that it entails. Moreover, when I speak of the functioning of Whiteness, I am addressing the subject in his or her particularity as a subject (of race) who has made specific investments in the order of race. In Orwell's case, because his investment is made as a self-proclaimed "liberal," even a "socialist" sympathizer of anti-colonial movements, the failure produces certain affects and ideational representatives (or unconscious thoughts) that further educe the psychoanalytic theory of race. In order to go beyond the observation of laughter to uncover its projected source, it is necessary to recall some of Freud's salient points about jokes, especially in their relation to the comic. This is necessary because laughter does not clarify easily whether a given statement or situation is to be understood as a joke, comedy, or a sign of humor.

In his *Jokes and their Relation to the Unconscious*, Freud elucidates the distinctions among jokes (the verbal artifact), the comic (scenarios of excess physical exertion), and humor (the process of making light of a grave situation), and above all insists on the necessity of analyzing jokes as distinct from the comic (1905c: 9–13). Freud insists that the distinguishing characteristic of jokes as opposed to the comic and humor is that of the three; jokes alone bear a direct relation to the unconscious, and while the others may overlap at times, the comic and humor, he contends, arise from the preconscious (208). Further:

> A joke is made, the comic is found, and first and foremost in people, only by a subsequent transference in things, situations, and so on, as well. As regards jokes, we know that the sources of the pleasure that is to be fostered lie in the subject himself and not in outside people.
>
> (1905c: 181)

Freud distinguishes between two types of jokes: those that are innocent (usually verbal jokes that play with words) and those that are tendentious (jokes usually engaging with a thought or concept). He further subdivides tendentious jokes into obscene or sexual jokes (also called "exposing jokes" [97]) that substitute for sexual contact (98) and hostile or aggressive jokes "that open sources of pleasure that have become inaccessible" (103). (Freud also includes cynical jokes that target institutions [113], and skeptical jokes that question the certainty of our knowledge [115] in the category of tendentious jokes, but he does not devote much time to analyzing either.) Freud's analysis of tendentious jokes is of course the most pertinent for an understanding of the anxiety entailed by Whiteness. However, one must examine the persistence of the comic in colonial or racial situations, and its relation to racial jokes, before one can discern the uncanny joke implied by Whiteness.

Most racial wit in the colony is, predictably enough, comic. On one hand the colonizer's inclination to infantalize the natives to sustain the logic of the civilizing mission, and on the other the colonized people's need to caricature their hated rulers, produce more comic stories than jokes. In colonial literature, the predominance of comic writing is well attested to by the existence of numerous novels, plays, poems and caricatures of natives. In a scenario of outright racial domination – be it colonialism or slavery – race relations are often represented as comic, and the prevailing modes of representation produce a narrative genre and cast of characters who acquire a stock value. As Freud implies, the characteristic aspect of comedy is that it is rarely ambivalent. Arising from the preconscious, it would be associated in Lacan's terms with the imaginary. For Freud, the comic is often direct in achieving its purpose, the most elementary form being slapstick or the exaggeration of physical movements. Freud elaborates various forms of comedy – the comedy of movement (or slapstick), comedy of character, comic speech, mimicry, parody, travesty, etc. – and suggests that they are all determined by a "standard" for appropriate responses. Thus:

> How is it that we laugh when we have recognized that some person's movements are exaggerated and inexpedient? By making a comparison, I believe, between the movement I observe in the other person and the one I should have carried out myself in his place. The two things compared must of course be judged by the same standard, and this standard is my expenditure of innervation, which is linked to my idea of movement in both of the two cases.
>
> (Freud 1905c: 191)

The function of the standard as the distinguishing feature of the comic locates it in the imaginary as the site where the ego ideal provides a norm of bodily unity and coordination that is perceived and incorporated as one's own. Thus Freud observes that children are entirely "without a feeling for the comic" (223). Taking up the comedy of movement as exemplary, Freud states:

> The comparison which provides the difference runs (stated in conscious formulas): "That is how he does it" and "This is how I should do it, how I did it." But a child is without this standard contained in the second sentence. ... The child's upbringing presents him with a standard: "this is how you ought to do it." If he now makes use of this standard in making the comparison ... he laughs at the other person.
>
> (1905c: 224)

The comic plays an essential function in negating whatever ambivalence the subject may feel with regard to the gap separating the experience of his own body from that of his ego ideal. Another important differentiation that Freud makes between comedy and jokes pertains to the "contingency or relativity" (220) of comedy with regard to the particular situation. Jokes, on the other hand, are "absolute;" they are made independent of time and place. Moreover,

> in the case of the comic, two persons are in general concerned: besides myself, the person in whom I find something comic. ... The comic process is content with these two persons: the self and the person who is the object. ... Joking as a *play* with one's own words and thoughts is to begin with without a person as an object.
>
> (1905c: 144)

The absolute nature of the joke and the fact that it requires not two but three persons for its success are indicative of the joke's origin in the unconscious.

> Generally speaking, a tendentious joke calls for three people: in addition to the one who makes the joke, there must be a second who is taken as the object of the hostile or sexual aggressiveness, and a third in whom the joke's aim of producing pleasure is fulfilled ... it is not the person who makes the joke who laughs at it and who therefore enjoys its pleasurable effect, but the inactive listener.
>
> (1905c: 100)

According to Lacan, the latter requirement of the joke for three persons demonstrates the essential splitness of subject, as a subject in language:

> Nowhere is the intention of the individual more evidently surpassed by what the subject finds – nowhere does the distinction that I make between the individual and the subject make itself better understood – since not only must there have been something foreign to me in what I found for me to take pleasure in it, but it must also remain this way for this find to hit its mark. This takes place from the necessity, so clearly marked by Freud, of the third listener, always presupposed, and from the fact that the witticism does not lose its power in its transmission into indirect speech.
>
> (E: 60)

The third listener is in the position of the Other, the unconscious, which signals the alienation of the subject in language. As Lacan states: "everything relating to wit takes place on the vacillating level of speech. If it weren't there, nothing would exist" (II: 234). Thus the joke must be understood as being founded on the essential ambiguity of the unconscious, which according to Lacan is an effect of language. He says:

> *Jokes and their relation to the Unconscious* remains the most unchallengeable of his [Freud's] works because it is the most transparent, a work in which the effect of the unconscious is demonstrated to us in its most subtle confines; and the face it reveals to us is that of the spirit in the ambiguity conferred on it by language, where the other side of its regalian power is the witticism of "conceit" [*pointe*], by which the whole of its order is annihilated in an instant – the "conceit", in fact, where its domination over the real is expressed in the challenge of non-sense.
>
> (E: 60)

Structurally speaking, the joke has a disruptive effect; not only does it thrive on the ambiguity of the unconscious, thus "playing" with its internal contradictions, but as Lacan points out, it threatens to annihilate the order of language with its non-sense. In the colonial context, the contradiction of bureaucracy and of race as a discourse – the constitutive tension between difference and sameness – is the fertile site for jokes. But it is precisely this contradiction that must not be acknowledged in order to protect the subject from anxiety. In such a situation of political vulnerability where anxiety can be potentially fatal, the comic works overtime to protect the subject of race from jokes.

Freud himself notes, albeit in an existential way, the essentially subversive nature of "tendentious" jokes. A rebellious attitude, he suggests, is the optimal condition for the joke. His examples of hostile or tendentious jokes are usually those made by "powerless" and "inferior" people against the "great, the dignified and the mighty" who cannot be directly disparaged in any way. Moreover, he suggests that most hostile jokes are also self-inflicted, whereas comedy is always directed at others:

> A particularly favourable occasion for tendentious jokes is presented when the intended rebellious criticism is directed against the subject himself, or, to put it more cautiously, against someone in whom the subject has a share – a collective person, that is (the subject's own nation, for instance). The occurrence of self-criticism as a determinant may explain how it is that a number of the most apt jokes … have grown up on the soil of Jewish popular life. They are stories created by Jews and directed against Jewish characteristics.
>
> (Freud 1905c: 111)

This notion of the joke as principally dissident and of the comic as reproductive of power relations, then, explains why there seems to be a predominance of comedy in colonialism and why jokes can become deeply suspect. It is a commonplace to observe that jokes and wordplay are never tolerated by totalitarian regimes, primarily because linguistic ambivalence may expose the hollow absolutism of regimes based on political and psychological repression. But jokes are not simply "subversive," that is, they are not always the weapons of the weak against the strong. According to Freud, jokes can thrive only when and where there is an inhibition or repression of instincts, and insofar as tendentious jokes are concerned, it is the inhibition of aggression that fuels the witticism. However, there is the species of joke called the "racist joke," whose relationship to aggression is rather more complex than Freud seems to acknowledge. Insofar as they are extreme examples of tendentious jokes, racist jokes reveal in greater detail the way in which they are determined by a certain attitude to aggression – its inhibition and its expression – within a particular society. A brief examination of aggression in jokes in general, and in "racist jokes" in particular, will serve the purpose of situating in a precise fashion the all-important function of ambivalence and aggression for the uncanny joke, which is characteristic of the scenario of colonialism.

Jokes thrive on the ambivalence of the unconscious, but they also rely on the inhibition of aggression, which is an essential ingredient of that ambivalence. In other words, aggression pertains to the primary ambivalence of love when at the earliest stage the desire to incorporate the love object is expressed as devouring and annihilating the object.[1] Lacan distinguishes between aggression and aggressivity. In Seminar III, he speaks of the "aggressive relation" with regard to the conflict between the drives and the ego. In conformity with Freud, Lacan suggests that aggression is constitutive of the ego insofar as it "sets itself up in a duality internal to the subject" (III: 93). Aggression in this seminar is said to inform every relation, and determines the function of exclusion and mastery that is endemic to inter-subjectivity. In his essay "Aggressivity in psychoanalysis," aggressivity is bound up with the ambivalence that obtains in the gap of the specular relation between the ego ideal and the body in pieces (E: 11). It is precisely this gap, I have suggested, that the comic attempts to conceal, thus working as a "safety valve" for narcissistic aggression. Such a localization of aggression, however, cannot address Freud's insight about repressed aggression and the unconscious origin of the joke. In Seminar II, however, aggressivity is not merely narcissistic or imaginary; it is also connected to the subject's desire and particularly to the death drive. Speaking of desire and its lacking object as an inadequate and ultimate explanation of life, Lacan says:

> The significance of *Beyond the Pleasure Principle* is that that isn't enough. Masochism is not inverted sadism, the phenomenon of aggressivity isn't to be explained simply on the level of imaginary identification. What Freud's primary masochism teaches us is that, when life has been dispossessed of its speech, its final word can only be the final malediction. ... Life doesn't want to be healed.
>
> (II: 232–3)

It is this aggression, this will to resist meaning, that as Freud implies is displaced by force of the symbolic law and is thus expressed in an inverted form by the nonsense within the envelope of the joke.[2]

In his analysis of hostile jokes, especially the "ethnic" or "racist" joke, Freud discusses the role of the juridical law in displacing aggression. This seeming discrepancy in emphasis is, perhaps, the result of his presumption that "racism" is a form of aggression pertaining to the aversion of (native) insiders for (alien) outsiders. He writes:

> [All] moral rules for the restrictions of active hatred give the clearest evidence to this day that they were originally framed for a small society of fellow clansmen. In so far as we are all able to feel that we are

members of one people, we allow ourselves to disregard most of these restrictions in relation to a foreign people.

(Freud 1905c: 102)

In other words, hostile jokes substitute for the violence that is forbidden expression in a homogeneous, civil society, just as obscene jokes substitute for the spontaneous touching that is also forbidden by moral law. Thus jokes which thrive on symbolic and legal interdiction are only possible, in Freud's view, when the joker, victim, and listener share the same nationality or race, whereas with "a foreign people" there is no necessity to displace the aggression into a joke; we permit ourselves to express it physically.[3] Thus, in Freud's seemingly narrow conception of hostile jokes, "racist" jokes, whether in a modern sovereign state or in colonialism, become redundant if not actually impossible. Thus, on the subject of anti-Semitic jokes, for instance, Freud is quite perfunctory: "The jokes made about Jews by foreigners are for the most part brutal comic stories in which a joke is made unnecessary by the fact that Jews are regarded by foreigners as comic figures" (111). The peculiar disavowal of the "racist" joker (he implies that there is no such person, as there are no racist jokes, *per se*), or more properly the comedian as a foreigner(!), once again nullifies the existence of "racist" jokes *per se*. But there are "racist" jokes that are not merely comic stories. There is enough wordplay in racist jokes to qualify them technically as jokes and not comic stories. A cursory glance at a popular collection of jokes such as Blanche Knott's *Truly Tasteless Jokes VI* (1985) proves that one can make hostile jokes about foreigners, and that racial or cultural difference *within* a given society is no hindrance to joking either. Freud's peculiar "blind spot" with regard to this brand of hostile jokes pertains to his inability to conceive of (or acknowledge) a multiracial society. Thus we have to resituate the function of aggression and its relation to jokes in the disparate contexts of a modern multiracial society and in colonialism.

A study of "racist" jokes in a multiracial society should not be undertaken as a sociological inquiry into race relations. Christie Davies (1990) and Elliot Oring (1992) have usefully criticized attempts to read ethnic jokes as crude indicators of social relations and levels of hostility against specific groups, as founded on inaccurate and inconsistent assumptions. While their arguments are generally persuasive in that they wish to preserve the spontaneity of the joking relationship, the debate itself is largely misconceived insofar as it focuses on the content of jokes rather than on the mechanism of joking, which reveals how Whiteness functions. Assertions to the effect that jokes are responsible for or innocent of racial oppression displace the emphasis from the joke's unconscious dependence on the prohibition of the law to intentionality and the conscious deployment of the joke as insult. (Indeed, to debate this issue is perhaps to be deflected by the comic and to miss the joke.) Such a deflection would considerably impoverish an understanding of how variations in the dialectical pressure of aggression and inhibition (from which the joke originates) produce differing joke situations, which are indicative of shifts in the working order of race as common sense.

Racist jokes in a multiracial society are often the outcome of ethnic heterogeneity and mark social boundaries. They usually emerge at the cusp of the inside and the outside insofar as they seek to treat citizens as foreigners. One view of such jokes is that they are a healthy sign of a civil society where interracial aggression is forbidden. Arthur Asa Berger (1993), for instance, adopts this rather libertarian position with regard to the US when he argues:

> America is a nation of immigrants – each with different customs and traditions and values – and is, par excellence, a breeding ground for ethnic jokes. Among other things, these jokes help release aggressive and hostile feelings in people and, in so doing, help facilitate the relatively peaceful coexistence of different ethnic groups in America.
>
> (Berger 1993: 65)

A related view, which emphasizes the functionality of humor in general, concerns the "racist" joke as a "safety valve," a point discussed by Jerry Palmer in his *Taking Humour Seriously* (1994): "In the 'safety valve' thesis the observation of a relationship between taboo and humor leads to the conclusion that humor operates to release the pressure of inhibition without affecting the application of the inhibition in non-comic circumstances" (61). In other words, the joke contains as it releases anti-social impulses. But as Palmer points out, there is no reason why the joke cannot possess the agency to overturn rather than uphold social norms or inhibitions against hostility. In other words, it is conceivable that the official prohibition against the expression of aggression can perpetuate an economy of violence, wherein the displacement of hostility into jokes engenders another level of further differentiation and hatred. Such a view of the "racist" joke as a "recycler" (rather than a defuser) of social violence is compatible with Freud's view of jokes as inherently dissident. It is important to acknowledge the particular mode of a "racist" joke's "dissidence" as not only "the weapon of the weak" that Freud suggests of racially homogeneous, class-differentiated societies, but possibly as symptomatic of the general subversion rather than fortification of inhibition against hostility. Not to do so is to idealize race relations as fully contained and regulated by civil(ized) inhibition.

The scene of colonialism, on the other hand, presents a variation of the relationship of ambivalence and aggression to jokes. The following "elephant joke" illustrates the difference:

There was once a Texan who had an unreasonable dislike of elephants. Realizing it bordered on a phobia, he consulted a psychiatrist, who told him it was a fairly common problem. "The cure is straightforward," said the shrink. "You have to go to Africa and shoot one." The idea appealed to the Texan, so he flew to Kenya and hired a guide to take him on an elephant hunting safari. The hunter's right hand man turned out to be a native who in turn hired a bunch of his fellow tribesmen to spread out in a long line, beat drums and blow horns, and drive the elephants toward the blind where the hunters were waiting. As they waited, the noise grew louder and louder until out of the bush with much clanging and shouting burst the head beater. The Texan drew a bead and shot him right between the eyes.

"What the hell'd you do that for?" bellowed the guide. "He's my best beater – I've worked with him for twenty years!"

"If there's anything I hate worse than elephants," drawled the Texan, "It's big, noisy niggers."

(Knott 1985: 86–7)

As this meta-joke (about the mechanism of jokes) illustrates so well, racial aggression demands displacement onto elephants (or into jokes) in societies where the law prohibits its expression. It is only in the colonial scene – in Africa – that this particular Texan can free himself from the pressure to displace his aggression. Thus racist jokes in societies like the US are produced in an economy of juridical prohibition and inflammation of differences through jokes. This is a model that would be more compatible with Foucault's notion of power/discourse than with Freud's theory of the displacement of aggression. But what if the interdiction against the free expression of aggression were ambivalently enforced, as most openly with "a foreign people" that one nevertheless governs – the scene of colonialism and slavery? Freud, of course, does not consider such a possibility. For instance, while the enactment of aggression is ostensibly forbidden by law in a society such as the US, it is nevertheless significant that the compensatory notion of "free speech" enables jokes to reiterate racial identity and engender hostility. In colonial regimes, on the other hand, the attitude to the expression of hostility is contradictory. While official rhetoric may prohibit the free expression of violent tendencies under the banner of higher civilization and moral development, in the actual practice and dispensation of the law, the opposite, as Hannah Arendt has pointed out, is often true. Consider the institutionalized form of violence in the colonial state, such as "administrative massacres," police interrogations, and technologies of obtaining confessions that were invented in such regimes. Thus the ambivalence of colonialism, or the regime of Whiteness, both can and cannot produce jokes. In fact, insofar as jokes emerge from that ambivalence that we have been describing as constitutive of colonialism, we witness a situation in which the practical use of violence to "contain the natives" makes jokes redundant; one can simply "draw a bead and shoot them between the eyes." The comic, meanwhile, serves as an additional outlet for aggression, or a buffer against ambivalence or "guilt." But insofar as the expression of aggression is officially prohibited as contradictory of the civilizing mission, a fact that a liberal such as Orwell might take very seriously, the juridical law and the symbolic law join forces to contain the ambivalence expressed by jokes. Jokes in such a context do not have the option of working through the displacement of aggression, as they can in modern civil societies where the law simply prohibits "racism." But in colonial society where aggression is both officially prohibited and sanctioned, jokes become truly "subversive" and uncanny in that they expose the contradiction of the order of Whiteness. In Orwell's "A hanging" (1968a), the sudden intrusion of the playful dog which interrupts the solemn rituals of colonial violence is described as uncanny. In this essay, a native, "a puny wisp of a man," is prepared for execution for an indeterminate crime. Orwell describes the solemn procession to the gallows thus:

> Suddenly, when we had gone ten yards, the procession stopped short without any order or warning. A dreadful thing had happened – a dog, come goodness knows whence, had appeared in the yard. It came bounding among us with a loud volley of barks, and leapt round us wagging its whole body, wild with glee at finding so many human beings together. It was a large woolly dog, half Airedale, half pariah. For a moment it pranced round us, and then, before anyone could stop it, it had made a dash for the prisoner, and jumping up tried to lick his face. Everyone stood aghast, too taken aback even to grab at the dog.
>
> (Orwell 1968a: 45)

I suggest that we read this "dreadful" occurrence, which in Orwell's peculiar syntax "had" already happened before the perception of its cause, as indicative of the presence of the unarticulated joke engendered by the ambivalence of Whiteness that must be contained. In colonialism, the joke, in the strictest sense in which Freud defines tendentious jokes, is always on the verge of being cracked. Freud writes:

> What is a joke to me may be merely a comic story to other people. But if a joke admits of this doubt, the reason can only be that it has a façade – in these instances a comic one – in the contemplation of which one person is satiated while another may try to peer behind it. A suspicion may arise, moreover, that this façade is intended to dazzle the examining eye and that these stories have therefore something to conceal.
>
>   In any case, if our marriage-broker anecdotes are jokes, they are all the better jokes because, thanks to their façade, they are in a position to

conceal not only what they have to say but also the fact that they have something – forbidden – to say.

(Freud 1905c: 105–6)

In a colonial situation, jokes, of course, will "say" that Whiteness is contradictory, and to permit the expression of such an envelope of witticism containing the nonsense core of Whiteness would be rather uncanny and threatening for the subject of race. Orwell was only too aware of this possibility, given his keen intuition regarding the colonial regime and its contradictory discourse of Whiteness. Orwell's set of candid observations on racial visibility, which he expresses as a source of puzzlement not so much at the fact of difference, but as something bewildering about himself, offers a rich insight into the nexus of relations among anxiety, visibility, and the signifier that I have been sketching throughout. Here it will be the threat of the joke that will set in motion the relay action among these elements in an endless circle of anxiety, visibility, and the signifier. A certain perception of racial difference leads to anxiety, that leads to encountering the historicity of the signifier, and that leads to cathecting the marks, etc.

In his essay "Marrakech" (1953b), Orwell seems aware, and painfully so, of the contradiction of Whiteness – the dialectic between the "neutral" order of race and its secret core of Whiteness as humanness. He writes:

> When you walk through a town like this ... it is always difficult to believe that you are walking among human beings. All colonial empires are in reality founded upon that fact. The people have brown faces – besides, there are so many of them! Are they really the same flesh as yourself? Do they even have names? Or are they merely a kind of undifferentiated brown stuff, about as individual as bees or coral insects? They rise out of the earth, they sweat and starve for a few years, and then they sink back into the nameless mounds of the graveyard and nobody notices that they are gone.
>
> (Orwell 1953b: 181)

Orwell admits that he finds this invisibility of "brown" people "strange," in other words inexplicable, even unrepresentable. When he does recognize the other's humanity (which he theoretically "recognizes" but of which he has no "knowledge"), it is always a surprise to him and *almost* uncanny. Again, in "Marrakech," he speaks of this discrepancy between recognizing and knowing with regard to a file of old women which regularly carries firewood past his house. Previously, he had registered the old women only as "Firewood ... passing." Then one day, "for the first time," he says, when walking behind these old women, he sees them:

Every afternoon a file of very old women passes down the road outside my house, each carrying a load of firewood. ... It was only that one day I happened to be walking behind them, and the curious up-and-down motion of the load of wood drew my attention to the human being beneath it. Then for the first time I noticed the poor old earth-coloured bodies, bodies reduced to bones and leathery skin, bent double under the crushing weight. Yet I suppose I had not been five minutes on Moroccan soil before I noticed the overloading of donkeys and was infuriated by it.

(Orwell 1953b: 185–6)

Orwell's surprise at himself is significant here; he seems to confront the fact that his perceptual schema, informed as it is by Whiteness as a regime of looking, is founded on a notion of humanness that primarily demarcates between who counts and who does not. It is a revelation that is always on the verge of being made and is thus just a bit uncanny. Lest we begin to translate this perceptual schema, racial difference, as pertaining more to class differences, Orwell corrects us. He writes:

All people who work with their hands are partly invisible, and the more important the work they do, the less visible they are. Still, a white skin is always fairly conspicuous. In northern Europe, when you see a labourer ploughing a field, you probably give him a second glance. In a hot country, anywhere south of the Gibraltar or east of Suez, the chances are that you don't even see him. I have noticed this again and again. In a tropical landscape one's eye takes in everything except the human beings. It takes in the dried up soil, the prickly pear, the palm tree and the distant mountain, but it always misses the peasant hoeing at his patch. He is the same colour as the earth, and a great deal less interesting to look at. ... People with brown skins are next door to invisible.

(1953b: 183–4, 186)

Note here that Orwell's emphasis is on his own perception: he notices that he does not notice the farmer, and that is what is potentially uncanny. In fact, on the relationship between race and class in the colony, Orwell is particularly useful. As an ambivalent colonizer, he recognizes that the dominant method of ordering human beings is founded on a law that privileges so-called "white" people as possessors of "Whiteness." Thus he acknowledges in *The Road to Wigan Pier* (1982):

In an "outpost of Empire" like Burma the class-question appeared at first sight to have been shelved. There was no obvious class-friction here, because the all-important thing was not whether you had been to one of the right schools but whether your skin was technically white. As a matter of fact most of the white men in Burma were not of the type who in England would be called "gentleman" ... [but] they were "white men", in contradistinction to the other and inferior class, the "natives."

(Orwell 1982: 123–4)

The issue here is not so much that of Orwell's identification with his own Whiteness. Such a reading would merely reproduce the colonialist presumption about "race." It is more interesting to note that Orwell is not speaking in terms of his belonging to Whiteness. Rather, underlying his more commonplace designation of white versus non-white people, he speaks of Whiteness not merely as a property of particular human beings, but as a technicality – that is, a system of ordering the world, a discourse of differences which institutes a regime of looking. Also, in "A hanging," Orwell is surprised by his own responses when he recognizes the humanity of the emaciated native prisoner. Walking ahead on his way to the gallows, the man avoids a puddle, and Orwell is astonished by this simple human gesture in the face of death: "It is curious," he admits, "but till that moment I had never realised what it means to destroy a healthy, conscious man. When I saw the prisoner step aside to avoid the puddle, I saw the mystery, the unspeakable wrongness, of cutting a life short when it is in full tide. This man was not dying, he was alive just as we were alive" (1968a: 45). What Orwell articulates repeatedly in his brief essays about his tenure as a police officer in colonial Burma and his sojourn in Morocco is the uncanny surprise and shock at his own responses in discovering a shared humanity. Orwell's essays are not naive articulations about encountering the humanity of the "other," in which case the horror of difference (the fetishizing of hair, skin and bone) would have been the predictable response. Rather, the shock is in discovering that the continuity of humanness can be surprising, thus signalling the profound alienation or split within his own psyche between what he recognizes and what he knows. In other words, in the extremity of the colonial context, Orwell seems to risk encountering the aspiration at the heart of the system of race, and that is founded on a core notion of wholeness (promised by the signifier "Whiteness") that mandates the very notion of humanness. In other words, what is uncanny for a subject such as Orwell is the discovery that at the core exists the untenable, unassimilable notion that the very assumption of a human subject position is to be implicated in a racial economy of meaning.

The elephant joke

Let us now address a question I have postponed till now: where and what exactly is the joke in "Shooting an elephant"? In this essay (1953a), Orwell is very aware of the ambivalence of colonial discourse and the contradiction of Whiteness, especially with regard to aggression. He expresses his own ambivalent hostility as a vacillation between wanting on the one hand "to drive a bayonet through a Buddhist priest's guts" (1953a: 149) and on the other sympathizing deeply with the Burmese hatred of colonialism (148). Thus his own job as a police officer trying to uphold colonial law was nose up against the unbearable contradiction of Whiteness. Doing his job meant, above all, containing that ambivalence and any expression of it. For Orwell in "Shooting an elephant," killing the elephant is, of course, the containment of such a moment of potential discharge of aggression through the joke which actually threatens to annihilate him as a subject of race. In that oft-quoted scene from the essay, he speaks of the colonizer as

> a sort of hollow, posing dummy, the conventionalized figure of a sahib. For it is the condition of his rule that he shall spend his life in trying to impress the "natives". ... He wears a mask and his face grows to fit it. I had got to shoot the elephant. I had committed myself to doing it when I sent for the rifle. A sahib has got to act like a sahib; he has got to appear resolute, to know his own mind and do definite things. To come all that way, rifle in hand, with two thousand people marching at my heels, and then to trail feebly away, having done nothing, no, that was impossible. The crowd would laugh at me. And my whole life, every white man's life in the East, was one long struggle not to be laughed at.
>
> (Orwell 1953a: 152–3)

In Orwell's own words, the key issue for the maintenance of the order of race and the promise of Whiteness is the disavowal of ambivalence – one must "appear resolute" and "know one's own mind," be fully in control of oneself and the situation. To fail to contain ambivalence would be not so much to risk ridicule from the natives, which is the popular interpretation of this scene (how after all can he "know" that?), as to let the joke slip out. The laughter of the Other, of one's own unconscious, could decimate his subjectivity in Whiteness. As he is the joker, victim, and listener of this uncontainable joke, it could expose the contradictions of the order of race and in the process destroy his (false) unity as a subject. As Freud tells us, the joking subject is always a "disunited personality":

> If one has occasion as a doctor to make the acquaintance of one of those people who, though not remarkable in other ways, are well known in their circle as jokers and originators of many viable jokes, one may be surprised to discover that the joker is a disunited personality, disposed to neurotic disorders.
>
> (Freud 1905c: 142)

And Orwell's anecdote, after all, is about a crisis averted: the successful consolidation of the order of race as the desire for Whiteness.

"Shooting an elephant" is in some ways the paradigmatic text of the relationship of aggression and ambivalence to jokes, and of jokes to the order of Whiteness. In this essay, the joke is always on the verge of being cracked when the threat of violence or aggression is paramount. Orwell speaks anxiously of the irruption of uncontrollable laughter at two moments: first when he is afraid that he may not be able to shoot the elephant and contain (unconscious) ambivalence, and next when he fears being trampled upon like the coolie. Orwell writes:

> A white man mustn't be frightened in front of "natives"; and so, in general, he isn't frightened. The sole thought in my mind was that if anything went wrong those two thousand Burmans would see me pursued, caught, trampled on and reduced to a grinning corpse like the Indian up the hill. And if that happened it was quite probable that some of them would laugh.
>
> (Orwell 1953a: 153–4)

In both cases, Orwell fears that laughter will ensue from violence – that is, killing or from being killed – thus implying that the expression or suppression of the "uncanny" joke of Whiteness depends on his ability to manage this violence. Indeed, in "Shooting an elephant," the dead coolie who had been ground underfoot by the elephant also generates uncanny dread in his grotesqueness: he is first described as devilish, and grinning, and then produces overwhelming fear when Orwell realizes that he could become like the coolie – his skin too could be "stripped clean," so he would not be identifiable anymore – were he to test the elephant's *must* first instead of shooting it. What turns uncanny here, or in the scenes quoted above from "Marrakech," is not the simple fear and dread of difference, or even the loss of his identity. What is precisely anxiety-producing is not necessarily the possibility of becoming like the other; rather, Orwell's anxiety is confronting the ambivalence or contradiction of Whiteness – here its core of "nonsense." To elaborate: in "Marrakech," what is uncanny is not difference itself, but realizing that shared humanity can be unexpected where it should not have been so. One could articulate it as: "I am surprised by my own surprise to discover that he and I are the same." The contradiction of Whiteness – its uncanny effects *do not* obtain from a simple encounter with difference as it supposedly does in so-called "racist" parlance. What is really at the core is discovering that one finds sameness in the place where sameness should be and has been all along, not as the extinction of difference but as its support, and that somehow one had not expected that. This is perhaps what Lacan means by saying that "the real is something one always finds in the same place, whether or not one has been there … the real is what keeps turning up where one expected it" (II: 297). Thus the encounter with the dead coolie, I suggest, is indicative of an encounter with an unexpected (and therefore uncanny) "homeliness," a certain sameness or continuity that the subject of race consciously recognizes but does not know except in the face of death. Thus what could produce laughter is that the Burmese natives might see (what he perhaps now "knows") that under the mask of Whiteness he too is just like them, their (in)human double, and *that* is uncanny. It would be utopian to idealize this moment of de-authorization or "exposure" in the discourse of Whiteness as a site of the political subversion of the regime of race. It is more properly a moment of the extinction of the order of language and meaning, as it promises not the possibility of traversing the fundamental fantasy of mastery and sameness as the extinction of difference, but, oddly enough, of its reproduction.

The elephant is the ambivalent figure of this "meaninglessness," thus of the joke nonsense, thereby rendering Orwell's anecdote a huge over-determined elephant joke. Paradoxically, the elephant, this mammalian substance with its "grandmotherly air" (1953a: 153) functions as the core – the void, or the hole – which the formations of the unconscious, here the joke, attempt to reach. From this perspective, it is impossible to ignore the series of condensations and displacements which, in ways that are characteristic of joke work, begin to aggregate around the elephant. The elephant is both the condensation of the Burmese crowd, and a figure of displacement for his own aggression. For instance, there are two moments in the anecdote when a marked slippage occurs between the threat posed by the elephant and the crowd. When speaking of his decision to send for an elephant rifle after encountering the gruesome corpse of the coolie, Orwell admits: "It made me vaguely uneasy. I had no intention of shooting the elephant – I had merely sent for the rifle to defend myself if necessary – and it is always unnerving to have a crowd following you" (151). The substitution or, more properly, the condensation of the natives with the elephant, occurs in Orwell's sentence at the second dash, for the peculiar ampersand that follows connects two entirely unrelated clauses. Again in the passage above, when Orwell fears that his being trampled on like the coolie might induce laughter, Orwell's phrasing is quite ambiguous: "The sole thought in my mind was that if anything went wrong those two thousand Burmans would see me pursued, caught, trampled on and reduced to a grinning corpse like the Indian up the hill" (153–4). The agency of pursuing, catching and trampling, in this instance, seems to belong more to the Burmese than to the elephant. For it is unlikely that an elephant in *must* would pursue, let alone "catch," its prey with such single-minded determination. On the other hand, the elephant is also the locus of displacement of Orwell's contradictory impulses. Given his perceived loss of agency in Burma, caught as he was between a theoretical hatred of the British Empire and the more quotidian hatred of the Burmese who jeer at him, the elephant's rampage seems to displace his own aggressive instincts:

Early one morning the sub-inspector at a police station at the other end
of town rang me up on the 'phone and said that an elephant was
ravaging the bazaar. Would I please come and do something about it? ...
The Burmese population had no weapons and were quite helpless
against it. It had already destroyed somebody's bamboo hut, killed a
cow and raided some fruit-stalls and devoured the stock; also it had met
the municipal rubbish van and, when the driver jumped out and took to
his heels, had turned the van over and inflicted violences upon it.

(1953a: 149–50)

Orwell's displaced aggression is palpable in his ability to find comedy in
an account of the elephant's dangerous rampaging. The sudden tone of
levity after the racially strained opening of the essay and the endearing
description of the elephant as a "canny" creature release Orwell's racial
tension. When he encounters the elephant, however, Orwell's empathy with it
inhibits his duty to shoot it and thus protect the natives: "As soon as I saw
the elephant I knew with perfect certainty that I ought not to shoot him
[sic]" (1953a: 151). At this face-to-face encounter, the elephant that Orwell
had previously referred to with the neutral pronoun "it" is gendered as
"him," thus once again disclosing Orwell's powerful identification with the
creature as a figure that displaces the aggression that he forbids himself to
express. Thus for Orwell, a mixture of metaphors arises with regard to the
elephant: for instance, he describes it in the peculiar abstraction of "a costly
piece of machinery," which however seems to him to possess a "grandmotherly air" (153), such that "it seemed to me that it would be murder to
shoot him" (153). After the first shot, however, the elephant becomes
"immensely old" (154) – as archaic as the joke itself that has once more been
repressed. This notion of the elephant as the nonsense figure around which
signifiers aggregate becomes more apparent at the end of the story, when
there are "endless discussions" about doing the right thing. As if to materi-
alize the contradictions within colonial discourse, Orwell says that "among
the Europeans opinion was divided. The older men [the dragon slayers in
Arendt's formulation] said I was right, the younger men [the bureaucrats]
said it was a damn shame to shoot an elephant for killing a coolie, because
an elephant was worth more than any damn Coringhee coolie" (155–6).
Orwell himself, with his more liberal "instincts," is of course "very glad that
the coolie had been killed; it put me legally in the right and it gave me a
sufficient pretext for shooting the elephant" (156), thus articulating in one
incredible stroke the reticulation of colonial law and bureaucracy – that is,
the ideology of colonial rule and its pathological residue as unaccountability
and violence.

   In order to discern the meaning of the joke in relation to Whiteness, it is
necessary that one not be captivated by the comic, which Orwell uses as a
disguise for his aggression. Instead, one must discern that the comic

functions in the colonial context not merely as a façade for the joke (Freud suggests this of jokes and the comic in general [1905c: 181]), but also as a cover, a veil that conceals as it reveals the anxiety and ambivalence of colonial Whiteness. As Freud argues with regard to the relation between the comic and jokes: "If we fail to detect the joke, we are once again left only with the comic or funny story" (205). To put this another way, all comic stories about natives carry within them the anxious joke of Whiteness. And it is the particular deployment of the joke, which in large part remains unspoken by mutual consent of the colonizer and the colonized, that determines the immediate relationship of subjects of race as "white" person and "native."

Chapter 4

Looking alike

Or the ethics of *Suture*

> Things are because we see them, and what we see, and how we see it,
> depends on the Arts that have influenced us. To look at a thing is very
> different from seeing a thing. One does not see anything until one sees its
> beauty. Then, and then only, does it come into existence.
>
> (Oscar Wilde, "The decay of lying": 79)

Is there an ethics that is specific to the subject of race? With this question, I
do not mean to open the topic of racism or of what may constitute anti-
racist practice. If racism is construed as immoral, then any action that aims
to correct or eliminate that immorality can be considered ethical. But this is
not a problematic that can address the question of ethics as it pertains to the
desire of the subject who is constituted as a subject in relation to the law of
racial difference. In the following, I take up the issue of ethics as that which
is "articulated from the point of view of the location of man in relation to
the real" (VII: 11) in order to explore its relation to the concept of race.
Specifically, I turn to the 1993 film by Scott McGehee and David Siegel,
Suture, as a particularly brilliant exemplum of the ethical project in relation
to race. This film, which has been overlooked by most film critics and
scholars, offers an attempt to think race in ways that aim at a fundamental
transformation of our ways of seeing. What we mean by ethics, and an
ethics in relation to the desire of the subject of race, should emerge in the
course of our discussion.

   The film, shot entirely in black and white, was made by a couple of
academics with no film industry contacts whatsoever.[1] It was received with
hostility or bewilderment at best. Even those critics who seemed to have
enjoyed the film's visual ploys expressed uncertainty about their position as
viewers. The fact that it generated much aggravation should be read as one
of the effects that the film produces through its technique of suturing.
Suture belongs to the genre of mystery films that relies on the plot device of
mistaken identity. The story revolves around two "identical" half-brothers,
Vincent Towers and Clay Arlington, who reportedly connect for the first
time at their wealthy father's funeral. Vincent (Michael Harris), the heir and

legitimate son, is a suspect in his father's murder. He attempts to escape criminal investigation by maneuvering Clay (Dennis Haysbert) to take his place in a planned car accident. Vincent plants a car bomb that is meant to kill Clay, in the hope that the authorities will mistake the victim for Vincent and call off the investigation. Clay, however, survives the accident; inevitably taken for Vincent, he is sutured back physically by Dr Renée Descartes (Mel Harris), the plastic surgeon, and psychologically by Max Shinoda (Sab Shimono). The only visitor at Clay's bedside who knew the unpopular and reclusive Vincent and seems to have had a special under-standing with him before the accident – the accountant Alice Jameson (Dina Merrill) – does not notice that it is the wrong man. Clay, who has lost his memory, largely enjoys his reconstruction as Vincent. Descartes apparently does a fine job of "restoring" his face disfigured in the crash. Clay, however, is haunted by flashes of memory of a working-class past, and feels dogged by the police whose case seems to have reached an impasse. It is when Vincent returns carrying a gun in the middle of the night and the two ostensibly "identical" men face each other, each with a gun in his hand, that memory comes flooding back to Clay. Clay shoots Vincent in the face, thus rendering him unidentifiable. Clay at this point chooses to retain his identity as Vincent, and despite the foreboding of his psychiatrist, seems to be living happily ever after with Renée. This is testi-fied to by the final montage of the film where Clay/Vincent and Renée appear in a series of still images enjoying themselves in varied locales and activities. This is of course no original plot; we can think of scores of films that utilize the device of the wrong man framed for a murder, such as Wolfgang Petersen's *Shattered*, Hitchcock's *The Thirty-Nine Steps*, and so on. But the sense of bewilderment that this film generates turns on that point where the traditional narrative would demand an absolute suspen-sion of our disbelief: the physical resemblance of the two brothers. In this film, however, it is not our disbelief that we are called to suspend, it is our credulity. We as spectators know what no one else in the film seems to know, recognize, realize, or care about, and this is that not only are the two men nothing alike (there is not the remotest resemblance, physical or other-wise, between them) but that Clay and Vincent are of different races. Vincent is white, and Clay is black. Like Magritte's famous painting *Ceci N'est pas une Pipe*, this film asks us to consider the relation between signi-fiers and visual images. When the bandages covering Clay's face are removed, we expect surprise on the part of the medical team. But there is none. The lack of surprise is a real surprise for us as viewers who have suspended our disbelief on the presumption of a shared knowledge and discourse. By requiring us to suspend our *belief*, the film, which largely deploys a traditional Hollywood neo-noir style, puts pressure on our suturing into the narration and forces a purchase of our visual pleasure at the price of our own raced subjectivities.

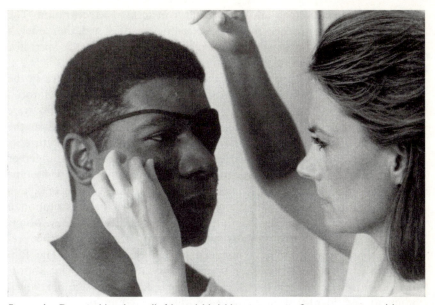

Figure 1 Dennis Haysbert (left) and Mel Harris star in *Suture*, presented by The Samuel Goldwyn Company. Courtesy of the Everett Collection, New York.

The Lacanian concept of suture (mentioned briefly in Seminar XI: 117–18) was elaborated by Jacques Alain Miller, who defines it in relation to "miscognition" as follows:

> Suture names the relation of the subject to the chain of its discourse; we shall see that it figures there as the element which is lacking, in the form of a stand-in. For, while there lacking, it is not purely and simply absent. Suture, by extension – the general relation of lack to the structure of which it is an element, inasmuch as it implies the position of a taking-the-place-of.
>
> (Miller 1977–8: 25–6)

In other words, suture names the process by which the subject comes to find a place for itself in a signifying chain by inserting itself in what is perceived as a gap, a place-holder for it. The subject appears in the chain as a signifier, thus making a subjective meaning possible. The concept was taken over in film theory in the mid-1970s to refer broadly to the transactions between the cinematic apparatus and the spectator in rendering the film intelligible.[2] As identification, as a process of narrative decoding, and as ideological interpellation, the analysis of "suture" focuses on the syntax and grammar of film in order to understand how a certain fiction of reciprocity is established between the camera/screen and the spectator in terms of recognition. The spectator recognizes him/herself on the screen or identifies with the camera's point of view, while the apparatus in turn recognizes the subject as spectator and gives him/her a place in the narrative.

In Siegel and McGehee's *Suture*, the term or the concept works in the film at several levels, which can be broadly categorized into the spectatorial and the diegetic. Though we will refer to the two registers as if they were separate moments, they are interconnected precisely at that point where the ethical subject of race emerges. Diegetically, the film plays on suture as sewing and as identity. Dr Descartes literally sutures Clay back together again. As a plastic surgeon, she works with photographs and a videotape of Vincent which permit her to restore the patient's face. However, Clay's suturing is more profound at the level of identity. Given a representation, a signifier that will give him a place in the chain of signification, Clay, who is entirely devoid of memory, finds himself being sutured into the pre-existing representation that is assigned to him as his place. The film suggests a constructionist reading of subjectivity at this point. Our knowledge of ourselves, it seems to say, is determined by the signifier which commands an identification. And even the visual fact of difference is bound and made possible by our identifications. We are posited entirely as symbolic subjects who are wholly determined by the signifier or language with no remainder. Well enough, but then why do we as spectators refute this claim? Why the aggravation, the incredulity, the citation of racial fact, of visible, physical evidence? We are put in the foolish position of naming the obvious to extinguish doubt about the facticity of the world. While on one hand the narrative movement of the film and its conventional focalization interpellates us as consumers of visual pleasure, the film's deliberate, seemingly perverse disavowal of this shared racial knowledge threatens to unravel the process of suturing. In the scene where Renée Descartes sedulously removes Clay's sutures – the shot is a close-up of their faces (Figure 1), enabling us to look deeply at the procedure as she pulls and snaps the stitches – she reassures him of his innocence on the basis of physiognomy and the "once complete science" of characterology. People with fine Greco-Roman noses and soft, straight hair do not commit murder, she assures him. They are inclined towards music, literature and the arts. The irony of the scene is multi-layered. The very profession of plastic surgery that Renée practices militates against the notion of physiognomy as destiny. Moreover, not only do we "know" that Vincent with his Greco-Roman nose and love of music, literature and the arts did attempt murder, but we also know that Clay does not fit the description in any sense. While we could find satisfaction in our superior "knowledge" that gives the lie to Renée's discourse, the film refuses to permit us this satisfaction. We are also troubled that the film does not avow this irony, and in fact refuses the conventional reciprocity of recognition entailed in cinematic suture. In literature, unstable narrators, of course, form a genre of their own, but a non self-reflexive, unstable camera is rather uncommon. As viewers, our suture comes apart as Renée Descartes sutures Clay into a racial narrative even as she removes the stitches from his epidermis, that momentous "lamella"[3] which figures as fate. This is a moment in the film that actualizes the discourse of race as a particular structure of anxiety. It is an anxiety (as I have been delineating thus far) that emerges in the encounter with the historicity of race (the signifier Whiteness), which then finds an object through the so-called pre-discursive mark: skin, hair and bone. I suggest that the effects of the film's disavowal of racial difference, and its demand that we do so as well to maintain our level of visual pleasure, are propositional. I will take up that aspect presently. In the following, I discuss the question of ethics as it is thematized by the diegesis of the film, before I invoke the issue as it functions spectatorially in the viewing of the film itself.

Love thy neighbor

In the foregoing précis of the film, it was suggested that *Suture* deploys a conventional narrative device of the innocent double framed for a murder. However, the film's conventionality exceeds even the codes of Hollywood; it is a profoundly Oedipal story, but it tells the story not of the Oedipus of Freud's *Interpretation of Dreams*, but the proto-Oedipus myth that Freud detailed in *Totem and Taboo*. Though both myths deal with parricide and the functioning of the law prohibiting incest, there are also some important differences between them. Freud's reading of Sophocles' *Oedipus Rex* assumes the pre-existence of the prohibition, whereas his tale of the primal horde attempts to account for the prohibition as a structural component of subject constitution. *Suture* very appropriately invokes the father of the primal horde, rather than Laius, to enable us to pose the question of the "function of desire" (Lacan, VII: 209) and of the supplementary object, the remainder of the law, in relation to race.

In the videotape of the father's birthday party, which according to Alice Jameson was "most productive politically of all his birthday parties," the father is depicted as possessing everything. The "home movie," with its limited visuals, grainy footage and foregrounded apparatus, evokes the sense of the ultimately uncapturable, unrepresentable nature of rich Mr Towers as he sits surrounded by admiring friends. Vincent stands beside him, glowering. Clay comments that he (Vincent, whom he now identifies as himself) doesn't seem to be having a very good time, and the next frame shows a rather giddy group of women toasting the old man. "He was very powerful, Vincent; people treated him with great respect," says Alice Jameson, who is clueing Clay/Vincent into his guilt, unlike Vincent, of course, who it is suggested had no friends. The father hoarded wealth, power, and seemingly the women. In the opening conversation with Clay at the bus station, Vincent conveys the "most simple and basic of lessons" to Clay. He responds with characteristic hauteur to Clay's comment about crime in cities:

> "Crime isn't so much a problem here as a fact. Each man has his own jungle. It's just a matter of understanding it and knowing where one fits in. ... Take me for example, Vincent Towers. I am a very wealthy man, with expensive things all around me, and I am forced to protect what's mine against people who might feed off my privilege, feed off what doesn't belong to them. It's the most simple and basic of lessons. It's the law our father lived by."

Hoarding women, wealth, and power, the primal father, in Freud's myth, incites the envy of the sons, and thus is born the conspiracy of the brothers to kill the father and share the women. According to Freud in *Totem and Taboo*:

> The dead father became stronger than the living one had been – for events took the course we so often see them follow in human affairs to this day. What had up to then been prevented by his actual existence was thenceforward prohibited by the sons themselves, in accordance with the psychological procedure so familiar to us in psycho-analyses under the name of "deferred obedience". They revoked their deed by forbidding the killing of the totem, the substitute for their father; and they renounced its fruits by resigning their claim to the women who had now been set free. They thus created out of their filial sense of guilt the two fundamental taboos of totemism, which for that very reason inevitably corresponded to the two repressed wishes of the Oedipus complex.
>
> (Freud 1913: 143)

But Vincent is not interested in participating in what Juliet MacCannell has termed the "regime of the brothers,"[4] if by that we mean the installation of the moral law: the twin prohibitions of incest and murder, the submission to the superego, and the pleasure principle with its notion of the good. However, as Vincent discovers, killing the (primal) father does not deliver the coveted enjoyment that he (as with the primal brothers) believed was denied to him by the father. As Lacan says: "Whoever enters the path of uninhibited *jouissance*, in the name of the rejection of the moral law in some form or other, encounters obstacles whose power is revealed to us every day in our experience in innumerable forms" (VII: 177). If "failure is far more propitious for a moral reaction than satisfaction" (Freud 1913: 143), in Vincent's case it is precisely his attempt to displace the futility of his action (his rejection of the moral law) that opens the film onto the problem of evil as Lacan construes it – the evil that is *jouissance* (VII: 184), and situates Vincent in relation to the drives: the death drive.

What are the relations among the moral law, *jouissance* and the death drive? The primal father is the necessary fantasy of the time before the law generated by the law itself. In Lacan's terms, without the fantasy of a remainder, there being at least a One who is not subject to the incest taboo, the taboo itself could not hold its sway as the superego. However, this "dead father," translated by Lacan into the "death of God," initiates a fundamental problematic as the signifier of the Other S(O):

> it signifies the final response to the guarantee asked of the Other concerning the meaning of that Law articulated in the depths of the unconscious. If there is nothing more than a lack, the Other is wanting, and the signifier is that of his death.
>
> It is as a function of this position, which is itself dependent on the paradox of the Law, that the paradox of *jouissance* emerges.
>
> (VII: 193)

The inability of the Other to provide a guarantee as to the meaning of the law, the fact that the Other is lacking, produces certain effects: namely, the paradox of *jouissance*, the possibility of transgression, and the death drive. This nexus of relations founded on the lack in the Other (the death of God) makes itself present as the cruel superego. Distinguishing between the ego ideal (the law of the pleasure principle as founded on the "good father" [VII: 181]), and the superego (founded on the "dead father"), Lacan suggests that it is the "sublation" of the law by the Christian commandment "love thy neighbor as thyself" that makes transgression as *jouissance* a possibility. The superego decrees a certain enjoyment. Rather than normalize desire as in Freud's ideal ("that patriarchal civility is supposed to set us on the most reasonable path to temperate or normal desires" [VII: 177]), its commandment to "love thy neighbor" literally invokes the drive as oriented towards *jouissance*. And *jouissance* is, of course, inaccessible except through transgression. "Transgression in the direction of *jouissance* only takes place if it is supported by the oppositional principle, by the forms of the Law" (VII: 177). (The subject's orientation towards the possibility of *jouissance* dictates the psychical structure of one's *desire*. That is, one can defend against it, pursue it in fantasy, reproduce its semblance in a bodily symptom, etc. The permutations are virtually infinite in that they are particular to each subject.[5] Thus one can reasonably conceive of desire as the aim, which must continually miss its goal, which is *jouissance*, in order to reproduce itself as desire.[6]) Lacan stresses that "this point of transgression has a significant relation to something that is involved in our inquiry into ethics, that is to say the meaning of desire" (VII: 207). The exemplar of such an "ethics" of transgression, transgression as "love thy neighbor," is Sade. Through his audacious pairing of Kant and Sade (VII: 188), Lacan suggests that it is Sade who "teaches us, in the order of symbolic play, how to attempt to go beyond the limit, and how to discover the laws of one's neighbor's space as such" (VII: 197). Lacan is, of course, expatiating on Freud's indignation in *Civilization and its Discontents* (1930) at the commandment to love thy neighbor. Freud termed it the "*credo quia absurdum*" (1930: 64) in view of the fact that

> men are not gentle creatures who want to be loved, and who at the most can defend themselves if they are attacked; they are, on the contrary, creatures among whose instinctual endowments is to be reckoned a powerful share of aggressiveness. As a result, their neighbor is for them not only a potential helper or sexual object, but also someone who tempts them to satisfy their aggressiveness on him, to exploit his capacity for work without compensation, to use him sexually without his consent, to seize his possessions, to humiliate him, to cause him pain, to torture and to kill him.
>
> (Freud 1930: 65)

Given this human drive beyond the pleasure principle, the commandment to love one's neighbor becomes diabolical. As Lacan puts it, "to love him, to love him as myself, is necessarily to move toward some cruelty. His or mine?, you will object. But haven't I just explained to you that nothing indicates that they are distinct?" (VII: 198). Interestingly, if one retreats from this commandment, it is not in the name of the law, but the imaginary, for we do not wish to assault the image "on which we were formed as an ego" (VII: 195). Vincent, like Sade, "proves the imaginary structure of the limit" (VII: 197) by heeding the commandment and loving his neighbor as himself. Loving him to death, Vincent invites his brother to take his place in death. Thus it would be a mistake to think that Vincent does not feel guilt; he is quite committed to his transgression. His last words to Clay before he sets off the remote car bomb are an apology and an explanation. In other words, he is not a psychotic who has foreclosed the Name of the Father – the signifier that institutes lack or desire, and subjects one to the law. Rather, Vincent wants to transgress the law, to cross its limit by separating out a double of himself (VII: 261) in Clay, his neighborly other, who will bear the burden of his will to create his world, and himself *ex nihilo*. Motivated by the death drive, Vincent is fixed on what Lacan calls the "sovereign good," the *das Ding*, the forbidden object (VII: 70). "When one approaches that central emptiness, which up to now has been the form in which access to *jouissance* has presented itself to us, my neighbor's body breaks into pieces" (VII: 202). On screen, we see the car explode on a television monitor in the airport. A screen within a screen, it is not clear if it is "the" car exploding with Clay in it, or "a" car explosion. In this brilliant Lacanian moment, the camera suggests the lethality of identical things: car explosions are not irreducible because they are identical; rather sameness indicates an emptiness, the extimate *das Ding* of evil, of *jouissance*.[7]

Not only does Vincent believe that he will obtain the *jouissance* that was denied him by his father, but he expects to create himself anew by ridding himself of the signifier that locates him in a narrative of guilt that he wishes to refute. This attempt to fashion himself out of nothing, by giving himself a new signifier, is unmistakably the "will to destruction," the will to go beyond the moral law, which Lacan specifies as endemic to the death drive.

> The death drive is to be situated in the historical domain; it is articulated at a level that can only be defined as a function of the signifying chain, that is to say, insofar as a reference point, that is a reference point of order, can be situated relative to the functioning of nature. It requires something from beyond whence it may itself be grasped in a fundamental act of memorization, as a result of which everything may be recaptured, not simply in the movement of metamorphoses but from an initial intention.
>
> (VII: 211)

This beyond, which in Freudian terms would be the trauma which compels its repetition and rememorization in order to secure the unbound cathexes, is the *ex nihilo* on which the signifying chain is "founded and articulated as such" (VII: 212). The death drive is the absolute "will to destruction. Will to make a fresh start. Will for an Other-thing, given that everything can be challenged from the perspective of the function of the signifier" (VII: 212). Such a "will" is exemplified by the Sadean hero who seeks not just the simple death of the organism, but its "second death," a death beyond death where the cyclical movement of nature can be interrupted, so that creation can begin anew, *ex nihilo*. Thus Vincent's "true" desire is to annihilate himself beyond regeneration. His name, identity, memory, material goods have passed on to an other, but more importantly, in the end even his body is unidentifiable, to the point that the very historicity of his life as once having had existence is erased. As Clay says, "It's a dead body that can't be identified, and in the most real way it's not the body of Vincent Towers." My argument is that, through his death drive, Vincent makes Clay, the ethical subject (of race), come into being in a certain relation to the limit, where "the problematic of desire" is raised as a desire in relation to death.

Vincent's death drive, exemplary of Sadean "ethics," makes possible Clay's ethical position as a *desire* for death. Lacan's ethics of psychoanalysis is not the simple ethics of the pleasure principle, but neither is it an advocacy of *jouissance* or the Sadean death drive. As Lacan himself states towards the end of his 1962 essay "Kant with Sade":

> Sade is not close enough to his own wickedness to recognize his neighbor in it ... Sade thus stopped, at the point where desire is knotted together with the law. ... Of a treatise truly about desire, there is little here, even nothing.
>
> (74–5)

Lacan insists that ethics pertains to the "freedom of desire" which will go beyond the law rather than merely support it through fantasy, or oppose it as drive. Such an ethics addresses death as the constitutive factor in both drive and desire. The conjunction between the desire for death and the death drive depends upon the differing functions of affirmation and negation in the subject's relation to the beyond – the *ex nihilo*, the void that is the cause of the signifier. If the death drive is the negation of negation, the desire for death is the affirmation of the subject as he/she assumes his/her own mortality. "It is in effect as a desire for death that [the subject] affirms himself for others" (E: 105). For Lacan, such an assumption of one's own mortality, where desire is constituted "in a fundamental relation to death" (VII: 303), is the proper site for the emergence of the ethical subject[8] who finds his/her location "in relation to the real" (VII: 11).

Dead again

> The function of desire must remain in a fundamental relationship to death. The question I ask is this: shouldn't the true termination of an analysis ... in the end confront the one who undergoes it with the reality of the human condition? It is precisely this, that in connection with anguish, Freud designated as the level at which its signal is produced, namely Hilflosigkeit or distress, the state in which man is in relationship to himself which is his own death – in the sense I have you to isolate it this year, and can expect help from no one.
>
> At the end of a training analysis the subject should reach and should know the domain and the level of the experience of absolute disarray. It is a level at which anguish is already a protection, not so much *Abwarten* [waiting] as *Erwartung* [anticipation]. Anguish develops by letting a danger appear, whereas there is no danger at the level of the final experience of Hilflosigkeit.
>
> I have already told you how the limit of this region is expressed for man; it touches the end of what he is and what he is not.
>
> (VII: 303–4)

In the opening sequence of the film, the voice-over of the psychiatrist Max Shinoda invokes the question of identity. "How is it that we know who we are?" On the screen we see the door being opened, stealthily. A "black" man in bed opens his one eye. Voice-over: "We might wake up in the night disoriented and wonder where we are." On screen, the "black" man discerns the entry of an armed intruder. "We may have forgotten where the window, or the door, or the bathroom is, or who is sleeping beside us." The man picks up the rifle. "We may think perhaps that we have lived through what we just dreamed of, or we may wonder if we are still dreaming." The man hides in the sunken bathtub with the curtain closed around him. "But we never wonder who we are." The intruder (a "white" man) enters, fires three shots at the now-empty bed, enters the bathroom, tears apart the curtain, and we see an explosion which dissolves into the analepsis that explains the events of the narrative thus far. This immensely suturing opening of the film, which affirms a "core" identity as it negates it filmically (in fact we do not know who we are in the film, and neither does Clay, as we soon discover) bears a striking "resemblance" to Lacan's anecdote in Seminar XI. Here Lacan underlines the connections among the concepts of reality, perception-consciousness, the unconscious, memory, and identity. In Seminar VII, he had already spoken of the necessity to conceive of reality produced by the so-called perception consciousness system as founded on the object and thus the relation of desire in the unconscious. In this later seminar, Lacan focuses on the subject of the unconscious as that which is known only in and as rupture, "between perception and consciousness." Lacan's anecdote follows:

> The other day, I was awoken from a short nap by [a] knocking at my door just before I actually awoke. With this impatient knocking I had already formed a dream, a dream that manifested to me something other than this knocking. And when I awake, it is in so far as I reconstitute my entire representation around this knocking – this perception – that I am aware of it. I know that I am there, at what time I went to sleep, and why I went to sleep. When the knocking occurs, not in my perception, but in my consciousness, it is because my consciousness reconstitutes itself around this representation, that I know that I am waking up, that I am *knocked up*.
>
> But here I must question myself as to what I am at that moment – at the moment, so immediately before and so separate.
>
> (XI: 56)

Contrary to Max Shinoda, the psychiatrist, the anecdote suggests that we do indeed wonder who we are, and it is in that wondering, that forgetting, that the subject's emergence as such is locatable. In Seminar VII, Lacan says that the subject of the symbolic order is nothing more than the fact that "he can forget. Strike out that 'he'; the subject is literally at his beginning the elision of a signifier as such, the missing signifier in the chain" (VII: 224). Rather than rendering him pathological as Shinoda claims in the initial voice-over, Clay's amnesia locates him fully within the law of the symbolic order. Having no memory of anything before the accident, lacking a signifier for himself, he submits entirely to the place that is assigned to him in a pre-existing signifying chain. As Max himself suggests, Clay's amnesia relies upon representations of forgetting. In one of his first meetings with Clay, Max says:

> "Research suggests that your own understanding of how, what an amne-siac forgets, whatever is seen in movies or TV has created a pattern by which you yourself have forgotten. If you had forgotten now how to talk, we wouldn't be having this conversation."

Clay's dilemma is to encounter as a question of identity ("Who am I?") the complex syllogistic relations between knowing and recognizing on one hand and remembering and forgetting on another. In a provocative scene with Alice Jameson, Clay is preparing to go home to figure out, as he says, "who I am, and figure out whether or not they [the police] are right." Alice's response is ambiguous, questioning whether he is ready to figure that out given his present lack of knowledge and memory. When Clay affirms that he doesn't know anything, with the stress on anything, Alice contradicts him, assuring him that he has the knowledge, but lacks memory of the man he was, and the man he needs to be. Clay's response to this seduction, that he does in fact have the necessary knowledge, is to remind her that he does not remember. Immediately after, even this evasion is subverted by Alice's attention to a scar on his back that she apparently does not remember, and inquires whether Clay acquired it in the accident. Clay seems to recognize that the scar is not associated with the accident, but he says, "it's another one of those things I can't remember." If knowing and remembering are means of ascertaining who one is, then as a form of forgetting, recognizing without knowing locates the subject in doubt. In Clay's case, as with the subject delineated by psychoanalysis, the encounter with doubt leads not to certainty but to the question of desire and its cause.

Clay's position in the symbolic is most apparent in his immediate and anguished acceptance of guilt. Interestingly, he accepts Vincent's guilt without being conscious of having committed the crime. He has neither memory nor knowledge of the crime. Like the Lacan who was awakened from his short nap by a knocking, Clay knows himself entirely through representation, but that is not all. His submission to the signifier is simulta-neously obedience to the moral law. There is no question of doubt where guilt is concerned for the subject of the symbolic; it is the necessary condi-tion of one's existence as a speaking subject. Thus Clay, at this point in the

film, occupies a position opposed to that of Vincent. He has a strong ego
ideal, submits to the moral law, and sets the pleasure principle and the good
in motion. Clay also fully cooperates with the law. He agrees to appear in a
police line-up of suspects for Mrs Lucerne, the sole witness to the murder, to
identify; he tries to piece his past back together, and he dutifully remembers
details from his dreams for Max's sake. However, though he assumes virtually all of Vincent's affections, his love of the opera, target shooting,
expensive clothes, etc., he significantly repudiates the "mother" – Alice
Jameson. Alice is an older woman, maternal and seductive at the same time,
and it is quite clear that not only did she play hostess at the elder Mr
Towers' house (the nominal wife and mother) but that she and Vincent were
having an affair. However, Clay too, of course, has his desire, a lack
produced by his very submission to the law. His fundamental fantasy, unlike
Vincent's, is not one of overcoming castration by taking the place of the
primal father, but of filling the lack in the other. Clay is pursued by
the object, an *objet petit a* in the shape of a St Christopher medal that was
given to him by his mother. The first "memory" that returns after he leaves
the hospital is significantly not of the object itself but of him looking for the
object. In fact, the first we hear about the medal, it is as something Clay has
lost. Clay is looking for it in the laundry hamper, and Vincent peremptorily
prohibits the search. "Clay! What are you looking for?" he barks, a little
unnerved by the good that Clay seeks, this unforeseen residue of his plans.
Clay looks a little guilty, and postpones the search. In his delirium after the
accident, the medal returns, along with flashes of heavy construction equip-
ment and crushed cars. Going "home" for the first time from the hospital,
Clay finds the object and promptly passes out. The next we hear about the
medal, it is lost again, and no one seems to remember having seen it. Clay's
recognition of the medal as his lost object places him within the ambit of
the law, in that it is the thing that will save him from his *jouissance* by being
perpetually lost. To coincide with it would be disastrous. One can do so
either through the drive as we witness in Vincent, or as Lacan says in the
epigraph quoted above, by the subject going through (or traversing) the
fundamental fantasy, where the object falls from its place as the cause of
desire, and the analysand thereby encounters his/her desire in its relation to
death. Lacan clarifies the connection between desire for the object and the
law thus:

> What we find in the incest law is located as such at the level of
> the unconscious in relation to *das Ding*, the Thing. The desire for the
> mother cannot be satisfied because it is the end, the terminal point,
> the abolition of the whole world of demand, which is the one that at its
> deepest level structures the man's unconscious. It is to the extent that the
> function of the pleasure principle is to make man always search for what
> he has to find again, but which he never will attain, that one reaches the

essence, namely, that sphere or relationship which is known as the law of the prohibition of incest.

(VII: 68)

How does race function at this moment in the film? Interestingly enough, the film signifies this radical non-identity with oneself, which is the condition of being a subject in the symbolic, through the device of racial difference. The uncanniness of Clay's suturing of himself to the signifier "Vincent" is heightened by his racial difference. Here racial visibility serves not so much as a compensatory object for the limit (the totality or historicity) of race, but for the limit of the symbolic itself. It points to the gap, the incompleteness of the Other as language. It is a moment when the racial mark seems to serve the function of reification (as that which escapes representation and is thus in the real) that it seeks to perform in the encounter with anxiety; however, it is precisely this function, as we shall see, that is carefully undermined by the particular ethicality celebrated by the film. Renée Descartes, the plastic surgeon, who evokes race most explicitly, functions as the limit of that certainty. Her name, as with other names in the film, is obviously a pun that we cannot ignore. In the transposition of Renée Descartes into a woman and a plastic surgeon no less, the film invites the viewer to employ a psychoanalytic perspective of Renée as a Cartesian subject who does not recognize the workings of her desire. Renée's understanding of Clay/Vincent seems to be based not on sense perception, but on pure intellection. She constructs a representation of the identity of Clay/Vincent purely on the basis of mental images and X-rays. Her attitude to the body is again Cartesian – it seems to be a carapace (XX: 6) which she claims to be able to fix, as opposed to the mind, "the electrical system," which she leaves to Max. Renée can view Clay as Vincent because she conceptualizes their identity. Her judgment of Clay as good, her claim to "know" Clay's true and fundamental personality, is again through the exercise of her will. The point at which Renée dispels Clay's doubt is also the point when we see why Lacan insists that "Freud's method is Cartesian – in the sense that he sets out from the basis of the subject of certainty" (XI: 35). Renée's certainty, which seems very sound, is seemingly based on a clear and distinct perception of Clay/Vincent's goodness. We as viewers know, of course, that her perception is both false and right. It is false because she has misrecognized Clay for Vincent, but it is also right, in that Clay is not what we know Vincent to be. Knowledge and perception split here to reveal the foundation of the subject of psychoanalysis in the subject of science. In "Science and Truth" (XIII: lesson one), Lacan stresses the correlation of the Cartesian subject with the subject of science for whom experience is repeatable and the world knowable as an object. He speaks of such a subject as the necessary point of departure for psychoanalysis' discovery of "the subject caught up in a constituting division" (XIII: 5). Because knowledge and truth are disjointed in Renée's discourse, we are made to see beyond the limits of Renée's certainty (the Cartesian subject as ego who is fully coincident with him/herself) to her desire. For Lacan, the "subject's division between truth and knowledge" (12) is the precise locus of the unconscious which has some other cause – the *objet a* of psychoanalysis.

Renée's object is localized in the signifier Vincent and its soaring consonants (VT),[9] which contrast with the more fetal and earthy Clay Arlington, "salt of the earth", as Renée says sarcastically at one point, referring to Vincent before she gets to "know" him. We see the moment of her cathexis, when the videotape of Mr Towers' birthday party plays in the background, while Renée works at her desk. A woman's voice on the tape laughingly calls Vincent insistently, at which point Renée looks up, herself hailed by the signifier. The screen then fills with her looking at the screen, while she rewinds and replays Vincent's 180-degree turnaround to face his interpellant and to turn back again. What we see is a mugshot: right profile, center, left profile. Renée plays the clip over and over again, ostensibly to get a better look at him. Renée's wish to be seen by him is apparent in her first visit to Vincent's house to look over photographs with Alice. She arrives rather heavily and impressively dressed, explaining that she would be meeting some friends at the opera later. It is not important that Vincent is not physically there to "see" her. It is rather his function as the gaze, and this is manifest in the half-veiled portrait of him, that she uncovers, for both her and Clay, that is relevant here. Vincent's photographs take on an object-like force, as later we see Clay obsessively playing the tape and gazing at Vincent's photographs; obviously his absence opens a space of desire that both Clay and Renée wish to fill. But Renée's desire is rather more complex than the structure of fantasy ($\$ \lozenge a$) would suggest.

It is not easy to determine Renée's love object. She seems to be in love with Clay/Vincent's being, a body beyond appearance. Her first glimpse of him is through his X-rays. "He looks like a mess!" is her first remark. When she visits Vincent's apartment, the first shot is a close-up of her hands around a plain spherical sculpture. It is a ball, an opaque ball, literally nothing. Later, when she makes love to an abstract Vincent, her hands shape and mold his body, and the scenes are intercut with X-rays of the parts Renée caresses. Clay is literally clay in Renée's hands as she fashions "Vincent" (the signifier) on the surgical table and the hotel bed, marking his body with her desire. What does it mean to create the object? To pose that question would be, in Lacanian terms, to raise the issue of sublimation, more properly artistic sublimation.[10] Of the relations between creation and the object, Lacan says: "An object insofar as it is a created object, may fill the function that enables it not to avoid the Thing as signifier, but to represent it" (VII: 119). Renée creates the object that will represent for her the "Thing," her sovereign good. Lacan invokes the example of the potter creating a vase out of the hole in the middle of the potter's wheel. Invoking Heidegger's famous meditation on the "vase,"[11] Lacan suggests that "it creates the void and thereby introduces the possibility of filling it. Emptiness and fullness are introduced into a world that by itself knows not of them" (VII: 120). But the void-producing vase is itself produced out of nothing. Lacan says,

> the potter, just like you to whom I am speaking, creates the vase with his hand around this emptiness, creates it, just like the mythical creator, *ex nihilo*, starting with a hole. ... *The fashioning of the signifier and the introduction of a gap or a hole in the real is [sic] identical.*
>
> (VII: 121, my emphasis)

The signifier "Vincent" that Renée creates out of clay, nothing, also produces the lack, represented here by "Vincent's" amnesia, that Renée can now properly aim to fill. To create, in other words, is to situate oneself in relation to the lack in the Other. For "Vincent's" amnesia is not his property, but the symptom of the failure of the symbolic, of language, which is his proper cause. Renée's love object then is more than an *objet petit a*; it is an object that is raised "to the dignity of the Thing." Her attachment to Clay/Vincent is neither the imaginary misrecognition that it may initially appear to be nor the simple genital fantasy that ensues in what Lacan terms phallic *jouissance*. Renée seems to open a space where *jouissance*, as tied to the Thing, the emptiness at the center of the real, is made manifest. Renée, in fashioning the signifier, also produces her own desire in relation to that lack in the Other. If Renée's desire begins as the desire of the Other, which we perceive in her initial encounter with the enigma that Vincent poses, in (re)creating that signifier, she gains access to a *jouissance* that will enable Clay as the ethical subject of race to emerge. In other words, Renée as a certain Descartes, her fantasy of self-identity, is precisely what Clay must preserve in order to continue being her cause of desire. And it is this recognition of her desire that contributes to Clay's ethical attitude to race. It is of course possible to read Renée as giving birth to Clay as Vincent, but that would be precisely to elide the fact that, in psychoanalysis, creation as sublimation is differentiated from birthing.[12] Whereas the latter refers to instinct and nature, the object created by sublimation is related to the drive. Renée's creation of the signifier points to something beyond the symbolic for its cause, thus setting in motion, at the spectatorial and diegetic levels, the dialectic between resemblance and similitude.

This is not a black man

In the scene we quoted earlier, where Renée undoes "Vincent's" stitches, even as she reassures him of his innocence on the basis of his elegant Greco-Roman nose and fine straight hair, what we are confronted with is a screen that behaves like a Magritte canvas. "This is not a black man," it seems to say, anymore than Descartes is Descartes. As a canvas, such a negative discourse can invite meditation on the relations between text and image, words and referents, signifiers and signifieds. But in a film that relies on the momentum of narrative for its coherence, such meditation is of course impossible. This is a moment when the visual attributes of film as such – its visual plenitude, or overspecification of detail, and its non-assertiveness where these details are concerned – are considerably narrowed and sharpened to something like a pure linguistic text.[13] In this scene, visual detail is at a bare minimum, for all we see is an extreme close-up, just the heads, partly in profile, of Clay and Renée. The effect of this elimination of extraneous detail so characteristic of cinema allows the camera to *assert* the visible difference between the two figures on screen. Our pleasure as spectators, insofar as it is enabled by our suturing to one of the other characters, is hijacked by a representational schema that suborns us into its discourse by the sheer pressure of its narrative, even as we are inclined to protest. There are several key things happening here at the diegetic and spectatorial levels that we can sort out with the help of Foucault's perspicacious little book on René Magritte, *This Is Not a Pipe* (1983).

When confronted with a direct, flat denial such as "This is not a pipe," our response, as Foucault points out, could be "My God, how simple-minded! The statement is perfectly true, since it is quite apparent that the drawing representing the pipe is not the pipe itself" (Foucault 1983: 19). Acknowledging our common-sense understanding that representations and the things they represent are not the same, Foucault examines the convention of language that nevertheless persists in collapsing visual image and referent to suggest "the impossibility of defining a perspective that would let us say that the assertion is true, false, or contradictory" (20). With film, however, the conventions of representation work a little differently. Though it is acknowledged that the person playing the part is not the same as the character he or she is representing, our suturing into the filmic narrative is designed to deny the discrepancy between the actor and real or fictional character. Within the logic of cinematic suture, then, the truth of the character depends upon the adequacy of the actor to define the role. Renée's assertion of Clay's Greco-Roman nose plays false with regard, not only to the character Clay, but with reference to Dennis Haysbert, "the black actor" in question. It's not a question of miscasting, an inappropriate or unconvincing Scarlett O'Hara, or Hamlet, but a seemingly fundamental and radical misidentification of a black man for a white man. Haysbert is not failing in his role as Vincent "the white man" (as one could say for example about Alec Guinness in brown make-up playing an Arab King Faisal, etc.); he is being one. *Suture*, unlike Magritte's canvas, does not deny; rather, it affirms what is apparently a lie: "This is a white man." It is at this level of the enunciation as *lying* rather than of its *difference* from the enounced, that the film unsettles the viewer and demands, even enjoins, a certain enjoyment.

Foucault's discussion of Magritte focuses on the mutual non-relation between the verbal and the visual, text and image, to interrogate not only the transparency of either as mediums of representation, but to restore to each its autonomy through negation. In Magritte's canvas, the pipe resembles a pipe, but the text denies it, thus invoking three types of ambiguity generated by the pronoun "this." In *Suture*, however, we have no such apparent ambiguity of the pronoun. The shifters "I" and "you" have the relative stability necessary for signification to occur. What becomes problematic, then, is the status of resemblance and its inevitable function as the affirming of presence.

According to Foucault, one of the principles governing "classical" painting

> posits an equivalence between the fact of resemblance and the affirmation of a representative bond. Let a figure resemble an object (or some other figure), and that alone is enough for there to slip into the pure play of the painting a statement – obvious, banal, repeated a thousand times yet almost always silent.
>
> (Foucault 1983: 34)

Magritte is of course the painter who militates against such commonplace reinforcements. Though his paintings bear a great fealty to resemblance, they nevertheless refuse mastery of the object that accompanies the assertion of visual reality. The resemblances in Magritte's canvases are thus radically in excess. Resemblance, then, gets realigned with repetition rather than with affirmation. "The ship at sea will not resemble merely a ship, but the sea itself, even to its hull and sails being composed of waves (*Le Séducteur*)" (Foucault 1983: 35). For Foucault, this technique subverts resemblance as affirmation and establishes instead the relations of similitude where resemblances multiply themselves, thus effecting "a cruel separation between the graphic and plastic elements" (35). The argument for similitude, over resemblance is quite straightforward. The latter presupposes an original, a primary reference. It aims toward a transparent representation of the object as visible, which "orders and hierarchizes" according to the exactness of the copy. Similitude, Foucault argues, "serves repetition" (44); in multiplying resemblances, the original vanishes, leaving only the simulacrum. Referring to Magritte's *Décalcomanie* (which depicts the proverbial back of the gentleman in the bowler hat blocking the view of the sea, which is then visible in the curtain beside him, which seems to have been cut out in exactly his shape), Foucault says:

> And thanks to *Décalcomanie* the advantage of similitude over resemblance can be grasped. The latter reveals the clearly visible; similitude reveals what recognizable objects, familiar silhouettes hide, prevent from

being seen, render invisible. ("Body" = "curtain," says mimetic representation. "Right is left, left is right; the hidden here is visible there; the
sunken is in relief; flatness extends into depth," say the similitudes of
Décalcomanie.)

(Foucault 1983: 46)

Though similitude denies the reality affirmed by resemblance, it is nevertheless itself affirmative of the simulacrum. Thus what we have is a series of
affirmations "which reject the assertion of resemblance" (47). For Foucault,
such affirmation (he uncovers seven kinds of affirmation in *This Is Not a
Pipe*) posits a radically reconfigured relationship between the verbal and the
visual. Representation as resemblance can only affirm reality by introducing
the excluded element of language into its domain. "Hence ... classical
painting spoke – and spoke constantly – while constituting itself entirely
outside language" (53). Thus it could establish a common ground between
signs and images. Magritte, on the other hand, "knits verbal signs and
plastic elements together. ... He brings pure similitudes and non affirmative
verbal statements into play within the instability of a disoriented volume
and unmapped space" (53–4). For Foucault, it is this relation to discourse
that is of importance in Magritte's painting, where signification becomes
denatured to the point that it unravels to expose the futility of representation as perception.

If we apply some of Foucault's insights to *Suture*, the first problem we
encounter is the automatic linking of resemblance with affirmation. As
"subjects of race," "we," as spectators, perceive that Clay does not resemble
Vincent, but the text, the screenplay, nevertheless affirms a resemblance that
"we" simply do not see. Rather than assert autonomy from the image, the
linguistic text (Renée's speech) in this scene, and in the film as a whole, seemingly subordinates itself to the image in the manner of conventional
representations. To affirm a reality on the basis of non-resemblance can
conceivably constitute the definition of the common lie. However, there is no
conspiracy, diegetically speaking, to mislead Clay. The film simply registers
a hiatus between the so-called original (Vincent), the representation of that
original (photographs), and its reconstitution, or rediscovery (Clay). Thus
Clay looks at the video of Vincent at his father's birthday party and recognizes himself in it. And Clay looks at himself in the mirror and also
recognizes himself as Vincent in the reflection. This set of *non-similitudes as
resemblances* is made even more confounding in the scenes with Mrs
Lucerne, the sole witness at the scene of Mr Towers' murder. Mrs Lucerne,
in her conversation with Lt Weismann, claims, first, to have an extraordi-
nary ability to distinguish people's faces; she can even tell her two pet birds
apart; and second, to have superb recall in general. She boasts of her powers
of memory. However, when Weismann gives her several photographs of
suspects, among which she is to distinguish and identify Vincent, the camera

moves over to her right shoulder, and we see along with her the police records of several men. Mrs Lucerne at first seems intimidated by the similarity amongst the photographs. "All these men look so similar ..., " she exclaims, "I don't think I recognize any sort of distinction. Photographs are different from people, you know." However, the photos "in fact" depict markedly dissimilar faces: thick-set men, wide-jawed men, men with broad foreheads and others with narrow ones, etc. The confusing similarity that Mrs Lucerne perceives is registered by the camera as a set of *non-similitudes*. Surprisingly, however, Mrs Lucerne does pick out Vincent's photograph from the pile, as if to confirm the original in the face of insistent simulacra. Later, at the police line-up when Clay (as Vincent) with an eye patch and expensive clothes is standing along with the other suspects, "we" perceive him as the only "black man" in the line-up. Mrs Lucerne, on the other hand, in conformity with the film in general, does not notice his race. Though she unfailingly picks out "Vincent," here incarnated by Clay as the person most resembling the man at the murder scene, she remarks: "I must say it's uncanny how much this man looks like the man who shot me." When asked to confirm identity, however, she says, rather oddly: "As I told you Lieutenant, you cannot tell from pictures. [On screen, we see Clay's impassive face.] Looking at the photograph, I would have thought I knew. But now, I'm not so sure." Weismann says: "But you thought the picture looked familiar, didn't you?"

"Yes, yes I did," says Mrs Lucerne, "and there's a striking similarity there, but he's different." The peculiarity of this conversation lies in the fact that both Weismann and Mrs Lucerne try to establish similarity in relation to a photograph. By focusing on whether this man resembles the photograph, they both invoke the spectre of simulacra. The man who did the shooting, she says, "had very different eyes. They were farther apart. And his nose was different. His ears were lower. His look was just different. I don't think this is him." Lt Weismann assures her that the small details don't matter, as the subject had recently undergone extensive plastic surgery. At which Mrs Lucerne bursts out: "Well, then how do you expect me to identify him?" To which Officer Callahan replies: "Precisely! It boggles the mind!"

Lt Weismann and Mrs Lucerne, of course, hold widely discrepant aesthetic theories. For Weismann, the original is always unmistakable; no amount of plastic surgery can disguise the identity of the subject. Similitude as produced by surgery is a hoax. Mrs Lucerne, on the other hand, seems to believe that all there are are similitudes. Telling people apart, then, can only be an approximation of the original. In fact, by picking out Vincent's photograph and Clay's face as bearing a similarity to her memory of the man who did the shooting, she radically calls into question the veracity or originality of her memory. What is the image imprinted in Mrs Lucerne's memory? The film suggests that it is impossible to know. And this impossibility is founded at the point of *intersection*, which is really a *disjunction*, between the spectatorial and the diegetic levels. Lt Weismann perceives resemblance; Mrs Lucerne perceives similitude, but the camera sees neither. All "we" see, or that the camera seems to register, is a set of non-similitudes which are nevertheless affirmed by the diegesis as resemblance. What we encounter in *Suture*, then, is a revision, even a deconstruction of the opposition established by Foucault. The pairing of resemblance with affirmation and similitude with negation is not simply reversed but radically reconfigured. The film asserts the following formula: resemblance is non-similitude, and affirmation is repetition without resemblance. In other words, dissimilar objects are supposed to resemble (an original), while what is affirmed is the repetition of the original but without resemblance. This formula, of course, presumes the experience of the spectator as that of perceiving the non-similitude and the repetition. For in the film itself we have no acknowledgment of non-similitude or repetition. The overt discourse is of resemblance as affirmation. Thus the "knitting" together, to use Foucault's phrase, of the spectatorial and diegetic levels of the film takes place in a disoriented space (like Magritte's). It is the space, in fact, where we find a place for ourselves in the film narration as subjects of race. Thus what is properly disrupted and interrogated is our suturing of ourselves as raced.

But what of the "advantage" of similitude over affirmation that Foucault argues for? If affirmation produces bodies as opaque objects that are visible and conceal or block out what is behind or below them, similitude has the advantage of revealing the hidden and reversing the inside into the outside. In *Suture*, this opposition is also called into question through attention to the mark and the part object in the *absence* of the gestalt. The body, particularly Clay's body, here has neither the simple positivity of the object in representation as affirmation nor the negativity implied by similitude in its indication of the "mystery" of the thing represented. Clay's body is seemingly both transparent and opaque, but what makes it singular, gives it its specificity, is its distinguishing mark. Renée, for instance, works with the surface of the body, reshaping and moulding Clay. And it is the opaque materiality of his body that conceals his difference from Vincent. However, as our earlier discussion suggested, Clay's body is seen through the fluoroscope; he is utterly transparent to Renée, revealing to her *jouissance* a body beyond nudity. Thus the implicit opposition of surface and depth or outside and inside that prevails in the similitude vs. resemblance binary is recast as a continuum. Clay's body is akin to the Moebius strip invoked by Lacan as the topological metaphor for the "sexual reality of the unconscious" (XI: 149–60).[14] Moreover, when Vincent and Clay are distinguished, however minimally, it is not on the basis of resemblance or similitude but of the part object. Mrs Lucerne is troubled by parts of the body: the position of the ears, the placement of the eyes. Alice too is troubled by a scar on Clay's back, his distinguishing mark. I refer to the scene where she remarks on the scar on Clay's back that she does not remember Vincent as bearing, while

Clay despite his amnesia seems to know that somehow it is not related to the accident. There is a peculiar elision of what the subject of race would consider the more obvious differences for trivial ones. What then is the film proposing about the body? If racial visibility is a function of the gestalt, the permeation of color for instance, the film's refusal to countenance the wholeness of the racial body subverts our look. The film deploys an aesthetic strategy that invites us to meditate on the meaning and consequence of disrupting the racial gestalt.

We can better understand the strategy of *Suture* by pausing briefly over a scene in Mike Leigh's 1996 film *Secrets and Lies*. This film too deploys a potentially transformative strategy by maintaining a void throughout the diegesis, the impossibility of knowing who Hortense's father was and how he came to impregnate Cynthia, her white mother. This blank spot in the film functions as a point where our suture as subjects of race is produced symptomatically even as we navigate between the secret and the lie. Any attempt to manufacture a narrative to cover over that lacuna becomes a lethal exposure of the effect of the signifier upon our unconscious. We can only say too much about it, and it will never be quite enough. However, this strategy is rather limited in that it questions our suturing to race through what is essentially a mockery of our narrative compulsion, rather than an extended inquiry into the logic of racial knowledge and looking. In fact, on the question of racial visibility, the film reinforces the logic of racial gestalt in a moment when the possibility of similitude is raised. There is the scene where the mother and her "black" daughter sit side by side in a café having an amiable conversation about themselves. It is perhaps their second meeting. The mother, referring to her other (white) daughter Roxanne, who is mostly rude or indifferent towards her, says that she believes that she shares more of a resemblance with Hortense than with Roxanne. She says: "I'm more like you really," etc. At this the audience invariably bursts into laughter. In case this seems like unproven sociological evidence, let us look at the scene more closely. The camera angle, the frontal exposure of the two women, the *mise-en-scène* of the actors' expressions, and the speech act itself are all coded for comic effect. This scene is "too much" for the film, and thus the possibility of similitude "across races" is turned into a joke. There is something anxiety-producing in the notion that this mother and her daughter may share certain similarities. But the anxious joke here is not raised by the mere possibility of similitude. As I argued in the previous chapter, for that would entail the denial of their biological relationship which the film explicitly thematizes. It is not so much similitude itself that is uncanny as the discovery of one's own surprise in encountering similitude. The unconscious logic of the joke can be stated thus: The subject of race runs into his/her own splitness with regard to race. We are surprised by ourselves. We thought we knew that people across races could bear similarities. Then why are we surprised into recognizing it? To encounter something about ourselves that we knew but hadn't recognized is uncanny. The joke works to envelope this surprise of surprises to rescue us from admitting that we harbored the secret of pure difference without our own knowledge. And that pure difference is of course Whiteness as Being, which our own surprise dangerously uncovers as a sham. No such joke is possible in *Suture*, where the film resolutely refuses such racial looking. By returning our look, the film subverts the logic of racial gestalt implicit in both resemblance and similitude. By refusing our demand that black and white be recognized, the film radically subverts our suture as subjects of race. It does so by presenting the body not as gestalt (an imaginary construct) but as an impossible Moebius strip, or what Lacan terms the "interior 8," which can be discerned not all at once, but only in time, and that too only as a series of part objects. Thus the body must be understood in relation to the "sexual reality" of the unconscious, which is the nodal point of desire (XI: 154). As in the famous parable of the blind men and the elephant, the film suggests that the body is not susceptible to immediate perception. Thus its denial of racial gestalt should neither be reduced to a lie, nor be mistaken for a perverse disavowal. Neither would be consistent with the structure of race as I have been delineating it in previous chapters. Rather, what the film introduces into the symbolic of race, or more properly *against* it, is the question of the *jouissance* of the body, the truth that subjects are not determined wholly by signifiers (as the regime of Whiteness suggests), but that there is a "sexual reality" to the unconscious that race can never address. It opens the spectator as a "subject of race" to what Lacan suggests is the raw material of the psychoanalytic experience:

> the substance of the body ... as that which enjoys itself [*se jouit*]. That is, no doubt, a property of the living body, but we don't know what it means to be alive except for the following fact, that a body is something that enjoys itself [*cela se jouit*]. ... Enjoying [*jouir*] has the fundamental property that it is, ultimately, one person's body that enjoys a part of the Other's body.
>
> (XX: 24)

A measure of our action

What kind of an enjoyment does the film make possible, and how does it differ from the visual pleasure of narrative that feminists inveighed against in 1970s film theory? To return to the diegesis: it is the kind of enjoyment that Max explicitly warns against, even forbids. In his final interview with the psychiatrist, after Clay has recovered from his amnesia, he insists to Max's consternation that he is Vincent Towers:

Max:	But you just finished telling me that you are Clay Arlington.
Clay/Vincent:	No, I told you I remember another past when I was Clay Arlington.
Max:	If your memory has returned don't you think it would be useful to integrate that past into your life?
C/V:	Which past?
Max:	The past you know to be your own.
C/V:	It's all my past. Who was hounded by the police? Who was dragged through a line up?
Max:	That was a terrible mistake, but …
C/V:	When I look in the mirror I see Vincent Towers; when I go to the club, people call me Vincent Towers; Renée is in love with Vincent Towers.
Max:	Clay! We are talking about two distinct lives.
C/V:	And one is gone! It's a dead body that can't be identified and in a most real way it's not the body of Vincent Towers. I am Vincent Towers.
Max:	Clay, you're burying the wrong life; the one that isn't dead. This is a very dangerous game … You've made up your mind haven't you? You're not going back.
C/V:	No, I'm not.

Clay's decision to forget that he has remembered is, I would suggest, an "ethical" act. His analysis with Max terminates insofar as Clay/Vincent crosses from demand, to desire, and finally to the level of the drive, which enables him fully to assume his desire in relation to death. Lacan terms this moment, this looping, the traversal of the fundamental or the "radical phantasy," when the subject can contend with his/her drive (XI: 273–4).

To elaborate: Clay/Vincent accomplishes this "loop" in the following way. As an amnesiac, Clay is a perfect metaphor for the subject of the symbolic, racial or otherwise, who knows himself entirely through representations. As a dupe of the Other, the signifier promises him memory and self-knowledge, but it only alienates him more. In his "Rome discourse," Lacan situates the subject of the symbolic, the speaking subject, thus:

> For the function of language is not to inform but to evoke. What I seek in speech is the response of the other. What constitutes me as subject is my question. … I identify myself in language, but only by losing myself in it like an object.

> (E: 86)

Thus, for Clay, "needles" is a signifier that recurs in his unconscious, holding out the possibility of certitude. However, when Clay learns to read the signifier for what it is, the name of a small, working-class town in California, he revisits the place with Renée, but he experiences nothing but severe alienation. Oddly enough, what should have been familiar, homely, is on the contrary uncanny, and only aggravates Clay's repression. At this point, Clay is very much the subject of demand who repeatedly poses the question of his identity to Max, Renée, and Alice. He is, as Lacan says, constituted by his question. Renée, of course, answers his demand with the words: "Vincent, you are a kind and gentle person."

"I'd like to think that," says Clay, who believes he sees himself "as others see him – which will enable him to support himself in a dual situation that is satisfactory for him from the point of view of love" (XI: 268). But this sort of "identification" will not suffice to fill the lack that Clay suffers from. In the two dreams that Clay reports to Max, he narrates the trauma of the crash. In one, he is the car that explodes, and in the other he is the thing (lost in language like an object) upon which needles are stuck. Given that "Needles" turns out to be the name of his hometown, Clay's body at this point is literally written over with the signifiers of the Other. However, it is with the dream that Clay does not tell Max that we begin to perceive the shift from desire as lack to what Lacan calls "radical desire" (VII: 216). As Renée removes his sutures, Clay says: "I didn't tell Dr Shinoda this, but I had a dream last night that I killed my father. I had feelings of hate and anger and I just shot him." On screen, we see a gun going off three times. This scene is repeated in the conversation. Clay refrains from telling Max about this dream because he is too guilty, afraid that he will be perceived as a criminal. For Clay, the dream implicates him in his father's murder. It is a moment when his identification with Vincent is complete. (It is significantly not the imaginary identification with a mirror image, an ideal Clay has been pursuing so far.) In his unconscious, Clay has assumed the crime which makes the law possible; it is the crime that is associated with Vincent's death drive, the Sadean attempt to liberate nature from her chains. Of this drive, Lacan says: "It isn't for nothing that crime is one boundary of our exploration of desire or that it is on the basis of a crime that Freud attempted to reconstruct the genealogy of the law" (VII: 260). In assuming Vincent's crime in his unconscious, Clay has begun to explore the boundary of his desire. He has begun the arduous journey from the "normative" stance of alienation in the field of the Other, to move towards his excluded center – "the prehistoric Other," the "something strange to me, although it is at the heart of me," what Lacan calls the extimate core, the *das Ding* (VII: 71). Clay, then, is already situated at the limit of the law, where he must necessarily raise the question of what lies beyond. It is at the moment when Clay and Vincent face each other as doubles (alienating images of each other) that Clay's drives supervene. He must kill or be killed. In killing his brother,

Clay, of course is killing himself, "burying his life," as Max later puts it. Death here is not just the second death of the Sadean hero; it is itself doubled: Vincent dies twice, once in name and once in body, whereas Clay as Clay dies in both name and body, and chooses life after having fully come to terms with death. Speaking of Freud's notion of the "death instinct," Lacan says, using Freud's terminology, but referring to the death drive:

> How can man, that is to say a living being, have access to knowledge of the death instinct, to his own relationship to death?
>
> The answer is, by virtue of the signifier in its most radical form. It is in the signifier and insofar as the subject articulates a signifying chain that he comes up against the fact that he may disappear from the chain of what he is.
>
> (VII: 295)

While holding the phone, calling the emergency line, this is the very knowledge that Clay arrives at. A woman's voice urges him for his name, and Clay hesitates. And in that significant pause, before he pronounces the momentous words, "I am Vincent Towers," Clay finds his orientation as a "being for death." In that pause, which acts as the scansion of his discourse, Clay reaches that "domain and level of experience of absolute disarray" (VII: 304) that Lacan suggests is the necessary point at which the training analysis should terminate. This is the place where the problematic of desire is articulated in a fundamental relation to death. For Lacan, the paradigmatic subject of such an orientation is not so much Sophocles' Antigone, who must tragically cross the very limit of the law that she has established in order to uphold it, but the Oedipus of *Oedipus at Colonus*. Here it is the blind and exiled Oedipus who is "shown to be unyielding right to the end, demanding everything, giving up nothing, absolutely unreconciled" (VII: 310). This is the Oedipus who not only acquiesces to his malediction, but whose "engagement with annihilation … is taken to be the realization of his wish" (VII: 309–10). In other words, this Oedipus does not give ground relative to his desire, which Lacan says is the only thing the subject can be truly guilty about (VII: 319). Clay too, in a certain sense, arrives at this unassailable place. Such a posture should not be banalized as obstinacy or even contumacy; rather it is the ability to bear the gift[15] of "the signifying cut that confers on him the indomitable power of being what he is in the face of everything that may oppose him" (VII: 282). Clay/Vincent does not betray his desire for what Lacan calls "the good," a seemingly contradictory formulation given that what Clay visibly acquires, from a certain "materialist" perspective, is "the good life." But is it merely that? We must inquire into Clay's good. Lacan:

Something is played out in betrayal if one tolerates it, if driven by the idea of the good – and by that I mean the good of the one who has just committed the act of betrayal – one gives ground to the point of giving up one's own claims and says to oneself, "Well, if that's how things are, we should abandon our position; neither of us is worth that much, and especially me, so we should just return to the common path." You can be sure that what you find there is the structure of giving ground relative to one's desire.

(VII: 321)

The "good" here would be the refusal of dialectical struggle; it is a guilt-inducing abstention, rather than a renunciation, based neither on the love of life nor the love of freedom. But the struggle alone, which is waged until one or the other submits by forgoing freedom for life, or risking life for recognition, is not the guarantee of "freedom," or the proper site of the emergence of the subject of "radical desire." In his "Rome discourse," Lacan speaks of the "triangle of renunciation" within which one's "freedom" is inscribed. Rather than the familiar duality of the positions defined by the master and the slave, Lacan posits a third option: "the suicidal renunciation of the vanquished partner, depriving of his victory the master whom he abandons to his inhuman solitude" (E: 104). In this earlier formulation of the ethics of psychoanalysis, Lacan's example is not Oedipus or Antigone, but Empedocles, whose action "leaves forever present in the memory of men this symbolic act of his being-for-death" (104). But psychoanalysis is not a euthanasia; we should perhaps understand Empedocles as the scientist who wished to go beyond the laws of nature and whose "suicide" distinguishes the human subject as motivated, even constituted by the drive rather than the instinct that rules the organic world.

In choosing to remain Vincent, Clay affirms himself as a being for death, and more significantly, redefines his position in relation to the Other. To bear the gift of the signifying cut does not mean a meek submission to the law; rather, it means that one is no longer duped by the Other. Clay goes a step further: he not only stops being duped by the Other; he in turn dupes the Other. This is the true valence of Clay's relation to the law, especially the law of racial difference, as an ethical position. How does such a law manifest itself in the film? It does so as the psychiatrist's No! At the end of the film, we hear Max's voice again, this time over a montage. Max says:

"In a sense it has all worked out just as Clay said. He was right, but of course, he is ultimately wrong. For he is not Vincent Towers; he's Clay Arlington. He may dress in Vincent's fine clothes, drive Vincent's expensive car, play golf at Vincent's country club, or use Vincent's box at the opera. But this will not make him Vincent Towers. He can never be Vincent Towers; simply because he is not. Nothing can change this. Not the material comforts his life may afford him, nor the love Renée may provide. And if by some chance, over the cries of his true ego, he's able to achieve happiness, it will be false, empty, for he's buried the wrong life, the wrong past, buried his soul. He's lost all that makes life worth living. Of this we can be completely certain."

Max Shinoda, to invert his syntax, is wrong about Clay, but of course he is ultimately right. He is right, insofar as Clay/Vincent "is simply not." Clay is not Vincent, anymore than Clay or Vincent were themselves. Meanwhile on screen, we see a montage of images: Clay/Vincent and Renée enjoying themselves, looking absurdly satisfied with themselves.[16] As Lacan says:

> if there is anything resembling a drive it is a *montage*. ... The *montage* of the drive is a *montage* which, first, is presented as having neither head nor tail – in the sense in which one speaks of *montage* in a surrealist collage.
>
> (XI: 169)

The discontinuity of the drive (not in terms of its constant pressure, but in its source[17]) as a series of partial drives posits a subject that is "headless" (XI: 181). Like the composite figure of Thomas Mann's novella *Transposed Heads*, Clay, his identity and his history, contrary to Max's certitude about core identities, constitute a collage. Given that he is recreated physically by Renée as Vincent, and psychically by the law, it is not clear how he remains Clay Arlington. And this discontinuity is apparently the source of Clay/Vincent's "happiness." Towards the end of Seminar XI, Lacan poses a question, to which Clay/Vincent perhaps instantiates an answer:

> After the mapping of the subject in relation to the *a* [*objet petit a*], the experience of the fundamental phantasy becomes the drive. What, then, does he who has passed through the experience of this opaque relation to the origin of the drive, become? How can a subject who has traversed the radical phantasy experience the drive? This is the beyond of analysis, and has never been approached. Up to now, it has been approachable only at the level of the analyst, in as much as it would be required of him to have specifically traversed the cycle of the analytic experience in its totality.
>
> (XI: 273–4)

How do we understand Clay's traversal, and what is the fundamental fantasy that he has thus negotiated? The "traversal" that Clay accomplishes is one that is uniquely available to the subject of race and is intelligible only in the domain of race. Clay experiences his drive as the enjoyment derived in duping the Other. No longer will language dupe him; he will fully manipulate his position within language and therefore his desire, by passing. Passing, not as the *imaginary* passing of the black man as white, as witnessed in the genre of tragic mulatto novels, but the *symbolic* passing of the duped subject of race to the ethical subject as such. Such a subject will have fully confronted the structure of Whiteness in which he is implicated, where his/her desire is the desire of an Other that has no purchase on the body or its enjoyment. To confront the shallow totality of race is not to espouse "color blindness," for that is to foreclose the law of racial difference. Rather it is to traverse the fantasy engendered by Whiteness through symbolic passing. The significant difference between imaginary passing and symbolic passing lies in the relation one bears to the Other. In the former, one's identification with the signifier of Whiteness is never in jeopardy. One passes as a "negro" for what one is not, that is, "white." The object cause there is still enmeshed in a certain regime of visibility – skin, hair, bone. However, with symbolic passing as envisioned in *Suture*, it is one's relation to the signifier that is redefined. One neither submits nor resists its marking; rather, one assumes it and thereby makes it one's own. The (anxious) object of racial visibility has been traversed. It is "subjectified" to the point that it can no longer sustain the subject in the circuit of desiring Whiteness. One *passes* for what one *is* – a being in the world. The Other is simply snowed.

For us as spectators, our suturing to the film narrative is purchased at the price of our desuturing as subjects of race. The film requires that we learn to see differently. Clay's enucleated eye serves as a metaphor for the experience of the scopic drive *after* the fantasy has been traversed. Like Lacan's Empedocles, enucleation in relation to the regime of racial visibility is akin to that gesture of "suicide" by which the subject assumes his/her desire as a being for death. *Suture* inaugurates an adversarial aesthetics in relation to the scopic regime of race. It literally utilizes the visual medium against the visual regime of race. The *non sequitur* of racial visibility as a meaningful index of identity is exposed. The enjoyment the film affords is not the conventional "pleasure" entailed in what Laura Mulvey in 1975 termed phallocentric cinema (Mulvey 1989). Rather, what we experience is the very opposite of fetishism. Not disavowal of lack, and its displacement onto an imaginary object, but rather, a satisfaction derived from discontinuity and disarray. The question we are left with in the end is: can we cope with such an unraveling of our subjective support, or will we sew it all back again?

Chapter 5

What's in a name?

Love and knowledge beyond identity in "Recitatif"

> The kind of work I have always wanted to do requires me to learn how to maneuver ways to free up the language from its sometimes sinister, frequently lazy, almost always predictable employment of racially informed and determined chains.
>
> (Toni Morrison, *Playing in the Dark*: XI)

> It is not that words are imperfect or that, when confronted by the visible, they prove insuperably inadequate. Neither can be reduced to the other's terms: it is in vain that we say what we see; what we see never resides in what we say. And it is in vain that we attempt to show, by the use of images, metaphors, or similes, what we are saying; the space where they achieve their splendor is not that deployed by our eyes but that defined by the sequential elements of syntax. And the proper name, in this context, is merely an artifice: it gives us a finger to point with, in other words, to pass surreptitiously from the space where one speaks to the space where one looks; in other words, to fold one over the other as if they were equivalents.
>
> (René Magritte, cited in Foucault 1989)

> The signifier is nevertheless there in nature, and if we weren't looking for the signifier, we shouldn't find anything there at all. To extract a natural law is to extract a meaningless formula. The less it signifies anything, the happier we are. ... Every real signifier is, as such, a signifier that signifies nothing. ... Experience proves it – the more the signifier signifies nothing, the more indestructible it is.
>
> (Lacan, Seminar III: 184–5)

Using the racial signifier to designate a person ("the black guy over there") or appending it to a name ("so-and-so, the black poet") is a dominant mode of establishing identity, especially in the absence of visual evidence such as a photograph. However, it has of late become a questionable practice, at least in the news media, to cite someone's race when the story is apparently "neutral."[1] One may refer to a person's race only when the story warrants it.

We have thus learnt to be uncomfortable in invoking racial identity unnecessarily, especially when recounting an unsavory narrative. Most polite
and "sensitive" speakers prefer the ethnic or pseudo-technical term such as
"African-American" or "Caucasian." This is perhaps because color identities
aim at a descriptive accuracy that never finds their mark. Nevertheless, it is
still fairly routine to use racial signifiers as a necessary means to establish
identity. Personal ads that use abbreviations such as SWF or DBM, or references to achievements such as "Arthur Ashe, the first black Wimbledon
champion," seem to indicate that these signifiers are doing some work. But
what do we know, really, when we learn that someone has been designated as
the "first black" to win a tennis trophy, or when the "fit, dog lover" declares
herself a SWF? Are "black" and "white" in these statements on par with
"tennis champion" and "single, female, dog lover," or with Ashe and anony-
mous? In other words, are "black" and "white" descriptions, or are they
names? Are names descriptions? That is, of course, the more fundamental
question.

Actually, as descriptions, black and white do not say much about
identity, though they do establish group and personal *identifications* of the
subjects involved. It is customary in most cultural theory to distinguish
between identity and identification as social and psychical phenomena
respectively. In psychoanalysis, identification is the more privileged term
and is elaborated as a set of finite or incomplete processes by which identity
is constituted. Freud refers to identification in several related domains. In
Group Psychology and the Analysis of the Ego, Freud proposes identification
as "the earliest and original form of emotional tie" (Freud 1921: 39). The
division in psychology between group formations and the constitution of
the "individual" subject, he suggests, is artificial and untenable. For such an
opposition to work, it would entail the irreducibility of a notion such as
"social instinct," or "herd instinct," which Freud demonstrates can always
be broken down to its individual libidinal origins. Thus, even though identities such as racial, ethnic, national and cultural are primarily social or
group phenomena, Freud suggests that their composition is derived from
the modes of libidinal ties, or identifications, that subjects effect with
certain objects that replace their ego ideals.[2] Freud's examples of such
potentially lethal ties, or identifications, are of being in love and hypnosis,
themes that Lacan takes up in Seminar XI in relation to transference and
the gaze as *objet a*. Elsewhere, Freud invokes the concept of identification in
relation to objects of the drive, in mourning, in narcissism, in the formation
of symptoms. Identification is the key term in conversion hysteria and
obsessional neurosis, and it is not a negligible term in his theory of other
pathologies, including the perversions and psychoses.[3] In all of these discussions, identity is contingent on the vagaries of unconscious identification
and is not determined by either anatomy (biological differences) or destiny,
as in one's birth.

However, it is with reference to gender that identity as necessity emerges, and finds its support in a theory of identification that is quintessentially Oedipal. There is a marked difference here in the modality of relations between identity and identification, for Oedipal relations emphatically posit the issue of individual identity formation as a necessarily gendered phenomenon. In his essays on femininity, in "The passing of the Oedipus complex" (1924 [1963]), and other discussions of the familiar Oedipal scenario, Freud proposes that the boy resolves his castration anxiety by identifying with his father and displacing his love for his mother. The girl enters Oedipal relations by identifying with her mother and desiring a father substitute.

> The object-cathexes are given up and replaced by identification. The authority of the father of the parents is introjected into the ego and there forms the kernel of the super-ego. ... The libidinal trends belonging to the Oedipus-complex are in part desexualized and subli-mated, which probably happens with every transformation into identification; in part they are inhibited in their aim and changed into affectionate feelings.
>
> (Freud 1963: 179)

For Freud, this process of the subject's withdrawal of object cathexis and its transformation into identification is the proper mode of acquiring gender identity. One becomes a man or a woman, heterosexual or homosexual, by taking up pre-appointed positions along the axis of identification versus desire. This Oedipal narrative is, of course, the core site of contestation and critique for theorists of gender and sexuality, for it establishes in one stroke what Judith Butler, in *Gender Trouble* (1990), has identified as the sex-gender-desire nexus. One's mode of identification seems to establish not only one's gender identity on the basis of one's sex, thus implying a causality that has no logical necessity, but it also seems to regulate desire into compulsorily heterosexual channels. This is the node at which the most innovative work in feminism and queer theory has appropriately situated itself for the purposes of rethinking sexuality. However, our task in the following is not to engage in the particular problematic engendered by the Oedipal law. Lacan's more complex interpretation of the symbolic law and of sexual difference posits not a relation of necessity among sex, gender and desire, but actually one of impossibility. As Joan Copjec has powerfully argued in *Read My Desire* (1994), sexual difference is in the Real, and it appears in/as the failure of language and not as its effect. However, it would take us too far afield to examine these issues in detail. Rather, what I am here interested in is Judith Butler's procedure in interrogating identity. First, I want to mark at this point that though it is acknowledged that identifications constitute identities in psychoanalysis, the concept of identity as such is not much developed in that discourse. It is much more in the purview of psychology than psycho-analysis *per se*. This is perhaps because identity seems to reference a social or political entity which ultimately seeks representation, whereas "the subject" seems to refer more adequately to the effects and existence of the unconscious. However, the attribution of identity as a *social* inevitability, as differentiated from subjectivity (the unconscious formation) and the fact that signifiers of identity operate independently of psychical identifications suggests that we should probe the notion of identity more closely and not surrender it to the social sciences. An exploration of the discrepant discourses of identity and identification may show that identity in fact could work to block identification. And if identification has a certain ethical charge, in that it guarantees meaning and desire, then the grounds upon which identity posits a sense of sameness as substance or unity should be investigated.

The trouble with identity

Butler's *Gender Trouble* (1990) is pivotal in its interrogation of identity for feminist politics, and in its refusal of the opposition between the psychical and the social, which can be translated into the inside and the outside, private and public respectively. She begins her inquiry by unpacking the category of women as subjects of representation. Invoking Foucault, Butler argues that insofar as (juridical) power produces the subjects it purports to represent, the unitary category of "women" as seeking representation is itself an effect of power. Butler problematizes the identity of women as subjects of feminism by alluding to the political incoherence of the content of "women" and feminism. Rehearsing the debates between First World and Third World women on the potentially exclusionary and normalizing effects of a feminism that specifies its oppressor as a universal patriarchy, Butler suggests that "women" should remain an incomplete category, which can then serve "as a normative ideal relieved of coercive force" (1990: 15). Advocating an "anti-foundational coalitional politics," Butler homes in on the notion of women as a stable identity, based as it is on the sex/gender distinction. That is, she challenges the notion of gender as tendentious cultural inscription upon the natural sex of the person. Sex is not to nature and the "raw" as gender is to culture and the "cooked," she contends (37). Rather, it is the regulatory practices of gender that produce sexual difference as pre-discursive identity. Butler's examination of identity then proceeds along established lines of inquiry. She asks, in effect, what is this identity of "women" as the self same? Is there some substance to "women" that persists through time and across cultures? Does this identity possess a unity of properties or of experience that articulates a coherent and universal subject? Her inquiry leads her to undertake a genealogical analysis of the substance and unity of gender identity. She suggests, in what is now a famous pronouncement, that gender as a unity of experience is possible only when relations of necessity are assumed to prevail among sex, gender and desire. In other words, the assumption that gender identity follows from sex, which in turn entails the stabilizing of desire as heterosexual, is an effect of power.

> Gender is the repeated stylization of the body, a set of repeated acts within a highly rigid regulatory frame that congeal over time to produce the appearance of substance, of a natural sort of being. A political genealogy of gender ontologies, if it is successful, will deconstruct the substantive appearance of gender into its constitutive acts and locate and account for those acts within the compulsory frames set by the various forces that police the social appearance of gender. To expose the contingent acts that create the appearance of a naturalistic necessity. … is a task that now takes on the added burden of showing how the very notion of the subject, intelligible only through its appearance as gendered, admits of possibilities that have been forcibly foreclosed by the various reifications of gender that have constituted its contingent ontologies.
>
> (Butler 1990: 33)

Butler's procedure, then, is to unmask the relations of necessity as posited by power as purely contingent. This enables her not only to blow apart the sex-gender-desire nexus; it also permits resignification of identity as contingency. What is particularly attractive about Butler's procedure, whether one agrees with it or not, is its intuition about the necessity of power as the locus of the dominant iteration of identity as well as that of subversive repetition or pastiche. If one begins from the perspective of power as the ultimate productive force in the construction of categories – binary, monologic or differential – then one's task is usually focused on exposing the sandy bottom of power's foundational pretensions. One's critical task, to put it rather reductively, is to eliminate the modality of necessity and install in its place the contingency of all relations. There is a certain clarity of purpose here that psychoanalysis simply cannot achieve. For if we posit the unconscious (the locus of the symbolic and of its limits) as the cause of the subject, then the task of interrogating identity cannot rest content with the exposure of power's symbolic foundations. In other words, psychoanalysis cannot afford to collapse identity and identification as effects of power. Though the latter may imply the former, the notion of the incompleteness of language, rather than of identity, particularly sexual identity, in psychoanalytic discourse requires that identity cannot be fully thought or subsumed by a discussion of the necessity or contingency of relations among properties.[4] Analyzing *identity*, then, requires an approach that will not presume to know fully its contents or its cause.

In the following, I do not focus on the way identity, particularly racial identity, is produced by ideology – its investment and its regulation – but rather on the way identity is marked and thought. Thus I begin not with identity as a set of properties or attributes of a person; I do not pose the question of the substance of identity as it persists in time, or of its unity as it may be discerned spatially. The issues of racial essences and universals have been taken up elsewhere by others more competent than I in such discussions.[5] I begin with the signifier – identity as the investiture of name, and the marking of reference. What does it mean to point with the noun "black" or "white": "blacks have a higher mortality rate"; "whites have a lower risk of heart disease," etc.? What kind of words are these? Do they possess a meaning, or connote a concept, that remains identical with itself in all situations, or do their predicates determine the meaning of these words, thus making subject and predicate synonymous with each other? Is there any "sense" to naming someone black or white?

In his three Princeton lectures of 1970, later published as *Naming and Necessity* (1982), Saul Kripke argues against a dominant belief amongst analytic philosophers (he terms it the Frege-Russell thesis) that the reference of a proper name is determinable only through definite descriptions. Thus if someone were to mention a name such as Joe Doakes, the answer to the question "which Joe Doakes" would entail a description such as "the man who corrupted Hadleyburg" (Kripke 1982: 27–8). (In this case, the name is simply short for the description; thus, whoever fits the description would be the referent of Joe Doakes. The description gives the meaning of the name.) According to this view, *contra* James Mill who held that names were mere denotations, a proper name is not without "sense," i.e. connotation. It is to be understood as an abbreviation of a definite description which is its sense or its meaning. While acknowledging the power of this thesis, Kripke, however, asserts that it is wrong for reasons that have not been properly discerned until now. Though others have opposed the Frege-Russell thesis, Kripke suggests that they have in fact "abandoned its letter while retaining its spirit, namely, they have used the notion of a cluster concept" (1982: 30). The "cluster concept," attributable for instance to John Searle, would consider the referent of a name as determinable not by a single description, but by a family of descriptions. The cluster concept, though it may appear to controvert the notion of names as synonymous with a single description, in fact works in two ways: it can either consider the cluster of concepts as actually giving the *meaning* of the name, in which case the cluster of concepts would be synonymous with the name, or it can consider the cluster of concepts as that which determines *reference* and not meaning. In either case, the name is attached to certain properties either as meaning or as reference. After a brief discussion of various categories of truth including analytic, *a priori*, necessary, contingent, and essential, Kripke takes up the issue of identity as the definite description of properties. If a cluster of concepts, or a set of descriptions, establishes the meaning or reference of the name, then in what sense is that description a description of essential properties, and how essential are properties to the "sense" of a given name? As defined, "the question of essential properties so-called is supposed to be equivalent (and it is equivalent) to the question of 'identity across possible worlds'" (42). For Kripke, as for Butler, any invocation of identity as a set of properties involves the question of its stability, its universality, its "essence," in counter-factual space and time situations. While Butler refutes identity as pertaining to necessary properties, she does not question the assumption that a statement of identity requires properties of some sort for its meaning or for its reference. This is the fundamental assumption that Kripke questions. The notion that identity is a set of properties established through qualitative descriptions whether necessary or contingent, Kripke argues, is problematic: it implies that an object is known merely through description, whose corresponding qualities we then look for in counter-factual situations; the very difference between necessity and contingency is reduced to the way an object is described (39–40); and it is to misunderstand not only how identity is established, but also what is meant by the notion of the counter-factual. Kripke suggests that a counter-factual situation, or the notion of "all possible worlds," should not be thought of as a "foreign country" or something we perceive through a telescope. Possible worlds, Kripke suggests, are "*stipulated*, not discovered by powerful telescopes" (44). Thus, he says:

> Don't ask: how can I identify this table in another possible world, except by its properties? I have the table in my hands, I can point to it, and when I ask whether *it* might have been in another room, I am talking, by definition, about *it*. I don't have to identify it after seeing it through a telescope. If I am talking about it, I am talking about *it*, in the same way as when I say our hands might have been painted green, I have stipulated that I am talking about greenness. Some properties of an object may be essential to it, in that it could not have failed to have them. But these properties are not used to identify the object in another possible world, for such an identification is not needed. Nor need the essential properties of an object be the properties of an object used to identify it in the actual world, if indeed it is identified in the actual world by means of properties.
>
> (Kripke 1982: 53)

Thus the common-sense view that objects are identified by their properties is controverted by the notion of the name as purely a pointer. When translated to familiar debates in cultural theory about essence versus construction, of, say, sexual identity, Kripke's thesis produces radical effects. Identity in Kripke's logic is divorced from properties – essential or otherwise – thus potentially rendering the ancient quarrel between feminists and biologists moot. For him, identity is neither resemblance nor similitude (to invoke Foucault's work on Magritte again) nor a question of necessary or contingent qualities. Identity does not entail an assertion about the necessary attributes of a thing; it is rather a relation of "calling" that determines reference (1982: 70). For instance, "although someone other than the U.S. President in 1970 might have been the U.S. President in 1970 (e.g. Humphrey might have) no other than Nixon might have been Nixon" (48). Furthermore, though Nixon might not have been called Nixon, the name nevertheless rigidly designates that man who was not called Nixon. Identity is established by naming, and names do not necessarily have sense; i.e., they do not establish essential properties. Names are to be understood as "rigid designators" that establish reference rigidly across all possible worlds. Essence in these terms, then, is not a function of connotation, of a set of substantive and unified properties, but of denotation, of pointing and naming.

Before we extend Kripke's thesis about names as rigid designators to race, we must establish its correspondence with psychoanalysis. Lacan's notion of identity, particularly sexual identity, overlaps significantly with Kripke's. The rigid designator in Lacan corresponds to his notion of the letter (elaborated in Seminar XX) with two important implications: first, the letter leads to the discourse of the real; and second, to the proposition about sexual difference and woman, as entailed by the real. As an analyst, Lacan produces a discourse on the "emptiness" of rigid designators, and one must clarify this "discourse" before one begins to discuss racial identity as rigid designation.

In Lacanian terms, Kripke's rigid designators would be pure signifiers, such as S1, that establish reference, but do not entail concepts or signifieds. Already in 1957 in "The agency of the letter," Lacan had not only stressed the non-relation between signifier and signified, but had privileged the former over the latter by reversing Saussure's algorithm, which had suggested a relation of arbitrariness between the signified and the signifier. In *Encore* (Seminar XX), he says: "the signifier is posited only insofar as it has no relation to the signified" (XX: 29). Disarticulating signifier from signified, Lacan goes on to do the same with the signified and the referent: "what characterizes the relationship between the signified and what serves as the indispensable third party, namely the referent, is precisely that the signified misses the referent. The joiner doesn't work" (20). The seemingly unorthodox compatibility that I am arguing for between Kripke and Lacan turns on the dissociation of the signifier, or more properly the *letter*, from meaning.[6] For Lacan, disconnecting the elements of signification enables him not exactly to state the proposition about rigid designation, but to mark the "effect of writing" upon discourse, a notion that pertains to the letter, rather than to the signifier *per se* (XX: 36). In Seminar IX, "Identification," Lacan says: "there can be no definition of the proper name except insofar as we perceive the relation of the naming utterance to something that is, in its radical nature, of the order of the letter" (quoted in Grigg 1998: 75). Lacan stresses the function of the letter as the "material support that concrete discourse borrows from language" (E: 147). For Lacan, analytic discourse, insofar as it aims at discontinuity, must necessarily take recourse to the letter. The letter, he says, as it is made use of in mathematics, best reveals the grammar of the unconscious as a certain "writing" (XX: 44). The letter (A) is the locus of the signifier; thus the formula S(Ⱥ) (signifier of the lacking or barred Other) constitutes a "writing" or a notation (28). It is what enables the analyst to formalize the "truths" of analytic discourse. For Lacan "a letter is something that is read" (29); in other words, analytic work consists in deciphering "what these letters introduce into the function of the signifier" (29). I read the peculiar dehiscence that Lacan seems to be marking between the signifier and letter in this seminar as an attempt at clarifying the manner in which signifiers are subjectified by the unconscious in accordance with the logic of a certain "writing." Without this purely meaningless "writing," the function of the real cannot be discerned. Referring to his various symbols such as *a*, S, A, etc., he says "their very writing constitutes a medium [*support*] that goes beyond speech, without going beyond language's actual effects" (93). Formalization, insofar as it inscribes something beyond meaning, is thus also

> where the real distinguishes itself. The real can only be inscribed on the basis of an impasse of formalization. That is why I thought I could provide a model of it using mathematical formalization, inasmuch as it is the most advanced elaboration we have by which to produce signifier-ness.[7] The mathematical formalization of signifierness runs counter to meaning.
>
> (XX: 93)

About meaning itself, Lacan says aphoristically: "meaning indicates the direction toward which it fails" (79). What is interesting about Lacan's view of his mathemes is that they are themselves founded on the fundamental impossibility of the sexual relation which is the basis for the "effect of writing" on discourse as such. "Everything that is written stems from the fact that it will forever be impossible to write, as such, the sexual relationship. It is on that basis that there is a certain effect of discourse, which is called writing" (35). Thus what in Kripke is the signifier, or proper name, purely as a function of designation (not to be read, or interpreted), in Lacan, becomes the basis for the articulation of the (sexual) identity of the subject itself as founded on a failure of the symbolic – the fundamental "impossibility of telling the whole truth" (95).[8]

The Kripkean notion of identity is perhaps also comparable to Lacan's thesis about "woman." Lacan's statements in *Encore* about sexual difference and of woman as "not whole" can be understood better in the context of identity as naming that Kripke elaborates. About *the* woman, Lacan says: " 'Woman' [*la*] is a signifier, the crucial property [*propre*] of which is that it is the only one that cannot signify anything, and this is simply because it grounds woman's status in the fact that she is not-whole" (XX: 73). Thus what is essential about woman is not a cluster of descriptive properties, but the impossibility of attaching signifier to signified.[9] Using the vocabulary of set theory, Lacan suggests that women are "an open set," whose difference from each other is more than numerical. "From the moment there are names, one can make a list of women and count them. If there are *mille e tre* of them, it's clear that one can take them one by one – that is what is essential" (10). Sexual difference, then, cannot entail gender identity or heterosexual desire as Butler asserts, because "woman's" function as rigid designator escapes our attempt to fill the terms of sexual difference with necessary or contingent properties.

Racial identity, too, I would like to suggest – i.e., words like black and white, when used as nouns – works like names.[10] That is, they are rigid designators – they are signifiers that have no signified. They establish a reference, but deliver no connotations or meaning whatsoever. We can, of course, reasonably argue that race does not exist insofar as the identity of a person as "black" or "white" is contingent upon a cluster of concepts that are themselves too protean to be able to uphold anything like a necessary truth. We can cite historical evidence to show that groups that were once considered white are no longer classified as such for this or that reason, etc. But as my discussion in Chapter 1 specified, arguments leveled at race theory are highly ineffectual and possess insufficient explanatory power. Thus rather than lapse into the historicist argument, it may be more productive to view racial color designators as operating not unlike proper names. The proper name is neither wholly one's own (i.e., we are all named by others) nor is it meaningful. One inhabits the name as the reference of oneself, and as Kripke asserts, it bears no relation to a set of properties that establish either its meaning or its reference: Nixon is Nixon, or as he says, quoting Bishop Butler, "everything is what it is and not another thing" (Kripke 1982: 94). Is this not true for "black" and "white"? If someone is designated as one or the other, there is a necessary truth to that designation, *but does it mean*? What would be the cluster of concepts that could establish such an identity? Even in identity statements such as "blacks are people of African descent" or "whites are people of European descent," though the predicates supposedly define and give the meaning of black and white, establishing the necessity of these concepts in every counter-factual situation will not be possible if only because national designations, and the notion of descent, are historically volatile and scientifically invalid respectively. No set of qualitative descriptions can establish black or white identity across all possible worlds, but we cannot therefore say that black and white do not exist, which is the error that a number of critical race theorists fall into.[11] As Kripke says, it is not how the speaker thinks he got the reference, but the actual chain of communication, which is relevant. ... Obviously the name is passed on from link to link. But of course not every sort of causal chain reaching from me to a certain man will do for me to make a reference. There may be a causal chain from our use of the term "Santa Claus" to a certain historical saint, but still the children, when they use this, by this time probably do not refer to that saint. ... It seems to me wrong to think we give ourselves some properties which somehow qualitatively uniquely pick out an object and determine our reference in that manner.

(Kripke 1982: 93–4)

If we substitute "black" or "white," etc. for Santa Claus in the above quotation, we discern two things immediately: first, the paradigm of "black" as reaching back to "Africa," as Santa Claus could to a medieval saint, is the source of an insurmountable confusion in critical race theory. The idea that "black" means "people of African descent" leads into the thicket of debates about biological descent, which will inevitably run into the false contradiction between culture and biology. Second, we can now see that the notion of racial passing is nothing but an intervention into the passing of the name from link to link. Changing one's identity from black to white, or vice-versa, means that one passes from one chain of communication to another. For instance, when the "Ex-Colored Man" in James Weldon Johnson's *Autobiography of an Ex-Colored Man* decides to pass from black to white, he does so by passing from one chain to another: "I finally made up my mind that I would neither disclaim the black race nor claim the white race; but that *I would change my name*, raise a mustache, and let the world take me for what it would" (Johnson 1995: 90, emphasis added). In his last lecture, Kripke himself suggests the possibility of "black" and "white" as rigid designators by advocating the view that

terms for natural kinds are much closer to proper names than is ordinarily supposed ... *Perhaps* some "general" names ("foolish," "fat," "yellow") express properties. In a significant sense, such general names as "cow" and "tiger" do not, unless *being a cow* counts trivially as a property. Certainly "cow" and "tiger" are *not* short for the conjunction of properties a dictionary would take to define them.

(Kripke 1982: 127–8)

It should be noted that Kripke's use of "yellow" in the above quotation is a reference to color and not to a human race, which could not, according to the above logic, express properties. In this context, we can understand the utterance "black is beautiful" not as an attempt at substituting a negative cluster of concepts with a positive one in order to reclaim the properties attached to "black" identity; rather, it is intelligible as an attempt to preserve the rigid designation of "black," by displacing its so-called properties onto black as a color, to mark its function as a general name, than as a property of group identity.

We must ask what consequence race names as rigid designators have for the psychoanalytic examination of race identity. I suggest that insofar as race identity, unlike sexual identity, has no bearing on the real, such rigid designation is better understood not as an indication of the "failure" of the symbolic (a symptom that escapes meaning or the possibility of interpretation), which would be the Lacanian translation of rigid designation, but of its agency. Black and white and other racial signifiers do not *fail* to signify properties (as "the" woman does in her position as *objet a* or the symptom); they perform the only function they can: they designate rigidly this or that individual ("everything is what it is and not another thing"). Does this mean that race names as rigid designators cannot be translated into Lacanian terms, that they have no psychoanalytic valence? That race names are rigid designators is, first of all, a counterintuitive claim. If we consider how and why racial signifiers are used in everyday speech, we encounter not only the ideological production of specific racial content (usually referred to as stereotypes), but the fraught status of the racial referent as such. One points with a word – black man, white woman – but this pointing cannot be "innocent" in the sense that it "merely" establishes reference as in: "no other than Nixon might have been Nixon" (Kripke 1982: 48). The pointing in this case involves the whole regime of racial visibility which, as I have been delineating it, is founded on a certain anxiety. This relation between racial naming as meaning, or the description of properties, and racial naming as reference, or pure designation, is not one of misreading the logical functioning of names; rather, I suggest that racial naming as referring to properties (or the stereotype) acts as an envelope, a cover for the anxiety of racial reference which literally means nothing. (This is the very definition of the stereotype as a form of discourse that attempts to produce meaning where none is possible.) There is something anxiety-producing about the fullness of the signifier/referent relation that bypasses the signified, or the concept, that would properly produce meaning and thus desire.

This anxious relation between the racial signifier as rigid designation and the racial signifier as a cluster of concepts founded on anxiety is brilliantly disclosed in the only short story ever written by Toni Morrison, "Recitatif." In the following, I read the story's technique as a working out of the Kripkean logic of naming in relation to the Lacanian gloss on rigid designators as a certain "writing" which indicates the failure, or the limit, of the symbolic. I choose this text for its singular meditation on names, rigid and non-rigid, and its device of refusing to deploy the racial "name" for significant purposes. This story, which is about love between women as much as it is about race, demands that we read identity as a gendered and raced phenomenon simultaneously. The contrapuntal relation, which I have been

arguing for thus far, between race and sexual difference is sharply thematized in this narrative, with reference to a set of relations that will be
delineated among naming, the body, knowledge, racial ambiguity, love and
hatred. I shall be arguing that the import or the force of rigid designation in
relation to race serves not so much to point up the impossibility of language
founded on the impasse of sexual difference, but the anxiety of reference
inherent in racial visibility as meaningless designation. In "Recitatif," both
these themes – of rigid designation as an impossible writing, and as anxious
reference – are braided together as unconscious knowledge, or an ignorant
knowing. To expand on Morrison's musical metaphor: I read the story as
possessing the structure of an antiphony, where there is a responsive alterna-
tion between racial anxiety and the impasse of sexual difference.
Approaching the referent involves a *récitatif* with the impossibility of
language, and when the impasse of language seems most insistent, then the
referent performs an encore. The keynote being the letter of love figured as
an emptiness, a nothing to know. The two themes are reconciled only in that
space of hateloving, where the (w)hole of identity forms a paradoxical
ground for what Lacan calls "true love."

Reciting identity

"Recitatif" can be read as a literary working out of Kripke's thesis about
names as rigid designators. I shall pay close attention to how this logic, as
borne out by the narrative technique, bears on the referent, or the raced
body. Morrison's short story should be considered as a part of the adversarial aesthetics that I delineated in the last chapter as appropriate to the
ethics of the raced subject. If *Suture* is the unwritable text *par excellence*,
then "Recitatif" is the quintessential unfilmable text. It accomplishes a
similar effect of "symbolic passing," but raises questions that pertain more
to knowledge than to visibility *per se*. Like *Suture*, the narrative technique
produces symptomatic responses from readers who, more often than not,
find themselves either wanting to tell the truth or have the truth told about
racial identity.

The story, set through the 1950s, 1960s and 1970s, is about two girls,
Twyla and Roberta Fisk, who meet as eight-year-olds in a shelter (St
Bonny's) for orphaned and abandoned children. Twyla narrates the story as
an adult, and she establishes within a few lines that the two are of different
races, a fact that at first makes Twyla "sick to [her] stomach" (Morrison
1983: 243). However, Twyla does not disclose who of the pair is the "salt"
and who the "pepper" (244). The narrative is episodically constructed into
four segments which take place at dawn, mid-morning, afternoon and
evening, with a span of several years separating each. In the first episode at
the shelter, when they are eight, their mothers are introduced into the story.
Roberta's is "sick," and Twyla's "dances all night." When the mothers meet,

they are immediately contrasted as puritanical and unconventional, "sacred" and "profane" respectively. Roberta's mother is an enormous, bible-toting, cross-wearing figure who quite intimidates Twyla, while Twyla's mother, Mary, is girlish and lacks a sense of propriety in her dress and manner. The girls meet again about eight years later at a Howard Johnson's where Twyla is a waitress, and Roberta, who now sports a hippie style, is cool and ironic. When they run into each other, this time like long lost friends, about twelve years later at an upscale grocery store, they are both married with children. Twyla is married to a fireman and lives a modest suburban life, while Roberta, who has now cleaned up, is married to a wealthy man who works at IBM and can afford servants and fine clothes. They have another encounter the same year at a school bussing protest which pits them on opposite sides of the struggle for integration. At their final meeting, at the close of the story, in a small coffee shop around Christmas time, another eight years or so seem to have elapsed, and Roberta is remorseful and emotional about certain shared memories of the shelter. The narrative is tightly constructed, producing the sense of a day elapsing in what is really almost a lifetime, and the running theme in all four episodes is their mothers and Maggie. Maggie, the cleaning woman at the shelter: a mute woman in a "kiddie hat," whose disability fascinates as it repulses the children.

Part of the story's interest, as mentioned previously, results from the narrator's refusal to identify the characters racially. In *Playing in the Dark* (1992), Morrison explains her purpose: "The only short story I have ever written, 'Recitatif,' was an experiment in the removal of all racial codes from a narrative about two characters of different races for whom racial identity is crucial" (1992: XI). What does it mean for Morrison to assert that racial identity is crucial for the characters and yet deliberately deny the knowledge of this identity to her readers? Is Morrison suggesting that race is crucial, in that it produces certain effects, but not meaningful, in that it delivers no knowledge? Race names, she seems to be suggesting, are nothing but rigid designators, and if a story is about meaning and interpretation, then the elimination of these designators discloses a great deal about social pathology. Inevitably, the story incites our hermeneutic impulse. In an essay published in *Critical Inquiry*, Elizabeth Abel (1993) rises to this bait by playing the critic-as-detective trying to figure out who is white and who black. Her method, predictably, is to read the descriptive properties of Twyla and Roberta and their mothers as clues to racial identity. Abel is, of course, deploying the cluster-concept notion of identity, where black and white have certain meanings. Figuring herself as "white," and her inter-locutor Lula Fragd as "a black feminist critic," Abel and Fragd, as white and black respectively, pin signifiers of racial identity on Roberta and Twyla on the basis of their own identifications. Lula believes that Twyla is black, while Elizabeth believes the opposite, that Roberta is black and Twyla white. In the peculiar foursome of the characters and the critics that ensues from this exercise, what is revealed, according to Abel, is the content of racial fantasies that white women have about black women:

> If white feminist readings of black women's texts disclose white critical fantasies, what (if any) value do these readings have – and for whom? How do white women's readings of black women's biological bodies inform our readings of black women's textual bodies?
>
> (Abel 1993: 477)

These may be significant questions, and what they do is to extend the family of descriptions, the cluster of concepts that determine the meaning of black and white to include practices of reading and criticism. Abel's questions and her critical procedure ironically run counter to Morrison's. Whereas Morrison challenges the notion that the signifiers "black" and "white" can be filled with properties, or have meaning, Abel, in effect, adds more properties in order to stabilize or capture racial identity as meaning. In this case, to read as a white woman is to appropriate black writing, and to be black is to be subjected to dominant discourse, and so on. Abel's political impulse to confront the pervasiveness of discriminatory trends in all cultural practices, though admirable for its courage, is of a piece with the contemporary approach to the discourse of racial thinking as a dirty secret that must be ferreted out from its hiding place so that it can be eradicated. The mode of confession that this sanitary notion of identity requires immediately recalls Foucault's critique of power/knowledge in *The History of Sexuality* (1978), where he argues that power's productive capability inheres in its ability to proliferate discourse (about sexuality) through the device of confession. Foucault's thesis, when extended to race, discloses the confessional mode favored by some strains of self-identified "white feminism," and the notion of racial identity it presumes, as precisely an effect of the productive aspect of power. This is, of course, the notion of identity that Butler (using Foucault) critiques and rightly subverts. The Morrison-Lacan-Kripke reading of identity, on the other hand, insofar as it delimits identity as a signifier without a signified, radically undercuts the agency of power (as repressive or productive, *pace* Abel and Butler respectively) in the writing of identity as such.

If power produces any effects at all in Morrison's story, it is not as racial identity but as social class. What is interesting is that the contents of class identity here do not function as clues to racial identity, thereby reducing race to a social construction. Social class serves to make racial identity even more opaque by driving a wedge between signifier and signified. The volatility of class identity, especially given the historical information about the spouses' professions that Abel reports Morrison as providing in private correspondence (such as "IBM's efforts to recruit black executives and ... the racial exclusiveness of the firemen's union" [Abel 1993: 476]), works not as "evidence" for fixing the characters' racial identity, but to produce even further ambiguity. Are we to assume that Twyla is white because she is married to a fireman who is probably white? Historical and economic indicators may suggest one thing or another, but what the story underscores by its refusal to pin racial signifiers onto characters is precisely the hiatus that prevails between historical facts and the identity of subjects. We may recall Stuart Hall's consequential essay "Race, articulation, and societies structured in dominance" (1996), which poses the question thus:

> the problem here is not whether economic structures are relevant to racial divisions but *how the two are theoretically connected.* ... The problem here is to account for the appearance of this "something else" – these extraeconomic factors and their place in the dynamic reproduction of such social formations.
>
> (Hall 1996: 20, emphasis added)

Hall suggests the inadequacy of paradigms that deploy either a simple economic determinist approach or the sociological one that proposes a set of "plural explanations" that engage in description rather than analysis. Taking up various economic and sociological theories of the South African socio-economic formation, Hall assesses the hinge that each theory produces between race and class. The essay has an encyclopedic scope, and it will not do to attempt a précis. But what Hall finally argues, through a precise deployment of the Gramscian notion of "articulation," is that "race is ... the modality in which class is 'lived,' the medium through which class relations are experienced, the form in which it is appropriated and 'fought through'" (1996: 55). What Hall works through, with great materialist rigor, is the way in which the exploitative practices of capitalism require the development of ideologies such as race. The analysis of class then must be *articulated* with race. This sort of historical evidence about social formations, comprehensively theorized, may perhaps seem intractable in the face of certain Lacanian or logical readings of identity. The hard material fact is that we live class as race, and we enact our struggles through racial identification. That much is incontrovertible. Yet what does it say about the "nature" of racial identity? We no doubt act on the basis of powerful identifications, but contrary to a certain familiar psychological wisdom, identity cannot be subsumed by identification, as it simply cannot be thought as concept.

How does Morrison's delimiting of identity, her refusal to let racial signifiers signify, bear on the referent, on our notions of the body? How can we imagine Roberta and Twyla as physical presences in the absence of the all-important racial marker of color? This could potentially work as a barrier to narrative coherence for those readers whose reading practice entails imaginary identification with particular characters. Identification itself is not impossible in this story; one could be hailed by the class narrative, or the narrative tone, etc. What is impossible is identification on the basis of the image. In "Recitatif," our imagination of Roberta and Twyla is not thwarted but liberated. They change shapes in our minds even as we try to see Roberta and Twyla now as black, then as white, according to the codes we employ. As Abel suggests, if we begin reading the story with Roberta figured as black and Twyla as white (or vice versa), they seem to exchange colors, or identities in the second half of the story. But the narrative invites us to think bodies differently – it incites a new way of looking and imagining, the aesthetics of which have yet to be fully specified. Like an "etch-a-sketch," the possibilities are enhanced rather than limited by the narrative refusal.

The (w)hole of identity

> I am called Jacques Lacan, but as something that can be missing, for which the name will tend to cover over another lack. The proper name, therefore, is a moveable function.
>
> (Seminar IX, quoted in Grigg 1998: 77)

"Recitatif" problematizes the referent, or the body as a site of knowledge, thus radically undercutting the hermeneutic impulse of the literary critic. If names are purely rigid designators that do not establish qualitative properties, then Morrison's story seems to want to interrogate not the (non-)function of the signified, but of the referent itself. When the signifier "black" or "white" points to a specific body, what have we discovered about it? Is there some knowledge, something that we know, due to the function of the signifier? Let us shift the emphasis from rigid designation to the unconscious. In Seminar XX, Lacan specifies analytic discourse as that which "announces to us that there is knowledge that is not known, knowledge that is based on the signifier as such" (XX: 96). In this formulation, the signifier is the basis of an unknowable knowledge that, contrary to the presumption that there is a substantive knowledge that has its locus in the Other and can be acquired (96), suggests that even the Other does not know. As Lacan says: "the hitch is that the Other, the locus, knows nothing" (98). The issue of what knows, and what there is to know, seems to orient the trajectory of Morrison's narrative insofar as it determines the relationship between Roberta and Twyla. The issue of knowledge, asking questions, not asking questions, about each other's mothers, is what makes their friendship, their love. Twyla narrates:

> As soon as Bozo left she [Roberta] came over to me and said, "Is your mother sick too?" "No," I said. "She just likes to dance all night." "Oh," she nodded her head and I liked the way she understood things so fast.
>
> (Morrison 1983: 244)

This all-significant moment of understanding is never explained, neither to the readers nor to each other. What binds the two girls in an inexplicable bond, at least according to Twyla, is a certain reticence, even ignorance: "So we got along – what with her leaving whole pieces of things on her plate and being nice about not asking questions" (245). After the disastrous meeting between the two mothers at the shelter, when Roberta's mother refuses to acknowledge Mary, Twyla's mother, Twyla remarks about her friend:

> I think she was sorry that her mother would not shake my mother's hand. And I liked that and I liked the fact that she didn't say a word about Mary groaning all the way through the service and not bringing lunch.
>
> (248)

The girls' willingness to maintain silence, to refuse curiosity, then also becomes the point of vulnerability that the two use against each other. In the next episode, about eight years later at the Howard Johnson's, when Twyla reaches out to Roberta only to be met with condescension, Twyla decides to hit back with the question "How's your mother?" In fact, this question becomes the leitmotif of all their following meetings, even though the only answer it seems to warrant to both women's satisfaction is "fine," or at the most a confirmation of the status quo. Reflecting on their friendship that seems to endure huge gaps and hiatuses, Twyla explains:

> Maybe it was the thing itself. Just being there, together. Two little girls who knew what nobody else in the world knew – how not to ask questions. How to believe what had to be believed. There was politeness in that reluctance and generosity as well. Is your mother sick too? No, she dances all night. Oh – and an understanding nod.
>
> (253)

What is this *thing*, this knowledge that consists of not knowing, or not asking questions, that establishes the bond between Roberta and Twyla? Is it some shameful knowledge, an awareness of something unspeakable about their mothers that each girl must protect as a secret for fear of revealing that which would destroy their subjective support? Is there, in other words, something to know? It appears that there is not. What Roberta and Twyla seem to share is not the fact that each has some substantive secret; rather, it is that there is nothing at all to know or tell about their mothers. Their mothers are absent, and empty. This emptiness, this knowledge as a "nothing to know" which connects the two girls, appears to have a corporal dimension in the mute figure of Maggie.

Maggie, the mute "kitchen woman" at the shelter: she with the bow legs, "legs like parentheses," (245) and a hollow body, a body whose "semi-circle legs" seem graphically to figure hollowness, emptiness. Twyla recollects the names they called her:

> "Bow legs! Bow legs!" Nothing. She just rocked on, the chin straps of her baby-boy hat swaying form side to side. I think we were wrong. I think she could hear and didn't let on. And it shames me even now to think there was somebody in there after all who heard us call her those names and couldn't tell on us.
>
> (245)

Twyla's mature fantasy that there was "somebody in there," inside Maggie's hollow body, is contradicted later, by her admission that "Maggie was my dancing mother. Deaf, I thought, and dumb. *Nobody inside*. Nobody who would hear you if you cried in the night. Nobody who could tell you anything important that you could use. Rocking, dancing, swaying as she walked" (259–60, emphasis added). The connection between Maggie's emptiness and Twyla's mother as also empty and absent is made explicit here as she tries to sort out her memory of Maggie. For Roberta, too, Maggie is associated with her mother because "she'd been brought up in an institution like my mother was and like I thought I would be too" (261). A peculiar nexus of relations emerges amongst knowledge as ignorance, absent, empty mothers, and Maggie the hollow, deaf-mute, as a foundation for "love" between the two women. In Lacanian terms, Maggie is, of course, the Other that does not know. In fact, as a mute woman, who rocks and sways as she works, completely oblivious to the world of words and speech, she incarnates that enigma of woman, that Other *jouissance*, of which Lacan says woman will say nothing and "perhaps knows nothing" (XX: 74), as it exceeds the domain of the symbolic. This is also the aspect of woman that characterizes her as "not all" who has a relationship with the Other as "not-everything" or "not-at-all-knowledgeable" (98). But, if Maggie is "woman" with the definite article crossed out to indicate her not-wholeness, what does it have to do with the girls' association of her with their mothers? In the same session ("Knowledge and truth") where Lacan elaborates the relationship of the signifier to (non-)knowledge and to the Other, he goes on to argue that insofar as the Other's not knowing is posited in relation to the unconscious, the subjects know that they do not know everything, thus filling out the unconscious as a certain wholeness. And this is the wholeness that "men" see in women, and which woman as mother or Other is responsible for (98–9). As mother, woman has "unconscious effects," and though she is not responsible for everyone's unconscious, not much can be said about hers (99). Maggie's emptiness is, then, also her fullness; she is the empty/full "thing" that Lacan had elaborated in Seminar VII, and brings up again in this session, this time in relation to hatred.

Maggie is not only the emptiness of the signifier, the ignorance of knowledge – i.e., she knows nothing ("nobody who could tell you anything") – but as the "thing," she is herself an unknowable, hollow, no-body. The signifier – Maggie – can designate her, but it cannot deliver any knowledge. And this unknowability, "not all" aspect of woman/Maggie, is underscored by Morrison particularly in relation to race. In terms of the narrative, we could ask: is Maggie simply a blank screen for the girls to project their fantasies upon? Or, in more symbolic terms, is she an empty signifier that can be filled with the contents of the girls' desire for their mothers? It would not be wrong to answer in the affirmative to both questions; however, we must contend with the fact that Maggie not only figures the enigma of sexual difference by her figuration of the mothers' emptiness as literally *das Ding*, but that of racial difference as well. Twyla's early recollection of her is vague and unspecific: "she was old and sandy-colored and she worked in the kitchen" (Morrison 1983: 245). Later, after the Howard Johnson's meeting, Roberta troubles Twyla with the episode of Maggie supposedly "falling down" in the orchard, a vague though persistent memory that Twyla harbors. At the bussing protest, Roberta this time not only accuses Twyla of cruelty towards Maggie, but of bigotry toward "a black lady" (257). Twyla is shocked and astonished to hear Roberta characterize Maggie as "black," and later admits that when she thought about it she "actually couldn't be certain" (259).

Thus we can see how there are at least two threads that follow from the set of relations specified earlier (*à propos* knowledge as ignorance, mothers and emptiness) having to do with cruelty (or hatred), and with racial ambiguity. What bearing does Maggie's figuring of the emptiness of the mother have on her racially ambiguous status, and how does hatred figure in this set? How do these issues inflect the themes of knowledge as "nothing to know" and of the body as designated by the signifier?

For Twyla, Maggie's muteness makes her the object *par excellence* of hatred. She wonders: "what about if somebody tries to kill her? ... Or if she wants to cry? Can she cry?" (245). Again, killing is what Twyla thinks of most when Mary visits her. Though she says that "a pretty mother on earth is better than a beautiful dead one in the sky even if she did leave you alone to go dancing" (247), when Mary in her girlish way calls "Twyla baby, Twyla baby!" Twyla says: "I could have killed her" (247). In this instance, it appears that the expression is more than a simple colloquialism, for killing is what she thinks of twice more in that same afternoon. During service: "All I could think of was that she really needed to be killed" (248). Again, when it is clear that Mary has no lunch to provide, Twyla thinks, "I could have killed her" (248). Twyla's wanting to kill her mother, something her mother apparently needed, is thus what is seemingly at stake in the embers of the memory about Maggie "falling down" that Roberta stokes. Roberta contradicts Twyla's memory, saying that Maggie did not fall down, but was pushed by the older girls who then tore her clothes. Later, she not only accuses Twyla of participating in Maggie's assault, of kicking her, but of doing so to a "black lady":

> What was she saying? Black? Maggie wasn't black.
> "She wasn't black," I said.
> "Like hell she wasn't, and you kicked her. We both did. You kicked a black lady who couldn't even scream."
> "Liar!"
> "You're the liar! Why don't you go on home and leave us alone, huh?"
>
> (258)

In the exchange of accusations that fly between them about who is telling the truth and who is lying, Twyla comes to realize later that what really troubled her about that quarrel was not

> the kicking part. I know I didn't do that, I couldn't do that. But I was puzzled about her telling me Maggie was black. When I thought about it I actually couldn't be certain. She wasn't pitch-black, I knew, or I would have remembered that. What I remember was the kiddie hat, and the semi-circle legs. I tried to reassure myself about the race thing for a long time until it dawned on me that the truth was already there, and Roberta knew it. I didn't kick her; I didn't join in with the girls and kick that lady, but I sure did want to. We watched and never tried to help her and never called for help.
>
> (259)

Twyla's thought process here seems to work entirely through the logic of the unconscious, and it remains unclear what it is that she reassures herself of: that Maggie wasn't black? That she, Twyla, didn't know Maggie was black? Or is it that whatever race Maggie was didn't matter, because it all came down to Twyla's wanting to kick her? In Twyla's peculiar reasoning, quoted above, the truth about wanting to kick Maggie is somehow caught up in her not knowing what Maggie was racially. What else would reassuring herself about "the race thing" mean here?

Hateloving

Let us return to the set of relations delineated above: knowledge as ignorance, mothers, emptiness, racial ambiguity and hatred. It appears that in this narrative, hatred performs the function of conjunction amongst these terms. Hatred in Lacan's teaching is primordial and closely related to ignorance and to love. In Seminar VII, speaking of *das Ding*, the "cause of the most fundamental human passion," Lacan says:

Luther writes of the following – God's eternal hatred of men, not simply of their failures and the works of their free will, but a hatred that existed even before the world was created. ... That hatred which existed even before the world was created is the correlative of the relationship that exists between a certain influence of the law as such and a certain conception of *das Ding* as the fundamental problem and, in a word, as the problem of evil. I assume that it hasn't escaped your attention that it is exactly what Freud deals with when the question he asks concerning the Father leads him to point out that the latter is the tyrant of the primitive horde, the one against whom the original crime was committed, and who for that very reason introduced the order, essence, and foundation of the domain of law.

(VII: 97)

Hatred, in this formulation, is the necessary condition for the establishment of the dialectic of desire. Without the primordial hatred of the sons towards the tyrant father, neither the law nor transgressive jouissance of *das Ding* would be possible. This paradigm of hatred, as evinced by the Freudian myth of the primal horde, is always directed at what is perceived as the other's satisfaction. It is also related to what Lacan terms in Seminar XI as *invidia* (XI: 116), and in Seminar XX as "jealouissance" (XX: 100). In both seminars, Lacan invokes the example from St Augustine, who observes the small child pale at the sight of his baby brother at his mother's breast. In Seminar XI, he terms such hatred "true envy – the envy that makes the subject pale before the image of a completeness closed upon itself, before the idea that the *petit a. ... may* be for another the possession that gives satisfaction, *Befriedigung*" (XI: 116). The child at the breast is supposed by the little boy to have the *petit a*, which offers a semblance of being. And it is this notion, that the other is privy to some *jouissance*, that makes hatred as "jealouissance" spring forth.[12] Lacan suggests that

this is the first substitute jouissance. ... the desire evoked on the basis of a metonomy that is inscribed on the basis of presumed demand, addressed to the Other, that is, on the basis of a kernel of what I call *Ding*. ... the very neighbor Freud refuses to love beyond certain limits.

(XX: 100)

Thus the "hatred" that Twyla and Roberta experience towards Maggie is inevitable, considering the fact that what they both seem to lack is precisely the possibility of desire. Their mothers (and Maggie) in their emptiness are paradoxically also too full: dancing, being sick, being mute, these are the symptoms of *jouissance* and not desire, in the sense of lacking something which will in turn permit the girls to become subjects of desire. Thus hatred, a hatred that is prior even to desire, provides an entry to the symbolic that the mothers potentially block at the moment. In "The Direction of the treatment," Lacan, referring to the subject as a "want-to-be" (*manque à être*), i.e., one who lacks being (a condition that is the determinant of the desiring subject as such), suggests that not only is desire "hollowed out" within demand, but that demand

> evokes the want-to-be under the three figures of the nothing that constitutes the basis of the demand for love, of the hate that even denies the other's being, and of the unspeakable element in that which is ignored in its request.
>
> (E: 265)

Here it is demand that makes subjectivity possible through love, hate, and the unspeakable, thus bringing these elements into a necessary relation with each other. The modality of these relations is developed to some extent in *Encore*. Lacan conjoins hatred with the subject's (manque-à-être) demand for love, for which he coins the interesting term "hainamoration" (XX: 90), or "hateloving." At this conjunction, Lacan posits a knowledge that only analysis can properly grasp. One can know "nothing of love without hate," he says, and suggests that knowledge itself must be rethought in relation to hatred (91). For ignorance is but a condition of not knowing hatred, a condition that is characteristic only of God (91). At the end of *Encore*, Lacan says: "Doesn't the extreme of love, true love, reside in the approach to being? And true love ... gives way to hatred" (146). Thus if to be ignorant is to not know hatred, then insofar as one cannot know love without hate, ignorance can know nothing of love either. But if hatred is the opposite of ignorance, it cannot be equated, however, with knowledge. Unconscious knowledge, Lacan says, is "closely related to love" (144).[13] I take this to mean that when one approaches being through unconscious knowledge, one reaches the paradoxical point of hainamoration or hateloving, where love gives way to hate. This would mean that the point of hainamoration is not the place of primordial hate which makes the law of desire possible, but it is the condition that prevails when one approaches being through unconscious knowledge or love. In the language of the *Ethics* seminar, it would be to "love one's neighbor as oneself," the death drive which aims at a death beyond putrefaction.

Given these propositions, we can recontextualize the pact of ignorance-as-knowledge shared by Twyla and Roberta as not the simple ignorance of hatred attributed to God, but rather a shared unconscious knowledge which is significantly related to love and the "nothing that constitutes the demand for love." This ignorant-knowledge, or more properly this unconscious knowledge, they share which has a "good" understanding of hate, a hate directed toward Maggie and their mothers, potentially orients them in the direction of being, and true love as hateloving. But love for whom? And being as what? And how do racial ambiguity and identity figure in this movement toward being and true love?

Refrain

What kind of an identity statement is "Maggie is black"? I have cited Kripke's thesis regarding names as rigid designators, and we have extended that thesis to race designators such as "black" and "white" to suggest that these nouns also function as names, insofar as they merely determine reference without recourse to qualitative descriptions that may serve as criteria for identity. Like proper names, "black" and "white" have no meaning, and neither is their reference determined through a cluster of concepts such that they are true in all situations. Race identity, then, is not contingent; it is necessary, even "essential," insofar as it is a rigid designation without qualitative criteria that can be true in all situations. We have further extended the absence of the signified in this notion of the signifier to Lacan's notion of identity, particularly in relation to the place of "woman" in sexual difference, as something that exceeds the symbolic. If the signified is a symbolic construct, it is precisely in its absence or failure that identity is made possible. With reference to woman and sexual difference, this is the excluded possibility of *jouissance*, the lack in the Other, that determines the subject of desire as such. However, racial identity insofar as it is entirely symbolic has no bearing on the lack in the Other. Thus the absence of the signified here does not mean that the symbolic has failed; it is rather that it has succeeded too well. There is no question of mapping racial difference onto the graph of sexual difference. "Black," "white," etc. are rigid designators, and whatever qualities or signifieds we may attempt to attach to them will be determined by history. This does not mean that racial identity is contingent; it is so only if we think of identity in qualitative terms. And as Kripke says, everyone knows that there are contingent identities. Racial identity is necessary in that it rigidly designates a referent without need of qualitative properties. To return to the context of the story, what does it mean to say that Maggie is black? What effect does it have, especially in relation to the fact that such reference is precisely refused, by the narrator, for Twyla and Roberta? I have suggested that one of the effects of such narrative reticence is to exemplify racial names as rigid designators without qualitative properties. Therefore trying to decode the narrative to read one of the other characters as black or white is to elide the fundamental proposition of the story: racial signifiers do not mean anything in the strong sense of having "no sense." Therefore, what is the effect of Roberta's fixing of Maggie as black, given that Twyla was unaware of Maggie's identity as black?

I would suggest that what Roberta does by invoking the racial signifier in relation to Maggie is not so much uncover some qualitative truth about Maggie (as Abel for instance assumes) as add nothing to nothing. That is, given that Maggie is already hollow, "no body inside," Roberta, by adding yet another empty signifier to Maggie, not only reopens but widens the hole that Maggie graphically figures with(in) her semi-circle legs. Moreover, the rigid designation of race, as we may recall, is not innocent. It incites the regime of visibility that we have been arguing is founded on anxiety – the anxiety that ensues in the encounter with the historicity of race that produces the pre-discursive effect of visibility.[14] Twyla's incoherent memory of Maggie as "sandy-colored," then, is a testimony not to her naiveté – she after all is "sick to her stomach" when she first encounters Roberta, the girl from "a whole other race" – but rather to the fact that the regime of racial visibility, after a certain point, was not in operation for her. Maggie displaces Mary as a source of racial knowledge. At first, Twyla narrates that "every now and then she [Mary] would stop dancing long enough to tell me something important and one of the things she said was that they never washed their hair and they smelled funny" (243). Later, Maggie, who is explicitly associated with Mary, is characterized as "nobody who could tell you anything important that you could use" (259). Twyla's unconscious knowledge about Maggie, then, is not a simple repression of her blackness (as if blackness implies qualities that in itself demand repression) but of the nothingness, the emptiness, the rigidity of signifiers that mean nothing at all. Roberta thus not only recalls that nothing of Maggie, but she also incites the anxiety of racial visibility in Twyla. And so Twyla's reaction is properly one of outrage. She revenges herself on Roberta with the lurid signs she hauls up for Roberta alone at the bussing protest. Roberta's innocuous sign "Mothers have rights too!" is met with Twyla's "So do children," "How would you know?" and finally the most lethal sign of them all: "Is your mother well?" Roberta leaves the scene of protest for good shortly afterwards. Twyla's signs, of course, meant for Roberta alone, cite that unconscious ignorant-knowledge about mothers that the two women share. By asking Roberta how she would know about mothers, Twyla is suggesting that it is Roberta who has willed a certain ignorance, an ignorance that Lacan would say knows nothing of either love or hate. If Roberta conjures the anamorphotic spectre of Maggie with her "Maggie is black" assertion, then so does Twyla with her direct invocation of Roberta's knowledge of her mother's emptiness. In this exchange of signs, the two women clearly approach what Lacan terms as being, the emptiness where love gives way to hate and perhaps hate to love. When Roberta at the end of the story sobs: "Oh shit, Twyla. Shit, shit, shit. What the hell happened to Maggie?" we see the two women reach that level of hainamoration, or hateloving, where true love gives way to hate. What better way to express one's love but with that aggressive metaphor of "shit"? Roberta in effect can be translated as saying: "I hatelove you in my hateloving of Maggie." For the subject of race, "true love" is a necessary movement of oscillation between the two poles of meaninglessness. Fluctuating between the anxiety of empty reference and the impasse of sexual difference, the subject of "inter-racial" love approaches being precipitously through hateloving. Twyla's initial dyspepsia at meeting Roberta should not be discounted as a silly prejudice. As someone who couldn't remember what she had read or what was said, for Twyla meeting someone who couldn't read and didn't listen (Morrison 1983: 244) is to encounter one's counterpart in meaninglessness. Twyla's visceral reaction is properly the response of "true love" that makes up for the impossibility of all relationships.

Chapter 6

Discolorations

Thinking that does not make system and perception accord conflicts with more than isolated visual impressions; it conflicts with practice.
(Horkheimer and Adorno, *The Dialectic of Enlightenment*: 83)

In presenting my hypothesis to various interlocutors in formal and informal settings, I have been asked how my theory of race as a symbolic system sustained by a regime of visibility translates into social policy. How does it affect our thinking about affirmative action, about anti-discrimination legislations, about those particularly powerful modes of political mobilization that have aggregated around identity? It is sophisticated and easy to be dismissive of "identity politics" because it seems naive and essentialist. But the immeasurable weightiness of, say, the black power movement or the women's rights movement in pushing back the forces of exploitation and resuscitating devalued cultures through the redefinition of identity must give us pause. Identity politics works. However, the argument of this book is that it also ultimately serves to reinforce the very system that is the source of the symptoms that such politics confines itself to addressing. It is race itself that must be dismantled as a regime of looking. We cannot aim at this goal by merely formulating new social policies. In fact, my theory is anti-policy for two reasons: first, any attempt to address race systematically through policy, and by that I mean state policy, will inevitably end up reifying race. Second, the only effective intervention can be cultural, at the "grassroots" level. Such intervention can and should work, sometimes in tandem and at others in tension with state policy, but the project of dismantling the regime of race cannot be given over to the state. Gramsci speaks of the necessity of transforming the cultural into the political; where race is concerned, it is imperative that we turn what is now "political," an issue of group interests, into the "cultural," an issue of social practice.

We must develop a new adversarial aesthetics that will throw racial signification into disarray. Given that race discourse was produced in a thoroughly visual culture, it is necessary that the visual itself be used against the scopic regime of race. I have laid the basis for such an aesthetics in

Chapters 4 and 5, where the relation of the bodily mark to the sig thrown into perplexity. In *Suture*, we as spectators are asked to give investment in Whiteness, the signifier that promises access to absolute humanness. The film puts pressure on the purely symbolic origins of race by unraveling the relation between racial gestalt and one's identity. Clay is Vincent if he takes up his place in the signifying chain. Similitude is established not on the basis of the body's gestalt, but the part object – ears, eyes, etc. In Toni Morrison's "Recitatif," it is racial reference that is called into question. As with *Suture*, the relation between visibility and the signifier is refused, but for another purpose. By emptying the racial signifier of its properties, so that white and black have no connotations, Morrison renders meaningless the relations among the signifier, the body, and identity. For Morrison, it is such emptiness that makes love approachable.

I am proposing an adversarial aesthetics that will destabilize racial looking so that racial identity will always be uncertain and unstable. The point of such a practice would be to confront the symbolic constitution of race and of racial looking *as* the investment we make in difference for sameness. The confrontation has to entail more than an exploration of the fantasy, which process I detailed in Chapter 2 on "The secret sharer." There we took measure of the fantasy of wholeness as the obliteration of difference that Whiteness holds out to the subject of race. A simple rejection of this fantasy of self-inflation on a political or ethical basis, such as the repugnance we see exhibited by Orwell, in Chapter 3, cannot be adequate. In Orwell's case, his liberal rejection of mastery can only lead to the reproduction of the system of race. For it is not enough to be aware of the affect of anxiety that race invariably generates. One must traverse the fundamental fantasy of singular humanity upon which racial identity is founded. It is a question of resituating oneself in relation to the raced signifier.

Such a practice would not aim so much at a cross-identification, such as ticking the "wrong" box on a questionnaire, or passing for another race. It would confound racial signification by stressing the continuity, the point of doubt among the so-called races, to the extent that each and every one of us must mistrust the knowledge of our racial belonging. The idea would be to void racial knowledge by releasing the racial signifier from its historical mooring in a signified. Such practices can only be, and must be representational, as what they necessitate is a radical intervention into language and signification. This entails the reinvention of culture as organized by differences based on other kinds of "reasonings" than race. Every medium of representation can and must be harnessed for such a practice. In addition to those I have cited earlier such as film, painting and literature, we must consider the possibilities presented by that other mode of representation, namely representation by proxy. The possibility of unsettling political representation, for instance, or procedures of verification based on race such as the passport, the visa and the driver's license may renew and refresh questions of identity – what is worth preserving, what is not. The idea is not to erase identity, even if such a preposterous act were possible. Rather, we must rethink identity in tension with our usual habits of visual categorization of individuals. Ideally, the practice that I am advocating will deploy the visual against the visual. Such redefinition is thinkable only as a collective and *normalizing* project; it should be aimed at infiltrating normative bourgeois self-definition. The practice of "discoloration" will be more effective if it is not restricted to particular intellectual groups or artists. Gramsci suggests that a philosophical movement, even as it elaborates

> a form of thought superior to "common sense" and coherent on a scientific plane. ... never forgets to remain in contact with the "simple" and indeed finds in this contact the source of the problems it sets out to study and to resolve.
>
> (Gramsci 1971: 330)

In other words, we cannot voluntarily abandon the quotidian logic of race. To do so would be a form of vanguardism that will only reinforce the system as the necessary point of differentiation. Rather, it is to the common sense of race that we must appeal. Otherwise, we will fail to address social contradiction in its specificity. Thus producing a sub-culture of "discolorationists" or encouraging subjects voluntarily to refuse racial identity (as advocated for "white" people by the journal *Race Traitor*) possibly will not be effective. An anti-race praxis must aim at a fundamental transformation of social and political logic. It cannot be a mere "phenomenon of individuals" which, as Gramsci reminds us, only marks the " 'high points' of the progress made by common sense" (1971: 331).

As a praxis, psychoanalysis is the most appropriate discourse for the examination of why we or certain groups may resist such an adversarial aesthetics. Working through our fantasies will involve the risk of desubjectification that many of us dread. Such dread, such an encounter with our own limit, is the only means of articulating the possibility of an ethics beyond the specious enjoyment promised by Whiteness.

Notes

Introduction: on looking

1 The definitive statement on the relation of caste to *varna* is M. N Srinivas' (1962) brief essay "Varna and caste." His discussion of the limits of translating *varna* as color should also be noted. Louis Dumont also categorically differentiates caste from race in *Homo Hierarchicus* (1966). For an analysis of the politics of translating scripture, see Gayatri Spivak's *A Critique of Postcolonial Reason* (1999) especially 252–311.

2 Such critique can considerably vitiate any attempt to explore the concept of race as witnessed in, for instance, Ann Laura Stoler's *Race and the Education of Desire* (1995), which spends disproportionate energy upbraiding Foucault for neglecting colonialism.

3 This is an observation echoed by other critics as well, for example Colette Guillaumin (1995) and Naomi Zack (1997).

4 I am indebted to Joan Copjec's (1994) work in thinking through the specificity of Lacan's theory of desire.

5 Whiteness studies cannot be represented monolithically. There is the ethnographically oriented school that regards Whiteness as pertaining to white people or Caucasians where the attempt is to induce self-consciousness or awareness of one's racial privilege and racial embodiment. See for instance Ruth Frankenberg (1993; 1997), the *Critical Race Theory* volumes edited by Richard Delgado (1995; 1997), Vron Ware (1992), Wray and Newitz (eds) (1997), etc. There is also the more materialist analysis of Whiteness as an ideological construct, such as Alexander Saxton's, and David Roediger's. The journal *Race Traitor* invokes both these types of analyses.

6 Thus the repeated discovery of race as subtending culture or nation or ethnicity by cultural critics such as Walter Benn Michaels (1992), I would suggest, is largely redundant, even naive. Race is neither wholly nature nor nurture, essence nor construct. It is primarily culture behaving like nature. One may say that about sexual difference as well, but psychoanalysis teaches us that sex is primarily an index of the indeterminacy of the subject, and therefore the aforementioned opposition between nature and culture is not germane to it.

7 It is, of course, this common-sense perception that cases of racial passing supposedly contest. However, the concept or logic of passing itself only serves to reinforce visibility and the strict categories of difference it supports, insofar as passing always functions as the exception that defines the norm.

8 For an analysis of Nominalism and racial theory see Zack's "Race and philosophic meaning" (1997).

9 I am drawing upon Lacan's Seminar XX in making these claims.
10 Lacan discusses the object of desire, the minus phi as distinguished from the object cause of desire, the *objet petit a*, in Seminar X on Anxiety.

I Deciphering Whiteness

1 Throughout this book, I use the term "race" to indicate that I am referring not to race as an aspect of individual or group identity, but as a concept with its own coherent systematicity.
2 See Zack 1997, "Race and philosophic meaning," and other essays by Holmstrom and by Lang in the same volume. Appiah likens belief in races to belief in witches (1992: 277).
3 For an interesting study of social scientists and their beliefs in the existence of race, see Reynolds (1992). Reynolds suggests that there is a correlation between the socioeconomic status of scientists and their willingness to credit race as a reality. His studies also demonstrate a significant gender gap (fewer women "believe" in race) and a disparity among the disciplines, with more physical anthropologists and animal behaviorists crediting race, while the majority of sociologists and cultural anthropologists discredit it. I thank Amiee Van Wagenen Wrin for this reference.
4 See for instance Charles Shepherdson's "Human diversity and the sexual relation" (1998).
5 Appiah writes:

> In the biological conception of the human organism, in which characteristics are determined by the pattern of genes in interaction with environments, it is the presence of the alleles (which give rise to these moral and intellectual capacities) that accounts for the observed differences in those capacities in people in similar environments. So the characteristic racial morphology – skin and hair and bone – could be a sign of those differences only if it were (highly) correlated with those alleles. Since there are no strong correlations, even those who think that intellectual and moral character are strongly genetically determined must accept that *race* is at best a poor indicator of capacity.
>
> (1992: 37)

6 My argument will no doubt seem a part of the prejudice against ocularcentrism that Martin Jay (1993) inveighs against in his authoritative work *Downcast Eyes*.
7 See for instance Guillaumin's "Race and nature: the system of marks" (in Guillaumin 1995).
8 The anthropologist Keith has suggested a schema for racial visibility in his article "The evolution of human races." Cited in Allport (1954: 140).
9 Lacan's seminars will be indicated henceforth by number, and references to *Ecrits* (1977) will be abbreviated as E.
10

> This simple definition assumes that language is not to be confused with the various psychical and somatic functions that serve it in the speaking subject – primarily because language and its structure exist prior to the moment at which each subject at a certain point in his mental development makes his entry into it.
>
> (E: 148)

11 There is the simple reading of Lacan's early essay on the mirror stage "Some reflections on the ego" (1953) that posits the child, who experiences its body as in pieces, as jubilating at the sight of the specular image which it takes as a promise of its own future coherence. This moment of jubilation is usually understood as the moment of the misrecognition of the image as one's ego ideal. Thus the task of psychoanalysis would be to show that our ego ideals are false and imaginary. Race then could be mapped onto the mirror stage as the misidentification of oneself as white, black, brown or yellow, which are imaginary constructs that have no grounding in the symbolic.

12 See also Homi Bhabha, "The other question," in *Location of Culture* (1994); also Silverman 1996; Fuss 1995.

13 This reading of identification considerably revises the classical Freudian opposition between identification and desire, which supposedly founds heterosexuality. Lacan's emphasis on desire as the engine of identification is an inevitable consequence of discerning subjectivity as a function of language.

14 I recognize that by quoting the Lacan of 1962 on the Imaginary that I do not fully succeed in specifying racial visibility, for now all visibility seems to be an anxious process. My contribution here is to suggest that insofar as the affect of anxiety is highly particular, we could view racial anxiety as a type of anxiety that promotes a specific visibility.

15 See Serge André's essay, "Otherness of the body" (1994).

16 Balibar's thesis implicates racism, sexism, humanism, and nationalism in a complex network of ideological and material relations that cannot be summarized here. See his essays in *Race, Nation, Class* (1992) co-authored with Wallerstein.

17 See particularly 185–207.

18 Hans F. K. Gunther's *The Racial Elements of European History* was translated from the German in 1927.

19 For a reading that educes the ambivalence of Fichte's nationalist rhetoric, see Balibar's excellent "Fichte and the internal border" in Balibar (1994).

20 See also Balibar (1994) for a discussion of Fichte's argument regarding the suitability of Germans to develop the human as such (70–1).

21 As Arendt points out, the intra-European rivalry among races seems to acquire a momentum after Gobineau's *Inequality of the Human Races* (1854). See for instance Ripley (1896), Widney (1907) and most importantly Gehring (1908).

22 The "chain of being" paradigm can thus envision reversals of top and bottom. Thus it becomes possible for liberalism to conceive of reverse racism or mythical scenarios of role reversal, as in the recent film *White Man's Burden*, where the "Blacks" are effectively the "Whites."

3 Whiteness and the elephant joke

1 Speaking of the development of the "stages of love" and of the "sexual instincts," Freud says: "First amongst these we recognize the phase of incorporating or devouring, a type of love which is compatible with abolition of any separate existence on the part of the object, and which may therefore be designated ambivalent" ("Instincts and their vicissitudes," 102).

2 See Samuel Weber's essay on jokes in *The Legend of Freud* (1982).

3 Writing in 1941 about the "habitual subject-matter" of comic postcards, Orwell lists the various characters and themes that appear in jokes and remarks that "foreigners seldom or never appear" in them. See his short piece "The art of Donald McGill" (1968b: 108).

4 Looking alike: or the ethics of *Suture*

1 See for instance the review by James Bernardelli (1994).
2 For a synthetic account of the various theories of suture in film analysis, see Kaja Silverman's *The Subject of Semiotics* (1984).
3 Lacan speaks of the lamella as the thing figured by *objets a* in Seminar XI, 197–8, and in "The position of the unconscious." 273–5. I extrapolate Lacan's concept to designate skin as it figures in the scopic regime of race as an object that appears "immortal."
4 Though I borrow Juliet Flower MacCannell's (1991) phrase "the regime of the brother," which is also the title of her book, her argument as to its connotation is far more complex than the simple Freudian/Lacanian one I assume here. MacCannell's analysis pertains to contemporary "post-Oedipal" society. She speaks of the "fraternal superego" as a pseudo-Oedipus that has an imaginary, rather than a symbolic function. She suggests that such a pliant "fraternity" is far more arbitrary and narcissistic than the symbolic patriarchy of pre-modernity.
5

It is then in relation to the original *Ding* that the first orientation, the first choice, the first seat of subjective orientation takes place, and that I will sometimes call *Neuronenwahl*, the choice of neurosis. That first grinding will henceforth regulate the function of the pleasure principle.

(VII: 54–5)

6 Lacan uses the metaphor of archery to distinguish between the aim and the goal of the partial drive in Seminar XI (179).
7 See Lacan's meditation on his friend Jacques Prévert's collection of matchboxes (113–14) and of the mustard pot (120–1). He speaks of the row of mustard pots and of the lethality of sameness in Seminar VII (198).
8 In his "Rome discourse," Lacan explicitly invokes Heidegger:

The death instinct essentially expresses the limit of the historical function of the subject. This limit is death – not as an eventual coming-to-term of the life of the individual, nor as the empirical certainty of the subject, but, as Heidegger's formula puts it, as that "possibility which is one's ownmost, unconditional, unsupersedable, certain and as such indeterminable (*unüberholbare*), for the subject – subject understood as meaning the subject defined by his historicity."

(E: 103)

9 The house that Vincent says that he chose for "aesthetic purposes" after the death of his father is a postmodern circular structure that is encircled by linked V's of steel or stone. Vincent's attempt to "(re)make" himself is concretely represented by it.
10 The concept of sublimation has a wide reach, and it would be impossible to summarize or do proper justice to it in a note. It should be recalled, however, that Lacan speaks of sublimation in several contexts in the *Ethics* seminar, including courtly love, comedy, religion, science, the arts, and of course the death drive. Though sublimation as such is always related to the drives, and all drives are ultimately oriented towards death, the differences in the various modalities of sublimation cannot all be collapsed into the death drive, which in the *Ethics*

seminar is associated specifically with the will to destruction as exemplified by the Sadean hero.

11 "Vase" is translated as "jug" by Hofstadter to refer to its authenticity in "pouring out." See his essay "The thing" in *Poetry, Language, Thought* (1985); also Heidegger, *What is a Thing?* (1967).

12 In *Moses and Monotheism* (1939), Freud speaks of the civilizational advance implied in the shift from the figuration of God as mother to father. Lacan comments on this moment in Freud's text as an elaboration of the function of paternal power as sublimation (VII: 143).

13 For a discussion of the difference between film and literature, especially in relation to temporality and description, see Seymour Chatman's "What novels can do that films can't (and vice versa)" in *On Narrative* (1981: 117–36).

14 See also Elizabeth Grosz's *Volatile Bodies* (1994), where she deploys the Moebius strip as a way to think beyond the mind/body dualism endemic to classical philosophy and various forms of feminism.

15 In his "Rome discourse," Lacan speaks of "the gift of speech" as defining the privileged field of psychoanalysis (E: 106).

16 This is a particularly Magrittian moment in the film when the linguistic text contradicts the visual, thereby restoring both to their autonomy.

17 See André Green's question at the end of the session entitled "The deconstruction of the drive" in Seminar XI (170–1).

5 What's in a name?

1 For instance, the Radio and Television News Directors Association of Canada's Code of Ethics mandates that

> News and public affairs broadcasts will put events into perspective by presenting relevant background information. Factors such as race, creed, nationality or religion will be reported only when relevant. Comment and editorial opinion will be identified as such. Errors will be quickly acknowledged and publicly corrected.
> (available on the internet at *www.media-awareness.ca/eng/issues/minrep/ Legislation/Indust.htm.* last accessed 13 December 1999)

2 Freud's schema of hypnosis or fascination, provided in ch. VIII of *Group Psychology* (1945), is taken up by Lacan in Seminar XI in relation to transference. By stressing the function of the *objet a* as that which replaces the little other or the ego ideal, Lacan speaks of identification as a (mirror) plane that must be traversed by the patient and the analyst through the transferential relation where the radical phantasy is altered to the point where the *objet a* is separated from the ego and the ego from the ego ideal (XI: 273).

3 On identification in relation to the drives, see Freud's *Three Essays on Sexuality* (1905); in relation to mourning, narcissism, hysteria, and other pathologies: "Mourning and melancholia" (1917), "Narcissism" (1914), "Dora: fragment of a case of hysteria" (1901) and "A child is being beaten" (1919) respectively.

4 For an elaboration of the difference between the psychoanalytic and Foucauldian positions on sexual difference, see Joan Copjec's trenchant and virtually incontrovertible essay "Sex and the euthanasia of reason," in *Read My Desire* (1994).

5 See Teresa Brennan's "Essence against identity," in *Metaphilosophy* (1996).

6 In "On the proper name as the signifier in its pure state" (1998), Russell Grigg draws the same correspondence between Lacan and Kripke.

7 Lacan defines signifierness as follows: "it is that which has a meaning effect" (XX: 19).

8 Lacan also says more famously that

> the subject is nothing other than what slides in a chain of signifiers, whether he knows which signifier he is the effect of or not. That effect – the subject – is the intermediary effect between what characterizes a signifier and another signifier, namely, the fact that each of them, each of them is an element. We know of no other basis by which the One may have been introduced into the world if not by the signifier as such, that is, the signifier insofar as we learn to separate it from its meaning effects.
>
> (XX: 50)

The notion of the subject as an effect of the relation between signifiers may at first glance seem incompatible with Kripke's notion of rigid designation as a necessary truth about things. However, we should recall that Kripke proposes that "the name is passed from link to link" and that this has nothing to do with properties. While the link establishes a rigid reference between name and thing, Lacanian analysis maintains that rigid reference in effect leaves the place of the thing empty.

9 Lacan thus articulates necessity here with impossibility in order to delineate the function of the symptom. In the Seminar of 21 January 1975, Lacan speaks of the symptom as that aspect of the unconscious that can be "translated by the letter," the mathematical formula $f(x)$, but as something unreadable, nothing to do with meaning. Woman's place as symptom or *objet a* cause of desire is the mark of the impossibility of the sexual relation and the fact that she is inaccessible as the Other sex.

10 Though I use black and white as examples of race names that function as rigid designators, all other color identities, such as brown, red and yellow, should be read as being rigid in the same way. Naomi Zack, in her essay "Race and philosophic meaning" (1997), goes even further to suggest that race fails all philosophic theories of meaning, including reference theory. Her argument against considering race names as rigid designators rests on the core point that meaning in reference theory is grounded in notions of "underlying traits" (35), which race can never be said to possess.

11 About the contingency of descriptions and statements of existence, Kripke says:

> In particular, philosophers sympathetic to the description theory of naming often argue that one cannot ever say of an object that it exists. A supposed statement about the existence of an object really is, so it's argued, a statement about whether a certain description or property is satisfied. As I have already said, I disagree.
>
> (1982: 110)

12 In "Extimite," Miller (1994) elaborates on this notion of invidia in relation to racism:

> Racism calls into play a hatred that is directed precisely toward what founds the Other's alterity, in other words, its *jouissance*. … It is not simply a matter of an imaginary aggressivity that, itself, is directed at fellow

beings. Racism is founded on what one imagines about the Other's *jouissance*; it is hatred of the particular way, of the Other's own way, of experiencing *jouissance*.

(79)

13 These somewhat contrary formulations can be made to appear consistent by being abstracted into the following propositions: hate is *a priori* and necessary to the law of desire; it makes the subject as "want-to-be" possible; it is implied in love; it negates ignorance, but is not knowledge.

14 Roberta and Twyla, black and white as rigid designators, prompt reflection on other kinds of names in the story such as: "bozo," "dummy," "bow legs," "biddies," "fags," "baby," "the big cross and the big Bible," "Hendrix," "asshole," "swiss cheese," "bigot," "liar," and others we can no doubt add such as "nigger," "frog," "darling," "sweetheart," etc. How should we think about these names which call up both hate and love, sometimes simultaneously? Are they rigid designators as well, or are they synonymous with a concept, thereby fixing reference and providing meaning to the name? In *Excitable Speech* (1997), Judith Butler suggests that lists such as the one above, where one refers "to such terms as if one were merely mentioning them, not making use of them, can support the structure of disavowal that permits for their hurtful circulation" (38). She insists that such re-circulation is not necessarily in complicity with power, but given the excess of connotation that language inherently carries, such lists may nevertheless have unforeseen consequences that may defeat one's oppositional purposes. For Butler, such words are illocutionary speech acts that perform their action in the moment of their utterance.

Bibliography

Abel, Elizabeth (1993) "Black writing, white reading: race and the politics of feminist interpretation," *Critical Inquiry*, 19, 470–98.

Adams, Parveen (1996) *The Emptiness of the Image: Psychoanalysis and Sexual Difference*, London: Routledge.

Adorno, Theodor and Horkheimer, Max (1976) [1947] *The Dialectic of Enlightenment* (trans. John Cumming) New York: Continuum Publishers.

Allport, Gordon (1954) *The Nature of Prejudice*, Reading MA: Addison Wesley.

Althusser, Louis (1971) [1964] *Lenin and Philosophy and Other Essays* (trans. Ben Brewster) New York: New Left Books.

Amin, Samir (1989) *Eurocentrism*, New York: Monthly Review Press.

André, Serge (1994) "The otherness of the body," in M. Bracher *et al.* (eds) *Lacanian Theory of Discourse: Subject, Structure and Society*, New York: NYU Press.

Anon. (1985) [1968] "The phallic phase and the subjective import of the castration complex," in Juliet Mitchell and Jacqueline Rose (eds) *Feminine Sexuality: Jacques Lacan and the Ecole Fruedienne* (trans. Jacqueline Rose) New York: Norton.

Appiah, Anthony (1992) *In My Father's House: Africa in the Philosophy of Culture*, New York: Oxford University Press.

Arendt, Hannah (1973) [1951] *The Origins of Totalitarianism*, New York: Harcourt Brace.

Balibar, Etienne (1994) *Masses, Classes, Ideas: Studies on Politics and Philosophy Before and After Marx* (trans. James Swenson) London: Routledge.

Balibar, Etienne and Wallerstein, Immanuel (1991) [1988] *Race, Nation, Class: Ambiguous Identities*, London: Verso.

Banton, Michael (1998) [1987] *Racial Theories*, 2nd edn, Cambridge: Cambridge University Press.

Banton, Michael and Harwood, Jonathan (1975) *The Race Concept*, New York: Praeger.

Berger, Arthur Asa (1993) *An Anatomy of Humor*, New Jersey: Transaction Publishers.

Bergson, Henri and Meredith, George (1956) *Comedy: An Essay on Comedy by George Meredith and Laughter by Henri Bergson* (intro. by Wylie Sypher) New York: Doubleday.

Bernal, Martin (1987) *Black Athena: The Afro-Asiatic Roots of Classical Civilization*, New Brunswick: Rutgers University Press.

Bernardelli, James (1994) http://movie-reviews.colossus.net/movies/s/suture.html

Bhabha, Homi (1994) *Location of Culture*, London: Routledge.

Brennan, Teresa (1989) "Introduction," in T. Brennan (ed.) *Between Feminism and Psychoanalysis*, London: Routledge, 1–23.

—— (1992) *The Interpretation of the Flesh: Freud and Femininity*, London: Routledge.

—— (1993) *History After Lacan*, London: Routledge.

—— (1996) "Essence against identity," *Metaphilosophy*, vol. 27, nos. 1 and 2, January/April, 92–103.

Butler, Judith (1990) *Gender Trouble: Feminism and the Subversion of Identity*, New York: Routledge.

—— (1993) *Bodies that Matter*, New York: Routledge.

—— (1997) *Excitable Speech*, New York: Routledge.

Chatman, Seymour (1981) "What novels can do that films can't (and vice versa)," in W. J. T. Mitchell (ed.) *On Narrative*, Chicago, University of Chicago Press, 117–36.

Conrad, Joseph (1966) [1909] "The secret sharer," in *Great Short Works of Joseph Conrad*, New York: Harper and Row.

Copjec, Joan (1994) *Read My Desire: Lacan Against the Historicists*, Cambridge MA: MIT Press.

Davies, Christie (1990) *Ethnic Humor Around the World: A Comparative Analysis*, Bloomington: Indiana University Press.

Delgado, Richard (ed.) (1995) *Critical Race Theory: The Cutting Edge*, Philadelphia: Temple University Press.

Delgado, Richard and Stefanic, Jean (eds) (1997) *Critical White Studies: Looking Behind the Mirror*, Philadelphia: Temple University Press.

Derrida, Jacques (1975) "Le facteur de la vérité," in *The Post Card: From Socrates to Freud and Beyond* (trans. Alan Bass) Chicago: University of Chicago press.

—— (1998) [1990] "For the love of Lacan," in *Resistances of Psychoanalysis* (trans. P. Kamuf, P. A. Brault and M. Naas) Stanford: Stanford University Press.

Dumont, Louis (1970) [1966] *Homo Hierarchicus* (trans. Mark Sainsbury, Louis Dumont and Basia Gulati) Chicago: University of Chicago Press.

Equiano, Olaudah (1995) [1789] *The Interesting Narrative and Other Writings*, New York: Penguin.

Eze, Emmanuel (ed.) (1997) *Race and the Enlightenment: A Reader*, Cambridge: Blackwell.

Fanon, Frantz (1967) [1952] *Black Skin, White Masks* (trans. Charles Lam Markham) New York: Grove Press.

Feldstein, Richard, Fink, Bruce and Jaanus, Maire (eds) (1995) *Reading Seminar XI: Lacan's Four Fundamental Concepts of Psychoanalysis*, Albany NY: SUNY Press.

—— (1996) *Reading Seminars I and II: Lacan's Return to Freud*, Albany NY: SUNY Press.

Fichte, Johann Gottlieb (1979) [1807–8] *Addresses to the German Nation*, Westport CT: Greenwoood Press.

Fink, Bruce (1995) *The Lacanian Subject: Between Language and Jouissance*, Princeton NJ: Princeton University Press.

—— (1997) *A Clinical Introduction to Lacanian Psychoanalysis*, Cambridge MA: Harvard University Press.

Foucault, Michel (1983) *This is Not a Pipe* (trans. James Harkness) Berkeley: University of California Press.

—— (1990) [1976] *The History of Sexuality, Vol. 1* (trans. Robert Hurley) New York: Vintage Books.

Frankenberg, Ruth (1993) *White Women, Race Matters: The Social Construction of Whiteness*, Minneapolis: University of Minnesota Press.

—— (1997) *Displacing Whiteness: Essays in Social and Cultural Criticism*, Durham NC: Duke University Press.

Freud, Sigmund, *The Standard Edition of the Complete Psychological Works of Sigmund Freud, Volumes 1–24*, ed. and trans. James Strachey, London: Hogarth Press, 1964.

—— (1900) *The Interpretation of Dreams*, SE IV–V.

—— (1905a) *Three Essays on the Theory of Sexuality*, SE VII, 125–245.

—— (1905b) [1901] *Fragment of an Analysis of a Case of Hysteria*, SE VII, 3.

—— (1905c) *Jokes and their Relation to the Unconscious*, SE VII.

—— (1913) *Totem and Taboo*, SE XIII, 1.

—— (1914) "On narcissism: an introduction," SE XIV, 69. Reprinted in Philip Rieff (ed.) *General Psychological Theory: Papers on Metapsychology*, New York: Collier Books, 1963, 56–82.

—— (1915) "Instincts and their vicissitudes" SE XIV, 111. Reprinted in Philip Rieff (ed.) *General Psychological Theory: Papers on Metapsychology*, New York: Collier Books, 1963, 83–103.

—— (1917) "Mourning and melancholia," SE XIV, 255. Reprinted in Philip Rieff (ed.) *General Psychological Theory: Papers on Metapsychology*, New York: Collier Books, 1963, 164–79.

—— (1919a) "The uncanny," SE XVII, 219.

—— (1919b) "A child is being beaten," SE XVII, 177. Reprinted in Philip Rieff (ed.) *Sexuality and the Psychology of Love*, New York: Collier Books, 1963, 107–32.

—— (1920) *Beyond the Pleasure Principle*, SE XVIII, 7.

—— (1921) *Group Psychology and the Analysis of the Ego*, SE XVIII, 69.

—— (1923) *The Ego and the Id*, SE XIX, 3.

—— (1924) "The dissolution of the Oedipus complex," SE XIX, 173. Reprinted in Philip Rieff (ed.) *Sexuality and the Psychology of Love*, New York: Collier Books, 1963, 176–82.

—— (1925) "Some psychological consequences of the anatomical distinction between the sexes," SE XIX, 243. Reprinted in Philip Rieff (ed.) *Sexuality and the Psychology of Love*, New York: Collier Books, 1963, 183–93.

—— (1927) "Humour," SE XXI, 160–6.

—— (1927a) *The Future of an Illusion*, SE XXI, 3.

—— (1927b) "Fetishism," SE XXI, 59.

—— (1930) *Civilization and its Discontents*, SE XXI, 59.

—— (1931) "Female sexuality," SE XXI, 223. Reprinted in Philip Rieff (ed.) *Sexuality and the Psychology of Love*, New York: Collier Books, 1963, 194–211.

—— (1933) *New Introductory Lectures on Psycho-Analysis*, SE XXII, 3.

—— (1937) "Analysis terminable and interminable," SE XXIII, 211.

—— (1939) *Moses and Monotheism*, SE XXIII, 3.

—— (1940) "Splitting of the ego in the process of defence," SE XXIII, 273.

Fuss, Diana (1995) *Identification Papers*, New York: Routledge.

Gehring, Albert (1908) *Racial Contrasts: Distinguishing Traits of the Graeco-Latins and Teutons*, New York: G. P. Putnam.

Gobineau, Arthur Comte de (1967) [1915] *The Inequality of the Human Races* (trans. Adrian Collins) New York: Howard Fertig.

Goldberg, David (1993) *Racist Culture: Philosophy and the Politics of Meaning*, Cambridge: Blackwell.

Gramsci, Antonio (1971) *Selections from the Prison Notebooks* (eds and trans. Quentin Hoare and Geoffrey Nowell Smith) New York: International Publishers.

Grant, Madison (1970) [1918] *The Passing of the Great Race: or The Racial Basis of European History*, New York: Arno Press and the *New York Times*.

Grigg, Russell (1998) "On the proper name as the signifier in its pure state" (trans. Daniel Collins) *Umbra*, special issue on Identity and Identification no. 1, 73–7.

Grosz, Elizabeth (1994) *Volatile Bodies: Toward a Corporeal Feminism*, Indianapolis: Indiana University Press.

Guillaumin, Colette (1995) *Racism, Sexism, Power and Ideology*, London: Routledge.

Gunther, H. F. K. (1927) *The Racial Elements of European History* (trans. G. C. Wheeler) London: Methuen.

Hall, Stuart (1996a) "Race, articulation and societies structured in dominance," in Houston Baker *et al.* (eds) *Black British Cultural Studies: A Reader*, Chicago: University of Chicago Press, 16–60.

—— (1996b) "Minimal selves," in Houston Baker *et al.* (eds) *Black British Cultural Studies: A Reader*, Chicago: University of Chicago Press, 114–19.

Harkness, Bruce (1962) *Conrad's Secret Sharer and the Critics*, Belmont CA: Wadsworth Publishers.

Heidegger, Martin (1967) *What is a Thing?* (trans. W. B. Barton Jr and Vera Deutsch) South Bend: Gateway Editions.

—— (1971) *Poetry, Language, Thought* (trans. Albert Hofstadter) New York: Harper and Row.

Herrnstein, Richard J. and Murray, Charles (1996) *The Bell Curve: Intelligence and Class Structure in American Life*, New York: Free Press.

Hughes, Langston (ed.) (1966) *The Book of Negro Humor*, New York: Dodd, Mead and Co.

Hurston, Zora Neal (1990) [1937] *Their Eyes Were Watching God*, New York: Harper Collins.

Jay, Martin (1993) *Downcast Eyes: The Denigration of Vision in Twentieth Century French Thought*, Berkeley: University of California Press.

Johnson, Barbara (1980) "The frame of reference: Poe, Lacan, Derrida," in *The Critical Difference: Essays in the Contemporary Rhetoric of Reading*, Baltimore: Johns Hopkins University Press, 110–46.

—— (1987) *A World of Difference*, Baltimore: Johns Hopkins University Press.

Johnson, Barbara and Garber, Marjorie (1987) "Secret sharing: reading Conrad psychoanalytically," *College English*, 49, 6, 628–40.

Johnson, James Weldon (1995) [1912] *Autobiography of an Ex-colored Man*, New York: Dover.

Julien, Philippe (1994) *Jacques Lacan's Return to Freud: the Real, the Symbolic, and the Imaginary* (trans. Devra Beck Simiu) New York: NYU press.

Knott, Blanche (1985) *Truly Tasteless Jokes*, vols VI, VIII, New York: St Martin's Press.

Kripke, Saul (1982) *Naming and Necessity*, Cambridge MA: Harvard University Press.

Lacan, Jacques (1933a) "The problem of style and the psychiatric conception of paranoiac forms of experience" (trans. Jon Anderson) *Critical Texts*, vol. V, no. 3, 1988, 4–6.

—— (1933b) "Motives of paranoiac crime: the crime of the Papin sisters" (trans. Jon Anderson) *Critical Texts*, vol. V, no. 3, 1988, 7–11.

—— (1938) "The family complexes" (trans. Carolyn Asp) *Critical Texts*, vol. V, no. 3, 1988, 13–29.

—— (1945) "Logical time and the assertion of anticipated certainty: a new sophism" (trans. Bruce Fink) *Newsletter of the Freudian Field*, vol 2, no. 2, 1988, 4–22.

—— (1953) "Some reflections on the ego," *International Journal of Psychoanalysis*, vol XXXIV, 1953, part I, 11–17.

—— (1953–4) *The Seminars of Jacques Lacan Book I. Freud's Papers on Technique 1953–54*, ed. Jacques-Alain Miller (trans. John Forrester) New York: Norton, 1988.

—— (1954) *The Seminars of Jacques Lacan Book II. The Ego in Freud's Theory and in the Technique of Psychoanalysis 1954–1955*, ed. Jacques-Alain Miller (trans. Sylvana Tomaselli, notes by John Forrester) New York: Norton, 1991.

—— (1955–6) *The Seminars of Jacques Lacan Book III. The Psychoses 1955–56* (trans. Russell Grigg) New York: Norton, 1993.

—— (1958) "Guiding remarks for a congress on feminine sexuality," in Juliet Mitchell and Jacqueline Rose (eds) *Feminine Sexuality: Jacques Lacan and the Ecole Freudienne*, New York: Norton, 1985, 86–98.

—— (1959–60) *The Seminars of Jacques Lacan, Book VII. The Ethics of Psychoanalysis* (trans. Dennis Porter) New York: Norton, 1992.

—— (1961) "Metaphor of the subject" (trans. Bruce Fink) *Newsletter of the Freudian Field*, vol. 5, no. 5, 1991, 10–15.

—— (1962) "Kant with Sade" (trans. James Swenson) *October*, no. 51, winter 1989, 55–75.

—— (1962–3) "Seminar X: L'angoisse" ("Seminar X: Anxiety") unpublished manuscript.

—— (1963) Introduction to the "Names-of-the-Father seminar" (trans. Jeffrey Mehlman) in Joan Copjec (ed.) *Television: A Challenge to the Psychoanalytic Establishment*, New York: Norton, 1990.

—— (1964a) *Seminar XI: Four Fundamental Concepts of Psychoanalysis* (trans. Alan Sheridan) New York: Norton, 1978.

—— (1964b) "On Freud's 'Trieb' and the psychoanalyst's desire" (trans. Bruce Fink) in R. Feldstein, B. Fink and M. Jaanus (eds) *Reading Seminars I and II*, Albany: SUNY Press, 1996, 417–27.

—— (1964c) "Position of the unconscious" (trans. Bruce Fink) in R. Feldstein, B. Fink and M. Jaanus (eds) *Reading Seminar XI*, Albany: SUNY Press, 1995, 259–82.

—— (1965–6) "Science and truth" (trans. Bruce Fink) *Newsletter of the Freudian Field*, vol. 3, no. 3, 1989, 4–29.

—— (1966) "Of structure as an inmixing of an otherness prerequisite to any subject whatever," in R. Macksey and E. Donato (eds) *The Structuralist Controversy: The Languages of Criticism and the Sciences of Man*, Baltimore: Johns Hopkins University Press, 1970.

—— (1972–3) *Seminar XX: On Feminine Sexuality and Limits of Love and Knowledge* (trans. Bruce Fink) New York: Norton, 1998.

—— (1974–5) "Seminar XXII: R.S.I.," seminar of 21 January 1975 (trans. Jacqueline Rose) in Juliet Mitchell and Jacqueline Rose (eds) *Feminine Sexuality: Jacques Lacan and the Ecole Freudienne*, New York: Norton, 1982, 162–71.

—— (1974) "Television" (trans. Dennis Hollier, Rosalind Krauss and Annette Michelson) in Joan Copjec (ed.) *Television: A Challenge to the Psychoanalytic Establishment*, New York: Norton, 1990.

—— (1977a) *Ecrits: A Selection* (trans. Alan Sheridan) New York: Norton, 1992.

—— (1977b) *Speech and Language in Psychoanalysis*, (trans. with notes and commentary by Anthony Wilden) Baltimore: Johns Hopkins University Press.

—— (1985) *Feminine Sexuality: Jacques Lacan and the Ecole Freudienne*, eds Juliet Mitchell and Jacqueline Rose (trans. Jacqueline Rose) New York: Norton.

—— (1990) *Television: A Challenge to the Psychoanalytic Establishment* (various translators) ed. Joan Copjec, New York: Norton.

Lévi-Strauss, Claude (1969) *The Elementary Structures of Kinship*, Boston MA: Beacon Press.

Lukacs, Georg (1972) [1923] *History and Class Consciousness* (trans. Rodney Livingstone) Cambridge MA: MIT Press.

MacCannell, Juliet (1991) *The Regime of the Brother: After the Patriarchy*, London: Routledge.

Mehlman, Jeffrey (1975) "How to read Freud on jokes: the critic as *Schadchen*," *New Literary History*, 6, 439–61.

Melville, Herman (1981) [1851] *Moby Dick*, New York: Bantam books.

Michaels, Walter Benn (1992) "Race into culture: a critical genealogy of cultural identity," *Critical Inquiry*, summer, vol. 18, no. 4, 655–85.

Miller, Jacques-Alain (1977–8) "Suture (elements of the logic of the signifier)," *Screen*, vol. XVIII, no. 4, 24–34.

—— (1986) "Extimite," in M. Bracher *et al.* (eds) *Lacanian Theory of Discourse*, New York: NYU Press, 1994.

—— (1989a) "An introduction to Seminars I and II," in R. Feldstein, B. Fink and M. Jaanus (eds) *Reading Seminars I and II*, Albany: SUNY Press, 1996, 3–35.

—— (1989b) "A discussion of Lacan's 'Kant with Sade'," in R. Feldstein, B. Fink and M. Jaanus (eds) *Reading Seminars I and II*, Albany: SUNY Press, 1996, 212–37.

—— (1989c) "An introduction to Lacan's critical perspectives," in R. Feldstein, B. Fink and M. Jaanus (eds) *Reading Seminars I and II*, Albany: SUNY Press, 1996, 241–7.

—— (1989d) "On perversion," in R. Feldstein, B. Fink and M. Jaanus (eds) *Reading Seminars I and II*, Albany: SUNY Press, 1996, 306–20.

—— (1990) "Context and concepts," in R. Feldstein, B. Fink and M. Jaanus (eds) *Reading Seminar XI*, Albany: SUNY Press, 1995, 3–15.

Montagu, Ashley (1972) [1951] *Statement on Race*, 3rd edn, London: Oxford University Press.

Morrison, Toni (1983) "Recitatif," in Amiri Baraka and Amina Baraka (eds) *Confirmation: An Anthology of African American Women*, New York: William Morrow.

—— (1992) *Playing in the Dark: Whiteness and the Literary Imagination*, Cambridge MA: Harvard University Press.

Mosse, George L. (1985) [1978] *Toward the Final Solution: A History of European Racism*, Madison: University of Wisconsin Press.

Muller, John P. and Richardson, William J. (eds) (1988) *The Purloined Poe: Lacan, Derrida, and Psychoanalytic Reading*, Baltimore: Johns Hopkins University Press.

Mulvey, Laura (1989) "Visual pleasure and narrative cinema," in *Visual and Other Pleasures*, Bloomington: Indiana University Press, 14–26.

Nietzsche, Friedrich (1967) *The Will to Power* (trans. Walter Kaufmann) New York: Vintage Books.

Omi, Michael and Winant, Howard (1994) [1986] *Racial Formation in the United States: From the 1960s to the 1990s*, 2nd edn, New York: Routledge.

Oring, Elliott (1992) *Jokes and Their Relations*, Lexington: University of Kentucky Press.

Orwell, George (1953a) [1945] "Shooting an elephant," in *A Collection of Essays*, New York: Harcourt Brace, 148–56.

—— (1953b) [1939] "Marrakech," in *A Collection of Essays*, New York: Harcourt Brace, 180–7.

—— (1968a) [1931] "A hanging," in Sonia Orwell and Ian Angus (eds) *An Age Like This: The Collected Essays, Journalism, and Letters of George Orwell, Vol. I*, New York: Harcourt Brace, 44–8.

—— (1968b) [1941] "The art of Donald McGill," in Sonia Orwell and Ian Angus (eds) *An Age Like This: The Collected Essays, Journalism, and Letters of George Orwell, Vol. I*, New York: Harcourt Brace, 105–16.

Palmer, Jerry (1994) *Taking Humour Seriously*, London: Routledge.

Poliakov, Leon (1971) *The Aryan Myth: A History of Racist and Nationalist Ideas in Europe* (trans. Edmund Howard) New York: Basic Books.

Reynolds, Larry T. (1992) "A retrospective on 'race': the career of a concept," *Sociological Focus*, vol. 25, no. 1, February, 1–13.

Ripley, William Z. (1899) *The Races of Europe: A Sociological Study*, New York: Appleton and Co.

Roediger, David (1994) *Towards the Abolition of Whiteness*, London: Verso.

Said, Edward (1978) *Orientalism*, New York: Vintage-Random Books.

Schwab, Raymond (1984) *The Oriental Renaissance: Europe's Rediscovery of India and the East 1680–1880* (trans. Gene Patterson-Black and Victor Reinking) New York: Columbia University Press.

Silverman, Kaja (1984) *The Subject of Semiotics*, Oxford: Oxford University Press.

—— (1996) *The Threshold of the Visible World*, New York: Routledge.

Smith, Paul (1988) *Discerning the Subject*, Minneapolis: University of Minnesota Press.

Shepherdson, Charles (1998) "Human diversity and the sexual relation," in C. Lane (ed.) *The Psychoanalysis of Race*, New York: Columbia University Press, 41–64.

Spivak, Gayatri Chakravorty (1999) *A Critique of Postcolonial Reason: Toward a History of the Vanishing Present*, Cambridge MA: Harvard University Press.

Srinivas, M. N. (1962) "Varna and caste," in *Caste in Modern India and Other Essays*, Bombay: Media Promoters and Publishers, 63–9.

Stoler, Anne Laura (1995) *Race and the Education of Desire: Foucault's History of Sexuality and the Colonial Order of Things*, Durham NC: Duke University Press.

Taylor, Isaac (1889) *The Origin of the Aryans: An Account of the Prehistoric Ethnology and Civilisation of Europe*, London: Walter Scott.

Ware, Vron (1992) *Beyond the Pale: White Women, Racism and History*, New York and London: Verso.

Weber, Samuel (1982) *The Legend of Freud*, Minneapolis: University of Minnesota Press.

—— (1991) *Return to Freud: Jacques Lacan's Dislocation of Psychoanalysis* (trans. Michael Levine) New York: Cambridge University Press.

Widney, Joseph P. (1907) *Race Life of the Aryan Peoples*, vols I and II, New York: Funk and Wagnalls.

Wilde, Oscar (1954) [1889] "The decay of lying," in *De Profundis and Other Writings*, New York: Penguin Books, 55–87.

Williams, Raymond (1971) *George Orwell* (ed. Frank Kermode) Minneapolis: University of Minnesota Press.

Williams, Raymond (ed.) (1974) *George Orwell: A Collection of Critical Essays*, New Jersey: Prentice Hall.

Wray, Matt and Newitz, A. (eds) (1996) *White Trash: Race and Class in America*, New York: Routledge.

Zack, Naomi (1997) "Race and philosophic meaning," in Naomi Zack (ed.) *Race/Sex: Their Sameness, Difference and Interplay*, New York: Routledge, 29–44.

—— (1997) "Introduction," in Naomi Zack (ed.) *Race/Sex: Their Sameness, Difference and Interplay*, New York: Routledge, 1–14.

Zizek, Slavoj (1989) *The Sublime Object of Ideology*, New York: Verso.

Index

"A hanging" (Orwell) 94, 97
Abel, Elizabeth 145–6, 148, 155
accountability 80
Adorno, Theodor 158
aesthetics, adversarial 10, 131, 144, 158–60
affirmation and resemblance 112, 120–1, 123
aggression 89–94, 97–101
alienation 60, 64, 71, 88, 97, 126–7
Althusser, Louis 30
ambivalence, structural and colonialism 81, 83, 86–7, 89, 92–4, 97–100, 102
Amin, Samir 47, 48, 52
anatomy 40, 56
Anderson, John 70, 78
annihilation 7, 9, 57–61, 74–5, 77, 88–90, 98, 111, 128
anxiety: body 36–8; deciphering Whiteness 18–19; humor 81–6, 89, 95, 99, 102; identity 134, 143–4, 156; image 107, 116, 124; imaginary 32; moral law 38, 43, 45–6; object of Whiteness 59, 70, 78; race and identity 159; subject and symbolic 21, 23; visibility and race 6, 8
appearance, physical 1–2, 9, 13, 19
Appiah, Anthony 13, 14, 16, 17, 18
Arendt, Hannah 49–51, 52, 79–81, 93, 101
articulation of class and race 147
Aryanism 51–4
Ashe, Arthur 133
Augustine, St 153
auto-altero-referential systems 55

Balibar, Etienne 16, 18, 47

being: deciphering Whiteness 38, 41, 45, 54, 56; identity 154–5; image 125, 128–9; object of Whiteness 59, 61, 63–4, 71
belonging, racial 13
Berger, Arthur Asa 92
Bernal, Martin 48, 52
Bhabha, Homi 81
binary logic 27
biology 12–14, 16, 18–20, 39, 46, 49, 124, 133, 138–9, 141–2, 146
body: deciphering Whiteness 22, 29–30; image and raced 35–8; imaginary 32–3, 35; moral law 38–40, 43, 45–6
Bopp, Franz 51
Boulanvilliers, Comte de 50, 52
boundaries, racial 18
Brennan, Teresa 4–5, 8, 46–7
bureaucracy, colonial 79–81, 84, 89, 101
Butler, Judith 39, 134, 135–6, 138, 141, 146

capitalism 47–8
caste 1
castration 6, 37, 39–40, 44, 59, 71, 77, 84, 115, 134
certainty 60–4, 68, 71–2, 78, 116–17
chain: communication 142; signifying 4, 6, 26–9, 36, 39, 55, 105–6, 111, 114, 128, 159
Chamberlain, H.S. 53
character 13
civil society 9, 92–4
class, social 20, 46, 49–50, 53, 55, 96–7, 146–7
classification, racial 19, 48, 55–6
cluster concept 137, 141–3, 145–6, 155

cohabitation 42–3
colonialism 79–84, 98, 101–2; jokes and
  the comic 85–97
color: deciphering Whiteness 11–12,
  16–17, 19–20, 31–2, 35–6, 43, 49, 52;
  identity 132–3, 137, 141–3, 145–8,
  155; image 119, 125, 131; object of
  Whiteness 57–8; visibility and race
  1–2, 9
comedy 86–7, 89, 101
comic 85–97, 101–2
community 1, 14
confession 146
Conrad, Joseph, "The Secret Sharer" 10,
  60–1, 64–6, 68–78, 81
construct, race as social 7–8, 12, 17–20,
  22, 31–2, 59, 146
contingency-necessity and racial identity
  136–9, 141, 155
contract, social 7
contradiction of Whiteness 97–99
Copjec, Joan 6, 23, 44, 134
Cromer, Lord 80
culture: deciphering Whiteness 12–13,
  16–22, 25–6; historicity 46–7, 49, 54;
  identity 133, 135, 138, 142, 146;
  imaginary 32; moral law 40–1; race
  and 158–60; visibility and race 1–2, 4,
  8; Whiteness as 59–61
cure and "The Secret Sharer" 64, 71–2,
  77–8
Cutty Sark 69–70, 74
cybernetics 27

Davies, Christie 91
death drive 90, 109–12, 126–9, 154
deciphering Whiteness 11–56
democracy 79–80
denial, logic of 46
Descartes, René 61–3, 66, 116–17, 119
description, racial 133, 137–8, 141, 146,
  155
designation: deciphering Whiteness 15,
  19; names and identity 144–5, 148,
  151, 155–6; racial 132–3, 139–44
desire: body 36–8; humor 81, 83, 90, 98;
  identity 134–6, 141, 143, 151, 153–4;
  image 103, 107, 109–18, 125–9, 131;
  imaginary 33–4; moral law 38–41,
  44–6; object of Whiteness 59–61,
  63–8, 70–1, 78; subject and symbolic
  22, 24, 29; visibility and race 3, 6, 8

destiny 1, 13, 16–17, 56, 133
desubjectification 160
diegesis-spectator 105–7, 118, 119,
  121–2, 123–5, 131
difference, human 4, 8, 19–20, 25, 31, 49,
  56, 69
difference, racial: class 96; colonialism
  81–2; deciphering Whiteness 13,
  15–16, 18–20, 20–2, 25; historicity 49,
  51; humor 89, 91, 93; identity 151,
  155; image 103, 106–7, 116, 119, 125,
  129, 131; imaginary 30, 32; moral law
  44–6; visibility and race 5, 7, 9–10;
  Whiteness 57–60, 68, 75–7, 95, 97,
  99–100, 159
difference, sexual: identity 134–6,
  139–41, 144, 151, 155, 157; moral law
  38–40, 43–4; object of Whiteness
  76–7; race and 61; subject and
  symbolic 21–3, 28–9; visibility and
  race 3–7, 10
Ding, das 110–11, 115, 117–18, 127,
  151–3
discolorations 158–60
discrimination, racial 41, 45, 82, 146
Doakes, Joe 137
domesticity 75–6
domination, racial 7, 36, 79–80, 86, 91
dreams 82, 82–3
drive 22, 39, 60–1, 115, 118, 130; death
  90, 109–12, 126–9, 154
Du Bois, W.E.B. 13, 16, 17

ego 5, 24, 26, 29–38, 41, 70–2, 87, 90,
  109, 115, 117, 133
elephant joke, Whiteness and 79–102
embodiment 20, 43, 46, 58
emptiness 117–18, 144, 149–53, 156, 159
Enlightenment 47
Equiano, Oulandah 35
ethics 160
ethics of Suture 10, 103–31, 144
ethnicity 4, 17, 20, 31, 46, 49, 52–3
ethnocentrism 47, 55
Eurocentrism 47–9, 55
Europe 52–6
exclusion 14, 16, 18, 25, 31, 58, 90, 127,
  135
exploitation 147, 158
extimacy 58, 67–9, 73, 77, 127
eye and gaze 64–7

family 18–20, 42
Fanon, Frantz 1, 31, 32, 35, 36
fantasy: fundamental 4–5, 10, 109, 112, 115, 117–18, 126, 130–1; modernity 46–7; object of Whiteness 58–61, 63–4, 67, 69; racial 10, 71, 74, 77–8, 81, 146, 159
feminism 6–7, 39, 125, 134–5, 138, 146
Fichte, Johann Gottlieb 52–4
Fink, Bruce 34
forgetting 113–14, 114, 126
formlessness 57–8
Foucault, Michel 7, 15, 56, 93, 123, 132, 135, 139, 146; "This is not a Pipe" 119–21
Francis, John 70
free association 62
freedom 129
Frege-Russell thesis 137
French racial thinking 50–1
Freud, Sigmund: castration 6, 37; death drive 111–12; and Descartes 116; humor 82–95, 98, 101; identification 133–4; libido 39; love thy neighbour 110; meaning 26–7; moral law 42; object of Whiteness 59, 61–3; primal horde 153; psychoanalysis 23–4; sexual difference 6; *Totem and Taboo* 107–8; unconscious 23–4, 26

Garber, Marjorie 61
gaze concept 5, 59–60, 65–7, 69–72, 78, 117, 133
gender 6–7, 25–6, 39–40, 134–6, 139–41, 143, 150, 155
generalizations and psychoanalysis 24
genetics 13, 16–18
German racial thinking 50–4
gestalt, racial 10, 123–5
Gobineau, Arthur, Comte de 50, 53
Goldberg, David 13, 14–16, 18
good 108, 110, 115, 117, 128–9
Gramsci, Antonio 147, 158, 160
Greece, classical 48
Grigg, Russell 140, 148
Guillaumin, Colette 11, 13, 14, 15, 19, 55
Guinness, Alec 119
Gunther, H.F.K. 52, 55–6

Hall, Stuart 35, 147
Harkness, Bruce 69

Harris, Mel 104
Harris, Michael 103
hateloving 144, 152–5
hatred and identity 151–4, 156
Haysbert, Dennis 104, 119
Hegel, Georg Wilhelm Friedrich 72, 74
Heidegger, Martin 117
Herder, Johann Gottfried von 52
heredity 1–2, 4
Herrnstein, Richard J. 13
historicity: deciphering Whiteness 14–16, 18–21, 28, 38, 43, 45–56; humor 81, 95; identity 141, 156; image 107, 111, 116; object of Whiteness 59; visibility and race 7–10
Hitchcock, Alfred 104
Hobbes, Thomas 7
Holbein, Hans 66
homesickness 84–5
Horkheimer, Max 158
hostile jokes 86, 89–91
Hughes, Langston 79
humanness 7, 45, 54–6, 60, 74–5, 78, 81, 95–7, 99, 159
humor 79–102
Hurston, Zora Neal 46

identification: cross- 159; deciphering Whiteness 12; identity 133–6, 139, 147–8; image 105–6, 127; imaginary 30–5; subject and symbolic 24, 30; visibility and race 2, 4
identity: anxiety 59; body 35–6, 38; deciphering Whiteness 12–17; historicity 46, 49; humor 93, 99; mistaken and image 103–7, 111, 113–14, 116, 119, 122, 127, 130–1; moral law 46; names and "Recitatif" 132–57; object of Whiteness 77; politics 158–60; subject and symbolic 21, 23–4, 27, 29–30; visibility and race 2–4, 7–9
ideology 30–2, 36, 48–51
imaginary 30–8, 40, 86–7, 110, 131
incest 25–6, 39–44, 46, 107–9, 115–16
inheritance 12, 17–19
intermarriage 42–3
introjection 24, 32, 35
IQ measurement 13

Johnson, Barbara 61
Johnson, James Weldon 35, 142

jokes 10, 82–5, 85–97, 124–5
Jones, William 51
jouissance: gender and 150, 153, 155;
    image 108–12, 115, 118, 123, 125;
    moral law 40–1, 43–6; object of
    Whiteness 59–61, 68–9, 71, 74, 76, 78;
    visibility and race 6–7
Julien, Philippe 36

Kant, Immanuel 11, 39, 110, 112
kinship 17, 19–20, 25–6, 28, 41–3
Klaproth, Martin Heinrich 51
Knott, Blanche 91, 93
knowledge and identity 132–57
Kripke, Saul 137–8, 139, 140–2, 143,
    144, 146, 155

Lacan, Jacques: agency of the letter
    139–40; aggression 90; anxiety 45;
    color and subjectivity 57; *das Ding*
    110–11; desire 107, 115–16, 128–9;
    drive 72, 126–7, 130; elephant joke
    79; extimacy 58, 68; gaze 59–61,
    65–7, 69–71; hatred 152–4, 156;
    identification 133, 143, 146–8, 155;
    imaginary 30, 30–3, 35–7, 86; joke
    88–9; *jouissance* 108–9; love 144;
    moral law 39–40; Other 150;
    psychoanalysis 4, 61–3, 79, 111–12,
    129; real 99, 103, 113; sexual
    difference 3, 6, 10, 21, 76; sexual
    reality 123, 125; signifier 132, 148;
    subject constitution 2–3; suture 105;
    symbolic law 25–7, 29–30;
    unconscious 22–4, 26; *unheimlich*
    82–4; void 117–18; woman 140–1
lack: body 37–8; humor 84; identity and
    153–5; image 109–10, 115, 118, 127,
    131; imaginary 35; moral law 38, 42,
    44–6; object of Whiteness 59–61, 63,
    67–8, 71, 74, 76–8; subject and
    symbolic 22–3, 29; visibility and
    race 3
language: deciphering Whiteness 15–16;
    extimacy 68–9; historicity 48–55;
    humor 81, 83, 88–9, 100; identity 134,
    136–7, 140, 144; image 106, 116,
    118–21, 131; imaginary 32–4; moral
    law 44–6; race and identity 159;
    subject and symbolic 21–7, 29–30;
    unconscious 63; visibility and race 1,
    4–5, 7

laughter 85–8, 98–100
law: colonialism 81; difference and 56;
    identity 134, 153; juridical 90, 94;
    moral and humor 91, 93, 96, 98, 101;
    moral and image 103, 107–12,
    114–16, 127, 129; moral, race and sex
    38–46; moral and visibility 10; object
    of Whiteness 58, 60; racial 25–7,
    29–30, 41–5; social 9, 12; symbolic
    74–8, 94
Leigh, Mike 124
letter, agency of 23, 139–40, 143–4
Lévi-Strauss, Claude 25, 27, 40, 41, 42
libido 39–40
light, Whiteness as 58
looking alike, ethics of *Suture* 103–31
love, knowledge and identity in
    "Recitatif" 10, 132–57
love thy neighbour 107–12
Lubbock, Basil 69, 70, 73, 74, 78
Lukács, Georg 9
Luther, Martin 53, 153
lying 119, 121

McCannell, Juliet 108
McGehee, Scott 103, 106
Magritte, René 104, 118, 119–21, 123,
    132, 139
Mann, Thomas 130
mapping the body 13
marks, bodily: deciphering Whiteness
    12–13, 19, 21, 30–1, 36, 38, 44, 46;
    discolorations 159; humor 97; image
    107, 114, 116, 123–4, 131; object of
    Whiteness 59; visibility and race
    1–2, 8
"Marrakech" (Orwell) 95–6, 99
Marx, Karl 9
mastery 7, 58, 72–5, 77–8, 81, 90, 100,
    129, 159
meaning: identity and 135, 137–41,
    143–4; names and identity 146,
    155–7, 159; subject and symbolic 27
Melville, Herman 57–8, 67
memory 28–9, 113–15, 122, 126
Merleau-Ponty, Maurice 67
Merrill, Dina 104
Mill, James 137
Miller, Jacques-Alain 68–9, 77, 105
mirror stage 30, 30–8, 72
miscegenation 41–3, 45–6
miscognition 105, 116, 118

misrecognition 5, 31–2, 35–6, 72
Moby Dick (Melville) 57–8
modernity 4–5, 46–7
Moebius strip comparison 123, 125
Morrison, Toni 10, 132, 143–57, 159
movement, comedy of 86
multiculturalism 49
multiracialism 91–2
Mulvey, Laura 131
Murray, Charles 13

names and identity 1, 132–57
Napoleon I, Bonaparte 52
narrative: "Recitatif" 144–5, 147–8,
    151–2, 155; *Suture* 104–7, 111, 113,
    119, 123–5, 131
nation 14, 18–19, 31, 49–50, 52–4
natives, colonialism and humor 80, 85–6,
    90, 93–4, 97–102
neo-racism 18
Nietzsche, Friedrich 57
Nixon, Richard 139, 141, 143

object: identity 133–4, 138; image 107,
    110, 117–18, 120, 123; moral law
    39–41, 45–6; of Whiteness 57–78
objet a 22, 38, 46, 63, 65, 67–9, 70, 71–2,
    77–8, 117, 133, 143
objet petit a 37, 45, 60–1, 64, 115, 118,
    130, 153
obscene jokes 86, 91
Oedipus complex 107, 128, 134
optics 32–3, 66–7
organism and sexuality 39–40
Orientalism 48, 52
Oring, Elliot 91
Orwell, George 10, 82, 85, 94, 95–101,
    159
Other: body 36–7; extimacy 68–9; gaze
    59–61; historicity 48, 55; humor 88,
    98; image 109, 111, 116, 118, 126–7,
    129, 131; imaginary 31, 33–4; moral
    law 39–41, 43–6; names and identity
    148, 150, 153, 155; subject and
    symbolic 23–5, 28; unconscious 63

Palmer, Jerry 92
Pascal, Blaise 27
paternalism 76
perspective 33
Petersen, Wolfgang 104

phenotype 4, 8, 12, 21, 59
physiognomy 50, 55, 106
pleasure principle 109–11, 115
power 7, 9, 14–15, 17, 21, 35, 39, 58, 89,
    135–6, 146
primal horde myth 42, 107–9, 115, 153
properties: identity 135, 137–9, 141–3;
    qualitative and identity 146, 148, 155;
    racial 159
proxy, representation by 159
psychoanalysis: deciphering Whiteness
    14, 20, 24, 27, 38–41, 46;
    discolorations 160; humor 85;
    identity 133–6, 139, 143; image 111,
    114, 116–18, 125, 129; object of
    Whiteness 60–3; visibility and race
    2–3, 7–8
psychology 22, 24, 133, 135, 147

queer theory 39, 134

race: body 35–6, 38; colonialism 79–81,
    83, 89, 97, 101; deciphering
    Whiteness 11–12, 15–19; historicity
    46–56; identity 132–3, 139, 141,
    143–7, 151–2, 155–6; image 103, 116,
    122–5, 130–1; imaginary 30–1; sex
    and moral law 38–46; subject and
    symbolic 20–2, 24–7, 29–30; theory
    13, 16–17, 141–2, 158–60; thinking 1,
    18, 49–52, 54–5, 146; visibility and
    2–5, 7–10
racism 8–9, 12, 14–15, 18–20, 31–2, 38,
    44, 46, 48–51, 55–6, 68–9, 70–1, 73,
    78, 103
racist jokes 89–94, 99
real: body 36; gender 134; humor 99;
    identity 139–40, 143; image 103, 112,
    120–1, 125; imaginary 32, 34; moral
    law 40–1, 43–6; object of Whiteness
    59, 68, 71; sexual difference 6; subject
    and symbolic 22–3
"Recitatif" (Morrison) 10, 143–57, 159
recognizing Whiteness 71–8
referent 19–20, 137–9, 141–4, 147–8,
    155–6, 159
religion 1, 68
repetition 120, 123
representation 119–21, 126, 135, 159
resemblance 104, 113, 118, 120–1, 123–5,
    139
Road to Wigan Pier, The (Orwell) 96–7

Roediger, David 49

Sade, Marquis de 39, 109–12, 128
Said, Edward 48, 52
sameness 8, 10, 56, 58, 64, 69, 81, 89,
    99–100, 111, 135, 159
Sartre, Jean Paul 67
Saussure, F. de 139
Schlegel, Friedrich von 51
Schwab, Raymond 51–2
science and race 12–14, 16–17
Searle, John 137
secondariness, racial 35
"Secret Sharer, The" (Conrad) 10, 64–6,
    68–78, 81, 159
secret of Whiteness 61–9
Secrets and Lies 124–5
self-division 61–3
set theory 141
sex: race and moral law 38–46
sex-gender-desire nexus 39, 134–6
sexual jokes 86
sexuality 20, 22, 29, 38–40, 67, 134–5
share of Whiteness 69–71
Shimono, Sab 104
"Shooting an elephant" 97–101
Siegel, David 103, 106
signifier: body 35–6, 38; deciphering
    Whiteness 20–30; historicity 46, 48–9,
    54–6; humor 81–2, 83, 85, 95; identity
    132–3, 135, 137, 139–41; image 104,
    106–7, 110–12, 114, 116–18, 120–1,
    124–9, 131; imaginary 32, 34–5;
    moral law 40–1, 43–5; names and
    identity 145–8, 150–1, 155–6; object
    of Whiteness 58–61, 63–4, 69, 71, 74,
    77; race and identity 158–9; racial
    12–14, 17; visibility and race 3–8, 10
silence and psychoanalysis 63
similitude 118, 120–5, 139, 159
simulcrum, affirmation of 120–2
slavery 42–3
Smith, Paul 23
social policy 158
social and psyche 133, 135
sociality 40–1
Sophocles 107, 128
spectator-diegesis 105–7, 118, 119,
    121–2, 123–5, 131, 159
Srinivas, M.N. 1
status 1, 21, 34, 42–3
subject: body 35–6; deciphering

Whiteness 19; humor 88–9, 98, 102;
    identity 133, 135–6, 140; image 103,
    105–7, 111–14, 116–18, 121, 124–5,
    130–1; imaginary 34–5; moral law
    38–9, 41, 44–6; object of Whiteness
    59–63, 67–8, 71–2, 74, 77; symbolic
    21–30; visibility and race 2–3, 5–7
subjectivity 1, 28, 41, 45–6, 85, 98,
    104–6, 135, 154; inter- 5, 7–9, 23, 56,
    69–71, 74, 82, 90
sublimation 39, 117–18
subversion 89, 92, 94
suffering and psychoanalysis 63–4
superego 39, 41, 108–9
supremacy 60
surprise 83, 104, 124–5
Suture 10, 103–4, 106–11, 113–31, 144,
    159
symbolic: body 36–8; historicity 47, 49,
    54, 56; humor 81; identity 134, 136,
    140, 143; image 106, 113–14, 116,
    118, 125–6, 131; imaginary 32–4;
    moral law 38, 40–6; names and
    identity 144, 150–1, 153, 155; object
    of Whiteness 58, 60, 68, 71, 73–4,
    76–8; race and identity 159; subject
    21–30; visibility and race 2–6, 8–9
symptom, concept of 81, 144

taboo 92; *see also* incest
tendentious humor 83, 86, 89, 94
terror 57–8
totalitarianism 89
transgression 41, 109–10
tuche-automaton 82

uncanny 10, 37–8, 82–6, 89, 94–7,
    99–100, 116, 124–5, 127
unconscious: deciphering Whiteness 19;
    extimacy 68; historicity 56; humor
    81–4, 86, 88–9, 91, 98, 100; identity
    133, 135–6, 140; image 113, 115, 117,
    124–5, 127; imaginary 32; moral law
    39; names and identity 148, 150–2,
    154, 156; object of Whiteness 59,
    62–4, 78; subject and symbolic 21–30;
    visibility and race 2
unheimlich 82–4
universalism 47–8, 54

violence 80, 91–4, 99, 101

visibility: body 35–6, 38; deciphering
    Whiteness 17, 19–20; historicity 46,
    48–9, 54–5; humor 95; identity 143–4;
    image 116, 124, 131; imaginary 32,
    35; moral law 39, 43; names and
    identity 144, 148, 156; object of
    Whiteness 58–9, 70–1; race theory
    158–60; subject and symbolic 20–3,
    27, 29–30

Volney, C.F. 51

Wallace, Captain 70, 74–5, 78
wholeness 5, 7–10, 21, 37, 59–61, 97,
    124, 140–1, 144, 148–52, 159
Wilde, Oscar 103
Williams, Raymond 85

Zizek, Slavoj 81